A NEW APPROACH
TO LATIN — Part 2

A NEW APPROACH TO LATIN — Part 2

EDWIN G. MACNAUGHTON, M.A.

AND

THOMAS W. McDOUGALL, M.A., B.A., Ph.D.

OLIVER & BOYD

Oliver & Boyd
Robert Stevenson House
1–3 Baxter's Place
Leith Walk
Edinburgh EH1 3BB
A Division of Longman Group Limited

ISBN 0 05 002365 9

Printed in Hong Kong by
Wilture Printing Co., Ltd.

Preface

The second part of *A New Approach to Latin* provides the pupil with all the grammar and syntax and much of the reading material which is required for the O level GCE or O grade SCE examinations. The systematic approach to the subject is also designed to meet the needs of pupils who may be aiming at examinations of a higher standard.

In accordance with modern practice the main approach to the subject is through ample Latin–English translation. The passages are graded in difficulty, new grammar and syntax being introduced gradually and exercised adequately. Many teachers still feel that Latin constructions can best be taught by the use of English–Latin examples, and to meet their needs we have offered a number of such exercises. They may be omitted, without detriment to the course, by those who do not favour their use.

We have endeavoured to present the Latin passages—which for the most part are either adaptations from Latin authors or deal with real historical situations—in credible Latin. In order to do so it has been necessary to use a much wider vocabulary than was common in earlier Latin course books. Words to which special attention should be drawn are marked by an asterisk in the special word lists. The general word list contains all the words which are used in this book, including those which were also used in the first part of the course.

The subject matter has been arranged so as to provide a sketch of the history and life of the Roman Empire from Augustus to the barbarian invasions. A short section of medieval passages is intended to dispel the idea that the literary supremacy of Latin ended with the Empire in the West. Frequent 'link' passages in English are designed to preserve the unity of the scheme.

As in the earlier volume we are indebted to friends for generous help and advice. Professor W. S. Watt of the University of Aberdeen read the typescript in draft form and gave us the benefit of his meticulous scholarship. Mr W. C. Henderson, formerly rector of Airdrie Academy, a teacher of long and successful experience, also read the typescript and made many valuable suggestions. For any blemishes which may appear in the final form of the book we ourselves are, of course, entirely responsible.

E.G.M.
T.W.McD.

Acknowledgments

The authors are very grateful to the following for supplying the photographs used in this book:

L. Gliori (p. 163); Italian State Tourist Office (p. 113); The Mansell Collection (pp. 16, 41, 53, 54, 80, 83, 87, 96, 106); National Museum of Antiquities of Scotland (p. 167); Radio Times Hulton Picture Library (pp. 89, 161).

Contents

Preliminary Exercises

1 **Active and Passive.** *Turn into passive form.*

   Example. **Active:** scrīptōrēs Caesarem laudant.
               Passive: Caesar ā scrīptōribus laudātur.

   magister scelestus puerōs in castra hostium dūxit.
   discipulī tē, sceleste, in urbem trahent.
   magister doctus discipulōs Graecē scrībere docet.
   bonus senex cibum viātōribus dat.
   frāter puerum excitāvit.
   agricola multōs et magnōs canēs alēbat.
   sagitta mīlitem vulnerāvit.
   cīvēs vōcēs discipulōrum audīverant.

2 **Pronouns.** *Revise pronouns, pages 187-9 and translate into Latin the words in italics.*

   I shall walk; *you* will ride alone.
   We go to the seaside; where do *you* all go?
   We see *them*; they do not see *us*.
   I like *him*; *he* does not like *me*.
   You all blame *him*; but he does not blame *himself*.
   If *you*, my brother, are unwilling to go, I shall go *myself*.
   These men are Greeks, *those* are Romans.
   The man who warned Caesar was a prophet.
   I do not understand *the things which* you tell me.
   Brutus *himself* was a conspirator; later, he killed *himself*.

3 **Gods and Heroes.** *vērum an falsum?*
   Tarquinius Superbus ultimus rēx Rōmānōrum erat.
   C. Mūcius Scaevola Lartem Porsinnam occīdit.
   Fābricius pecūniam medicō Pyrrhī dare nōluit.
   Carthāginiēnsēs prīmī hostēs trānsmarīnī Rōmānōrum erant.
   Rōmānī ab Hannibale numquam superātī sunt.
   Hannibal urbem Rōmam capere nōn potuit.
   Vulcānus deus bellī erat.
   Iīppiter pater deōrum et hominum erat.
   Via Appia ad Alpēs ferēbat (*led*).
   C. Iūlius Caesar ā praedōnibus captus est.

4 **Prepositions.** *A selection exercise.*
Valerius amīcōs ad —— dūxit. (*forō, forī, forum*)
puerī et puellae in —— lūdunt. (*lītus, lītore, lītora*)
cīvēs in —— festīnant. (*templō, templa, templīs*)
post —— paulīsper dormiēmus. (*merīdiē, merīdiem*)
canēs per —— errant. (*viīs, viā, viās*)
dē —— nōn audīvimus. (*Papīrium, Papīriī, Papīriō*)
magister discipulōs ex —— dūxit. (*urbs, urbe, urbem*)
tandem in —— hostium vēnērunt. (*castrīs, castrōrum, castra*)
magister extrā —— discipulōs exspectat. (*porta, portīs, portam*)
omnēs praeter —— attentī sunt. (*Publiō, Publium, Publiī*)

5 **The Relative Pronoun.** *Revise the relative pronoun, page 189.*
  (*a*) *redde Anglicē :*
    ubi est servus cui epistulam dedī?
    nusquam servum videō quem ad Viam Lātam mīsī.
    ea quae scrīpsī aperta sunt omnia.
    cīvēs eum laudāvērunt quī ad urbem frūmentum mīserat.
    Caesar praedōnēs cēpit ā quibus ipse captus erat.

  (*b*) *Translate into Latin the words in italics only :*
    Scipio, *by whom* Hannibal was defeated, was called Africanus.
    Pompey laughed at the soldiers *whose* efforts were useless.
    The pirates did not know *the man whom* they had taken.
    We do not believe *the things which* you tell us.
    The men with whom I travelled told me many strange things.

6 **Comparison.** *Revise Comparison of Adjectives and Adverbs, pages 186–7.*
  A selection exercise :
    via est lāta; flūmen est ——. (*lātior, lātiōrem, lātius*)
    campus est ——. (*lātissimum, lātissimus, lātissimē*)
    magister est —— quam discipulī. (*doctus, doctior, doctissimus*)
    numquam canem vīdī —— quam Hylacem. (*maior, maiōrem, maius*)
    —— est sedēre quam ambulāre. (*facilis, facillimum, facilius*)
    Hylax est ācer sed Lacō est ——. (*ācrius, ācriōrem, ācrior*)
    Vēlōx est omnium ——. (*ācriōrem, ācerrimus, ācerrimē*)
    Marcus —— currit quam Sextus. (*celerius, celerior, celeriter*)
    domum rediimus quam ——. (*celeriter, celerrimē, celerius*)

7 **Infinitives.** *Revise infinitive active and translate into Latin the words in italics:*

Valerius seems *to have* many friends.

He is said *to be* very popular.

I seem *to have heard* this before.

The enemy seem *to be about to go away (depart)*.

This man is known *to have fled* from France.

He does not seem *to be likely to return* there.

What is he said *to have done*?

I seem *to hear* strange voices.

We intend *to go* to the baths.

Caesar seemed *to be likely to be* king.

8 **Irregular Verbs.** *Revise* **volō, nōlō, mālō, eō,** *pages 196–7.*

redde Latīnē:

Do you (*pl.*) wish to dine?

We prefer to sleep for a short time.

We wish to swim.

Marcus refuses to come with us.

He prefers to catch fish.

Do not swim in the sea, boys!

Do you not prefer to swim in the sea?

We shall go to the Forum ourselves.

Marcus wishes to stay at home.

'I am tired', he says, 'so I am unwilling to leave home.'

9 **School.** *Test your word-power.*

hodiē Marcus ad —— it. —— domō discēdit. —— per viās eum dūcit. —— librōs et cērās portat. —— discipulōs salūtat. prīmum puerī ē librīs —; deinde ——; posteā —— in —— scrībunt. magister —— laudat, ignāvōs ——. per quīnque annōs Marcus apud —— studēbit, deinde apud —— litterīs Latīnīs et Graecīs operam dabit (*he will devote himself*). posteā fortasse —— discet. ipse enim ōlim —— vel —— erit et in —— ōrātiōnēs habēbit.

The following are the missing words; choose the appropriate one for each space:

industriōs, recitant, Rōstrīs, māne, magister, cōnsul, grammaticum, stilīs, paedagōgus, lūdum, capsārius, numerant, praetor, cērīs, artem ōrātōriam, castīgat, litterātōrem.

11

I A Gallery of Emperors

From Republic to Empire

The Roman people did not like kings. Their unhappy experience of those who had ruled them in their earliest times had left a memory so bitter that the very suggestion that Julius Caesar sought a crown had been enough to justify his murder. The confused period of civil strife which followed his death, however, had brought so much misery that, at the end of it, they were ready to accept the rule of one man, so long as he brought them peace. That one man was Gaius Iulius Caesar Octavianus, the grand-nephew and adopted son of the great Julius. As you have read, he was later given the title Augustus, by which he has been known ever since.

When Augustus assumed control of the state he showed great tact and understanding of the republican prejudices of the Roman people. Unlike Julius, he did not allow himself to be called dictator, an office which under the Roman constitution could not be held for more than six months. Instead, he had himself elected to republican offices such as those of consul, tribune of the people, high priest, which gave him all the power he needed, but within the framework of the law. On more than one occasion he offered to give back his power to the people, only to have it restored to him with the addition of new powers by the grateful citizens who dreaded nothing more than a return to the confusion of the civil wars.

However, he did assume one title which gave him a standing above that of all other citizens—the title of **princeps,** first citizen—the word from which our *prince* is derived. It is interesting to note how closely the example of Augustus was followed by the dictators of Italy and Germany in the first half of the twentieth century. They did not usurp such titles as *king* or *president*, but held supreme power without challenge or restriction under such seemingly inoffensive titles as *il Duce* (Mussolini of Italy) and *der Führer* (Hitler of Germany).

The rule of Augustus was just and beneficial to all. Order was restored throughout the Empire; trade flourished; the provinces were governed in such a way that they were no longer exposed to the greed of dishonest governors.

Lesson 1

Exercise 1a

Two birds in the hand

nunc cīvēs Rōmānī sciunt mē facilem et adfābilem esse; sed ōlim, postquam mē ad Actium superāvisse Antōnium audīvērunt, nōnnūllī mē esse
ferōcissimum crēdēbant. multī tamen, dum post proelium Rōmam redeō,
mihi obviam vēnērunt. inter eōs erat senex cum corvō. dum praetereō,
corvus, 'salvē', cantāvit, 'Caesar, victor, imperātor!' attonitus mē velle 5
eum magnō pretiō emere dīxī. senex sē vīgintī mīlibus sēstertium libenter
venditūrum esse respondit. ego corvum ēmī, senex laetus discessit.
postrīdiē tamen vīcīnus quīdam, homō invidus, ad mē vēnit et senem
habēre corvum alterum affirmāvit. 'hic corvus', inquit, 'melius dīcere
potest.' 10

mē libenter illum corvum audītūrum esse respondī et ad mē ferrī
iussī. statim ea quae didicerat ēdidit—'salvē, Antōnī, victor, imperātor!'
senex perterritus sē ad utrumque cāsum parātum esse dīxit. ego tamen,
minimē īrātus, prōmīsī mē alterum corvum eōdem pretiō ēmptūrum esse.
senex attonitus mē hominem esse clēmentissimum exclāmāvit. 15

WORD LIST

*facilis, -is, -e, good-natured
adfābilis, -is, -e, approachable
*crēdō, -ere, crēdidī, crēditum, believe
*obviam venīre (*with dative*), to come to
  meet
corvus, -ī, *m.*, raven
praetereō, -īre, -iī, -itum, pass by
*pretium, -iī, *n.*, price
*emō, -ere, ēmī, ēmptum, buy

*vendō, -ere, -didī, -ditum, sell
vīcīnus, -ī, *m.*, neighbour
invidus, -a, -um, jealous
*affirmāre, to declare
*discō, -ere, didicī, learn
ēdō, -ere, ēdidī, ēditum, utter
*uterque, utraque, utrumque, each (of
  two), either
cāsus, -ūs, *m.*, chance, event

13

1 **sciunt mē facilem et adfābilem esse,** know me to be good-natured and approachable, i.e. know that I am. . . .

2 **ad Actium,** off Actium; the naval battle of Actium in 31 B.C. marked the end of the struggle between Antonius (Mark Antony) and Octavianus (later Augustus).

postquam audīvērunt, after they had heard. The perfect tense after **postquam** is usually translated into English by the pluperfect (*had* . . .).

mē Antōnium superāvisse, that I had defeated Antony; see Language.

3,4 **dum redeō, dum praetereō,** while I *was* returning, while I *was* passing.

5,6 **mē velle dīxī,** I said that I was willing . . . (there are several other examples of this construction in this exercise; see Language).

6 **magnō pretiō,** at a great price.

vīgintī milibus sēstertium, for 20 000 **sēstertii** (*lit.* for twenty thousands of **sestertii**; the ablative (**vīgintī milibus**) indicates the price (see page 208). The modern equivalent of 20 000 sestertii might be as much as £500.

11 **ferrī,** to be brought; present infinitive passive of **ferō, ferre, tulī, lātum,** see page 195.

14 **prōmīsi mē alterum corvum ēmptūrum esse,** I promised that I would buy, *or simply* I promised to buy.

Language

Indirect or Reported Speech

Compare the following pairs of sentences:

1 (*a*) Direct: **facilis sum.** *I am good-natured.*
  (*b*) Indirect: **cīvēs mē facilem esse dīcunt.**
       The citizens declare me to be good-natured.
       (i.e. *The citizens say that I am good-natured.*)
       cīvēs mē facilem esse dīxērunt.
       The citizens declared me to be good-natured.
       (i.e. *The citizens said that I was good-natured.*)

2 (*a*) Direct: **Antōnium superāvī.** *I defeated Antony.*
  (*b*) Indirect: **cīvēs mē Antōnium superāvisse audiunt.**
       The citizens hear that I (have) defeated Antony.
       cīvēs mē Antōnium superāvisse audīvērunt.
       The citizens heard that I had defeated Antony.

The Latin method of expressing Indirect Speech is known as the Accusative and Infinitive Construction. From the above examples you will understand why. The normal English method of translating the Accusative and Infinitive Construction is by means of a Noun Clause introduced by *that* (which may, however, be omitted).

Notes

1 The Accusative and Infinitive Construction is found not only after verbs meaning *to say*, but also after those meaning *to think*, e.g. **putāre, crēdere;** *to know*, e.g. **scīre;** and verbs of *the senses*, e.g. **audīre,** *to hear*, **vidēre,** *to see*, **sentīre,** *to feel*.

2 Study the following examples:

Direct: **fēlīx sum.** I am fortunate.

Indirect: **mē fēlīcem esse dīcō.** *I* say that *I* am fortunate.

nōs fēlīcēs esse dīcimus. *We* say that *we* are fortunate.

tē fēlīcem esse scīs. *You* know that *you* are fortunate.

vōs fēlīcēs esse scītis. *You* (pl.) know that *you* are fortunate.

sē pilā lūsisse dīcit. *He* says that *he* played ball.

sē dīligenter studēre dīcunt. *They* say that *they* are studying hard.

Exercise 1b

(*a*) *Change to Direct form.*

    Example. vīcīnus dīxit senem alterum corvum habēre.

          Direct: senex alterum corvum habet.

1 hanc fābulam novam esse putō.

2 mē facilem et adfābilem esse scīvērunt.

3 mē velle corvum emere dīxī.

4 dīxistīne tē corvum venditūrum esse?

5 vīcīnus corvum alia verba didicisse affirmāvit.

6 senex sē territum esse dīxit.

7 mē alterum corvum venditūrum esse prōmīsī.

8 senex Caesarem clēmentissimum esse crēdidit.

(*b*) *Change to Indirect form.*

    Example. facilis sum. (dīcunt)

          Indirect: mē facilem esse dīcunt.

1 clēmēns es. (cīvēs sciunt)

2 Caesar homō ferōcissimus est. (nōn crēdimus)

3 alterum corvum habeō. (affirmō)

4 vīcīnus homō invidus est. (putāmus).

5 Caesar corvum ēmit. (senex gaudēbat)

6 alter corvus melius dīcere potest. (vīcīnus affirmāvit)

Lesson 2

'Factum est autem in diēbus illīs, exiit ēdictum ā Caesare Augustō ut dēscrīberētur ūniversus orbis.' *St Luke* 2:1 (Vulgate—Latin Bible—version)

Who was the Caesar you read about in Exercise 1a? He was the same man of whom St Luke wrote—Caesar Augustus—His Imperial Majesty, Caesar, the first and perhaps the greatest of the Roman Emperors. He came to power in 31 B.C. and it was during his reign that Jesus was born.

The Emperor Augustus

Exercise 2a

Octavianus tells of his early life.

Rōmae nātus sum in domō in Monte Palātīnō sitā haud procul ā Viā Sacrā. illō diē nātālī meō pater Octāvius ad cūriam sērō pervēnit; adeō gaudēbat fīlium sibi nātum fuisse. patrem tamen minimē nōveram; mē enim parvulō periit, sed prō certō habeō eum virum bonum et probum 5 fuisse.

     māter mea Atia, fēmina mītissima, erat fīlia sorōris C. Iūliī Caesaris quī posteā mē adoptāvit et fēcit hērēdem. pueritiam in vīllā Albānā ēgī collibus silvestribus cīnctā. ibi nōnnumquam pilā lūdēbam vel in vīllā cessābam, sed saepius paedagōgus mē dīligenter studēre cōgēbat.

10   quīndecim annōs nātus togam virīlem sūmpsī. posteā in Hispāniā et Graeciā Caesarem adiūvī quī tum tōtum orbem terrārum regēbat. dum in Macedoniā sum, ā mātre epistulam accēpī illum in cūriā trucīdātum esse.

     eō tempore ūndēvīgintī annōs nātus eram neque quisquam crēdēbat 15 mē ōlim prīncipem futūrum esse. ab Antōniō tamen partem imperiī petīvī sed is mē dērīsit et sē datūrum esse negāvit. dum autem ille in Galliā abest, senātus mihi dedit exercitum. Rōmam contendī atque ibi cōnsul creātus sum.

WORD LIST

situs, -a, -um, situated
*haud procul, not far
diēs nātālis, birthday
*adeō, so, to such an extent
*nōvī, nōvisse, know (a person)
*prō certō habēre, to be sure
probus, -a, -um, honourable
adoptāre, to adopt
*hērēs, -ēdis, *m.,* heir
*pueritia, -ae, *f.,* boyhood
*agō, -ere, ēgī, āctum, spend (time)

*collis, -is, *m.,* hill
silvestris, -is, -e, wooded
cīnctus, -a, -um, surrounded
cessāre, to idle
*cōgō, -ere, coēgī coāctum, compel
*sūmō, -ere, sūmpsī, sūmptum, assume, take
*trucīdāre, to assassinate
*ūndēvigintī, nineteen
dērīdeō, -ēre, -rīsī, -rīsum, laugh at

NOTES

1 **Rōmae,** at Rome: locative case, see pages 37, 38.
  Mōns Palātinus, the fashionable residential district of Rome.
3 **minimē nōveram,** I hardly knew him. **nōvī,** the perfect indicative of **nōscere,** means *I have got to know,* i.e. I know; so the pluperfect tense means *I knew.*
4 **mē parvulō,** when I was a little boy.
10 **togam virīlem sūmpsī,** I assumed the toga of manhood.
12 **epistulam accēpī illum trucīdātum esse,** I received a letter (telling me) that he had been assassinated. Verbs and phrases which *imply* telling are followed by the Accusative and Infinitive construction.
14 **neque quisquam crēdēbat . . . ,** and no one believed . . . , *lit.* nor anyone . . . . **quisquam** (*neut.* **quicquam**) after a negative word means *anyone.*
16 **sē datūrum esse negāvit,** said that he would not give it (see Language).

Language

1   More about Indirect Speech

Antōnius sē mihi partem imperiī datūrum esse negāvit.
Antony said that he would not give me a share, *lit.* denied that he would give. . . . **negāre,** to deny, should normally be translated *say that . . . not.*
Further examples:
Antōnius sē umquam mihi partem datūrum esse negāvit.
Antony said that he would *never* give me a share.
Antōnius sē mihi ūllam partem datūrum esse negāvit.
Antony said that he would *not* give me *any* share.
Antōnius sē mihi quicquam datūrum esse negāvit.
Antony said that he would *not* give me *anything.*
Antōnius sē cuiquam partem datūrum esse negāvit.
Antony said that he would *not* give a share *to anyone.*

2 Table of Infinitives Active and Passive

CONJUGATION	PRESENT	FUTURE	PERFECT
1st Active	**laudāre,** to praise	**laudātūrus, -a, -um esse,** to be about to praise	**laudāvisse,** to have praised
Passive	**laudārī,** to be praised	**laudātum īrī,** to be about to be praised	**laudātus, -a, -um esse,** to have been praised
2nd Active	**terrēre,** to frighten	**territūrus, -a, -um esse,** to be about to frighten	**terruisse,** to have frightened
Passive	**terrērī,** to be frightened	**territum īrī,** to be about to be frightened	**territus, -a, -um esse,** to have been frightened
3rd (a) Active	**dūcere,** to lead	**ductūrus, -a, -um, esse,** to be about to lead	**dūxisse,** to have led
Passive	**dūci,** to be led	**ductum īrī,** to be about to be led	**ductus, -a, -um esse,** to have been led
(b) Active	**capere,** to take	**captūrus, -a, -um esse,** to be about to take	**cēpisse,** to have taken
Passive	**capī,** to be taken	**captum īrī,** to be about to be taken	**captus, -a, -um esse,** to have been taken
4th Active	**audīre,** to hear	**audītūrus, -a, -um esse,** to be about to hear	**audīvisse,** to have heard
Passive	**audīrī,** to be heard	**audītum īrī,** to be about to be heard	**audītus, -a, -um esse,** to have been heard

Exercise 2b

1 *redde Anglicē:*

dīcit Octāviānus sē in Hispāniā Caesarem adiūvisse.

sē fortem et validum fuisse negat.

Octāviānus nārrat domum suam in Monte Palātīnō sitam fuisse.

Antōnius partem imperiī iuvenī datum īrī negāvit.

Octāviānus prō certō habēbat exercitum sibi ā senātū datum īrī.

2 *redde Latīnē:*

We heard that you were coming to the city.

Some citizens believed that you would be merciful.

We hope that the city will be saved.

Octavianus says that Caesar ruled the whole world.

Many men thought that he would be assassinated.

They said that the Romans did not like kings.

Lesson 3

Exercise 3a

The timid Octavianus becomes the mighty Augustus.

Antōnius, postquam ē Galliā rediit, in grātiam mē recēpit. Imperium
Rōmānum in trēs partēs dīvīsum est. mihi sorte obvēnērunt Ītalia, Gallia,
Hispānia; Lepidō Āfrica; Antōniō Oriēns ubi Cleopātram, fēminam
pulcherrimam, vīdit et amāvit.

    paucīs post annīs, ubi bellum Cleopātrae indīxī, Antōnius ad Actium 5
superātus sē interfēcit. brevī post Cleopātra aspidem sibi admōvit et
venēnō necāta est.

    trīgintā duōs annōs nātus, tōtum imperium Rōmānum tenēbam;
cōnsilium tamen callidissimum cēpī; senātuī enim, 'opus meum', inquam,
'cōnfectum est. pāx est composita. imperium quod mihi mandāvit senātus 10
populusque Rōmānus, nunc reddō. nihil nisi quiētem quaerō.' cīvēs
tamen mē honōribus onerāvērunt; mē prīncipem, pontificem maximum,
tribūnum creāvērunt et cognōmen mihi dedērunt Augustum.

    sed nunc senex īnfirmus sum. hieme complūrēs tunicās et togam
dēnsissimam gerō. aestāte nusquam dormīre possum nisi in peristȳliō. 15
cum forās eō, petasum in capite habeō. amīcī rīdent, sed nimium aut
calōris aut frīgoris timeō.

    quamquam īnfirmus sum, semper officia dīligentissimē perfēcī. māne
ē somnō excitārī est mihi molestissimum, sed saepe ad multam noctem in
rēs pūblicās incumbō. 20

WORD LIST

*grātia, -ae, *f.*, favour
recipere, to receive back
*dīvidō, -ere, -vīsī, -vīsum, divide
*sors, sortis, *f.*, lot, chance
obvenīre, to fall to one's lot
*Oriēns, -tis, *m.*, the East
*bellum indīcō, -ere, -dixī, -dictum
  (*with dative*), declare war upon
*superātus, -a, -um, having been overcome
aspis, -idis, *f.*, viper, adder
admoveō, -ēre, -mōvī, -mōtum, place
  against

venēnum, -ī, *n.*, poison
*trīgintā, thirty
compōnō, -ere, -posuī -positum,
  arrange, settle
*mandāre, to entrust
*quiēs, -ētis, *f.*, rest, peace
onerāre, to load, burden
*cognōmen, -inis, *n.*, surname
*īnfirmus, -a, -um, weak
*complūrēs, -plūra, several
*dēnsus, -a, -um, thick
forās, out of doors (motion)
petasus, -ī, *m.*, hat

*frigus, -oris, *n.*, cold
*perficiō, -ere, -fēci, -fectum, perform,
carry out

incumbō, -ere, -cubui, -cubitum,
devote oneself to

NOTES

2 **Imperium . . . divīsum est.** In 43 B.C. Octavianus, Antony and Lepidus made an agreement to divide the government of the Roman Empire among themselves. This association is sometimes called 'The Second Triumvirate'.

3 **Cleopātra,** queen of Egypt and a famous beauty of antiquity, with whom first Caesar, then Antony fell in love.
amāvit, fell in love with.

6 **aspidem sibi admōvit,** pressed a viper to her body.

9 **inquam,** I say *or* said (first person of **inquit**).

12 **princeps,** first citizen, a title devised to describe the special position of Augustus.
pontifex maximus, president of the college of priests.

13 **tribūnus,** i.e. **tribūnus plēbis;** the tribunes of the people were officers whose special duties were to look after the interests of the working class.

13 **Augustus,** the equivalent of 'His Majesty'.

14 **tunica,** a garment worn under the toga; also the working garb of slaves and artisans.

15 **peristȳlium,** the formal garden surrounded by a colonnade which formed part of the house of the well-to-do.

16 **nimium calōris,** too much (of) heat.

20 **rēs pūblicās,** affairs of state.

Exercise 3b

redde Anglicē:

prōmittō opus mox cōnfectum īrī.
cīvēs mē prīncipem futūrum esse nōn crēdēbant.
Augustus sē officia dīligentissimē perfēcisse dīcit.
nēmō affirmābit officia ab eō neglēcta esse.
cīvēs Rōmānī sē ā rēgibus rēctum īrī negant.
sē tamen ā prīncipe regī nōn negant.
Augustus sē multīs honōribus onerātum esse dīcit.
eum multīs honōribus onerātum esse legimus.

Language

ferō, ferre, tulī, lātum, *bear, carry, endure*

INDICATIVE

	Active		*Passive*	
Present Tense:	ferō	ferimus	feror	ferimur
	fers	**fertis**	**ferris**	feriminī
	fert	ferunt	**fertur**	feruntur
Future Tense:	feram, ferēs, etc.		ferar, ferēris, etc.	
Imperfect Tense:	ferēbam, ferēbās, etc.		ferēbar, ferēbāris, etc.	
Perfect Tense:	tulī, tulistī, etc.		lātus sum, es, etc.	
Fut. Perf. Tense:	tulerō, tuleris, etc.		lātus erō, eris, etc.	
Pluperfect Tense:	tuleram, tulerās, etc.		lātus eram, erās, etc.	

IMPERATIVE	fer	ferte	ferre	feriminī

INFINITIVE

Present:	ferre	ferrī
Future:	lātūrus, -a, -um esse	lātum īrī
Perfect:	tulisse	lātus, -a, -um esse

It will be seen that, once the principal parts have been learned, only those parts of the present indicative which are printed in heavy type are not formed in the usual way.

Lesson 4

Exercise 4a

Augustus : superstitious or aware of his destiny?

nōnnūllī mē culpant et dīcunt nimis superstitiōsum esse. hanc fābulam
tamen audī et, sī volēs, mē culpā. quīndecim annōs nātus, Cūmās iter
fēcī quod Sibyllam, Dēiphobēn nōmine, cōnsulere volēbam. illa in
cavernā obscūrā et gelidā habitāns cōnsulentibus respōnsa ambigua dabat.
5 intrātūrum mē cēpit pavor ingēns et paulīsper stābam incertus, sed tandem
audācter intrāvī et Sibyllam exspectābam. mox illa in cōnspectum vēnit
rubrīs vestibus amicta et raucā vōce Graecē haec praedīxit: 'sine proeliō
triumphābis; lutum inveniēs, relinquēs marmor; eīs quī tē deum esse
crēdunt tēla invīsa fabricābis'. prīmō eius verba nōn intellēxī sed paulātim
10 mihi aperiēbantur.

vītam simplicem agō; paulum cibī sūmō, pānem domī coctum,
cucumēs, piscēs frīctōs, cāseum, fīcōs. simplicitātem enim et verecundiam
et benignitātem cognōvī semper bonō exemplō omnibus esse.

iam senex sum. ut meus amīcus Quīntus Horātius scrīpsit:
15   'nōn semper īdem flōribus est honor
       vernīs.'

iam fābula paene cōnfecta est, sed putō mē partēs meās honestē ēgisse
et plausū omnium esse dignum.

WORD LIST

*culpāre, to blame
*cōnsulō, -ere, -luī, -ltum, consult
obscūrus, -a, -um, dark
gelidus, -a, -um, icy cold
pavor, -ōris, *m.*, terror, dread
ruber, -bra, -brum, red
amictus, -a, -um, dressed
raucus, -a, -um, hoarse
*praedīcere, to foretell
lutum, -ī, *n.*, mud
*tēlum, -ī, *n.*, weapon
invīsus, -a, -um, unseen
fabricāre, to forge, fashion

*intellegō, -ere, -lēxī, -lēctum, under-
  stand
*paulātim, gradually
*aperīre, to reveal
simplex, -icis, simple
cucumis, -is, *m.*, cucumber
frīctus, -a, -um, fried
cāseus, -eī, *m.*, cheese
simplicitās, -ātis, *f.*, simplicity
verecundia, -ae, *f.*, modesty
*cognōscō, -ere, -nōvī, -nitum, learn
*dignus, -a, -um (*with abl.*), worthy of

NOTES

2 **Cūmae,** a city on the coast of Campania in western Italy, famous for its Sibyl or prophetess.
3 **Dēiphobēn,** accusative of **Dēiphobē,** a Greek name.
4 **habitāns,** living (see Language).
cōnsulentibus, to those consulting her or who consulted her (see Language).
5 **intrātūrum,** as I was about to enter.
11 **paulum cibī,** little (of) food; the genitive case is often used in this way with words denoting quantity, e.g. **multum,** much; **plūs,** more; **minus,** less.
coctum, baked or which had been baked; **domī coctum,** home-baked.
13 **bonō exemplō omnibus esse,** to be (for) a good example to everyone.
14 **Quīntus Horātius,** the famous Roman lyric poet whom we know as Horace. As a young man, he fought in the Civil War *against* Antony and Octavianus, but later was reconciled to Augustus and became his firm friend. He acted as a kind of poet laureate, praising the virtues and exploits of his patron.
15 **nōn semper . . . vernīs,** the flowers of spring do not keep their glory for ever.
17 **partēs meās . . . dignum, partēs agere** means to act a part in a play.
honestē, honourably; note that **honestus** does not mean *honest,* but *honourable.*

Language

Participles

1 **illa in cavernā habitāns cōnsulentibus respōnsa ambigua dabat.**
She, living in a cave, gave obscure replies to those who consulted her (lit. '*to people consulting her*').

habitāns (*nom. sing.*) and **cōnsulentibus** (*dat. pl.*) are examples of the present participle active.

Participles are verbal adjectives and agree in case, number and gender with the noun or pronoun to which they are attached. Thus **habitāns** is nominative, singular, feminine, like **illa** to which it refers.

   Like other adjectives, participles can be used as nouns: so, just as **omnēs** can mean *all people,* so in the above example, **cōnsulentibus** (*dat. pl.*) means *to (people) consulting,* i.e. *to those who consulted her.*

2 **intrātūrum mē cēpit pavor ingēns.** *As I was about to enter great terror seized me.* (lit. '*great terror seized me about to enter*'.)
intrātūrum is the accusative case of the future participle active of **intrāre.**

3 **Antōnius, ad Actium superātus, sē interfēcit.** *Antony, beaten at Actium, killed himself.*
superātus, *beaten* or *having been beaten,* is the perfect participle passive of **superāre.**

23

Verb	Present Participle Active	Future Participle Active	Perfect Participle Passive
superō, -āre, -āvī, -ātum	superāns, -antis	superātūrus, -a, -um	superātus, -a, -um
doceō, -ēre, -uī, doctum	docēns, -entis	doctūrus, -a, -um	doctus, -a, -um
dīcō, -ere, dīxī, dictum	dīcēns, -entis	dictūrus, -a, -um	dictus, -a, -um
capiō, -ere, cēpī, captum	capiēns, -entis	captūrus, -a, -um	captus, -a, -um
audiō, -īre, -īvī, -ītum	audiēns, -entis	audītūrus, -a, -um	audītus, -a, -um
sum, esse, fui	—	futūrus, -a, -um	—
eō, īre, īvī, itum	iēns, euntis	itūrus, -a, -um	—
ferō, ferre, tulī, lātum	ferēns, -entis	lātūrus, -a, -um	lātus, -a, -um

It will be seen that the future participle active and the perfect participle passive are both formed from the stem of the supine—the fourth principal part of the verb.

Note
Declension of Participles :
1 Present participles have the same endings as adjectives of the Third Declension like **ingēns, -entis.**
2 Future and perfect participles are declined as adjectives of the First and Second Declensions, e.g. **bonus, -a, -um.**

Exercise 4b

1 *redde Anglicē :*
Sibyllam ambigua dīcentem Octāviānus attentē audīvit.
Octāviānō in cavernā stantī Sibylla futūra praedīxit.
ab amīcīs forīs exspectantibus vōx audīta est.
cavernam intrātūrus paulīsper stābam.
māne ē somnō excitātus in rēs pūblicās incumbō.
mē Cūmās iter factūrum superstitiōsum esse dīxērunt.

2 *Translate into Latin the words in italics only, using the appropriate participle in each case.*
The boys *playing* in the yard are making a great deal of noise.
So I cannot hear the girl *singing* in the hall.
A stranger accosted me *as I was about to climb* the stairs.
As I was going to leave (depart) he gave me a letter.
The waves battered the ship *which had been abandoned* by the crew.
The crew of the *abandoned* ship have been saved.

Revision Exercises

Revise Infinitives, Indirect Statement, Participles.

A

Translate the following passage using only the help given below. Afterwards check the accuracy of your translation using the General Word List at the end of the book, if necessary.

elephantī mīra nōnnumquam discunt.

dē Elephantīs

ferunt elephantōs animālia esse sagācissima et nōnnumquam discere multa et mīra perficere. affirmāvit quīdam nōnnūllōs etiam per fūnēs ascendere doctōs esse; Mūciānus, ter cōnsul, dīxit elephantum quendam litterās Graecās didicisse et verba eius linguae saepe scrīpsisse.

quis nescit elephantīs memoriam esse tenācissimam? trāditum est elephantum quendam post multōs annōs senem agnōvisse quī iuvenis ōlim fuisset rēctor.

omnēs sciunt elephantōs prīmum ā Rōmānīs vīsōs esse Pyrrhī rēgis bellō. tum enim ille spērābat hostēs speciē elephantōrum territum īrī et prīmō proeliō terga versūrōs esse.

scrībit tamen Plīnius Maior (*Pliny the Elder*) elephantōs, quamvīs corpore maximō, strīdōre porcī vel aspectū mūris minimī ipsōs terrērī.

WORD LIST
ferunt, they say
fūnis, a rope
ter, thrice

trāditum est, it is recorded
quamvīs, although
strīdor, squeal

B

redde Latīnē :

We do not believe that we are safe.
Do you know that you are fortunate?
I think that he is learned.
He thinks that he is learned.
Many think that Augustus was the greatest of the Roman emperors.
He himself said that he was timid (**timidus, -a, -um**).
Antony said that he would not give him an army.
We hear that cities are being destroyed by the pirates.

C

Translate, using the appropriate participle, the words in italics :

While playing in the garden we saw a little mouse.
I was stopped by Publius *as I was about to enter* the house.
Did you see the dog *running* from the butcher's?
Frightened by the earthquake, we stayed indoors.
We saw the Green (**prasina**) *beaten* by the Red (**russāta**).
Dromo gave me the letter *while I was sitting* in the garden.
My friends greeted me *when I was going to leave* for the Forum.
We shall visit the cities *destroyed* by the earthquake.

The Successors of Augustus

Augustus died in A.D. 14 after a long reign of forty years during which the Roman Empire had enjoyed peace and prosperity. He was succeeded by his stepson and adopted son, Tiberius, who was then fifty-six years of age. He was a capable and hard-working ruler under whom order and justice were maintained throughout the Empire. However, he had the misfortune to be a man of unattractive personality who, because of his gloomy and suspicious nature, failed to command the loyalty of the people. For the last ten years of his reign he lived in seclusion in his villa on the island of Capri, exercising a remote control over the state, but leaving the actual administration to subordinates.

When Tiberius died in A.D. 37 he was succeeded by his grand-nephew Gaius, better known as Caligula—an affectionate nickname given him from the **caligae,** soldiers' boots, which he wore as a child in the camp of his father, the well-loved Germanicus. His accession was hailed with joy, and for a time there was an atmosphere of relaxation following the stern rule of Tiberius. Soon however, following a severe illness, he suffered some kind of mental disorder which changed him to a monster of vice and cruelty. Among the more harmless of his excesses was the appointment of his horse as a consul! He was murdered in A.D. 41 by officers of the Praetorian Guard.

It was the same Praetorian Guard who selected the next emperor— Claudius, uncle of Caligula, a man with little to recommend him for high office. He had been the butt of his nephew's wit, and was regarded in the court as an eccentric. However, he proved himself an energetic and competent emperor. He inaugurated great public works, reorganised the civil service and introduced a vigorous foreign policy. He undertook the conquest and settlement of Britain, which had been left unmolested since the visits of Julius Caesar in 55 and 54 B.C. He died in A.D. 54, poisoned, it was believed, by the orders of his wife Agrippina who coveted the imperial power for her son Nero.

Lesson 5

Exercise 5a

Festus autem volēns Iūdaeīs grātiam praestāre, respondēns Paulō dīxit: vīs Hierosolymam ascendere et ibi dē hīs iūdicārī apud mē? dīxit autem Paulus: ad tribūnal Caesaris stō ubi mē oportet iūdicārī . . . Caesarem appellō. tunc Festus cum cōnsiliō locūtus respondit: Caesarem appellāvistī: ad Caesarem ībis. (*Acts* 25:9–12)

Caesar is a name that most school pupils associate only with the famous Gaius Julius Caesar who invaded Britain and was assassinated on the Ides of March, 44 B.C., but it became one of the official names of the Roman emperors, beginning with Augustus.

The Caesar referred to in the Acts of the Apostles 25:10 was the Emperor Nero who ruled from A.D. 54 to A.D. 68 and about whom there have been different opinions. A few have called him genius, but more have named him monster or madman.

itinere dēfessus ad pedēs Nerōnis nūntius concidit. anhēlāns, 'domine,' inquit, 'ardet Rōma!' ūnus ex comitibus Nerōnis, ubi hoc audīvit, 'aliud incendium!' inquit. 'nōnne vigilēs id exstinguere possunt?'

primō Nerō rem parvī faciēbat, sed ubi alius post alium nūntiāvit
5 incendium magnō ventō dispergī, multās urbis regiōnēs vāstātās esse, plūrimōs cīvēs iam periisse, perturbātus prīnceps equum ad sē dūcī iussit. tōtam per noctem iter fēcit cum paucīs comitibus et, ubi prīmā lūce ad montēm Albānum pervēnit, fūmum incendiī procul cōnspexit.

regiōnēs vāstātās Nerō circumībat et promittēbat cibum in urbem
10 statim portātum īrī. cīvēs tamen eum neglegēbant. nocte et interdiū per viās ambulābat, sed paucī eum agnōvērunt. subitō quīdam, ubi eum vīdit, 'nōnne,' inquit 'tū Caesar es? nunc occīdēris manū meā, nam tuō iussū Rōma incēnsa est!' Nerō pectus nūdāvit, sed homō dubitāvit et tandem gladium abiēcit.

15 quārtā nocte incendiī Tigellīnus Nerōnī, 'quīn, domine,' inquit, 'dē incendiō Rōmae cantās?' ille statim citharam cēpit et in sōlārium ambulāvit. nesciōquis pauper, quī ad īmum collem habitābat, eum cōnspexit et brevī per urbem ferēbātur fāma Nerōnem ipsum Rōmam incendī iussisse: eum enim dē Rōmā ārdentī cantāre voluisse.

WORD LIST

*nūntius, -iī, *m.*, messenger
concidō, -ere, cidī, fall down, sink down
anhēlāre, to pant, gasp
*ārdeō, -ēre, ārsī, ārsum, be on fire
*comes, -itis, *m. or f.*, companion, comrade
*incendium, -iī, *n.*, fire, conflagration
*exstinguō, -ere, -īnxī, -īnctum, put out (a fire)
dispergō, -ere, -sī, -sum, scatter, spread
*regiō, -ōnis, *f.*, district
*vāstāre, to lay waste
*fūmus, -ī, *m.*, smoke

*cōnspiciō, -ere, -spexī, -spectum, catch sight of, see
circumīre, to go round, inspect
*prōmittō, -ere, -mīsī, -missum, promise
*interdiū, by day
*agnōscō, -ere, -nōvī, -nitum, recognise
*pectus, -oris, *n.*, breast
nūdāre, to bare
*dubitāre, to hesitate, doubt
cithara, -ae, *f.*, lyre, guitar
sōlārium, -iī, *n.*, sunny spot, terrace, balcony
*fāma, -ae, *f.*, rumour, report

NOTES

3 **vigilēs**, seven cohorts, chiefly of freedmen, who served not only as police, but also as fire brigade.

4 **parvī faciēbat**, considered of little importance, made light of: **parvī**, genitive of value. See page 79.

5 **multās regiōnēs**, Rome was divided into fourteen districts.

15 **Tigellīnus**, the most unpopular of Nero's favourites.
   quin, why . . . not?

17 **ad imum collem**, at the foot of the hill: **imus**, lowest.

Exercise 5b

An Early Aviator

ōlim Nerō, quī artis magicae studiōsus erat, audīvit Simōnem quendam Galilaeum affirmāre sē volāre posse. comitī quī adstābat, 'dūc eum ad mē,' inquit, 'nam eum ad documentum prōvocāre volō.' Simōnī, ut vēnit, multum pecūniae prōmittit sī rem bene gesserit.

spectāculum in parvō Nerōnis Circō datur. in tribūnālī stat Simōn et   5
postquam ālās paulīsper extendit, in āera īnsilit. ēheu, nōn diū volat; ad humum magnō fragōre cadit.

eō tempore tamen nōn periit, sed brevī post pudōre superātus dē tēctō domūs sē dēiēcit atque ita dēcessit ē vītā.

Nerō, ubi hoc audīvit, īrātus amīcīs 'neque astrologī,' inquit, 'neque   10
magī ea mē docēre possunt quae discere cupiō, sed illī tam miserī Galilaeī ea mē docēre cupiunt quae scīre nōlō.'

WORD LIST

Galilaeus, Galilean
magicus, -a, -um, magic
*studiōsus, -a, -um (*with gen.*), devoted to
*volāre, to fly
documentum, -ī, *n.,* proof
*prōvocāre, to challenge
tribūnal, -is, *n.,* raised platform
āla, -ae, *f.,* wing
extendō, -ere, -tendī, -tentum or **tēnsum,** stretch or spread out

īnsiliō, -īre, -uī, leap into
*fragor, -ōris, *m.,* crash
*pudor, -ōris, *m.,* sense of shame
*tēctum, -ī, *n.,* roof
*dēiciō, -ere, -iēcī, -iectum, throw down
astrologus, -ī, *m.,* astrologer
magus, -ī, *m.,* a learned man and magician

NOTES

3 **ut,** when.
4 **sī rem bene gesserit,** if he proved successful.
6 **in ǣra,** into the air: a Greek form of the accusative of **āēr, āeris,** *m.*

ēheu! nōn diū volābit.

30

Exercise 5c

(a) redde Anglicē:
Nerō nūntium anhēlantem ad sē dūcī iussit.
tandem sē Rōmam festīnātūrum esse dīxit.
urbem ingentī incendiō vāstārī invēnit.
homō Nerōnem occīsūrus gladium abiēcisse dīcitur.
crēdisne Nerōnem ipsum urbem incendī iussisse?
Nerōnem ferunt artis magicae studiōsum fuisse.
Simōn in tribūnālī stāns ālās extendit.
eum ad humum magnō fragōre cecidisse dīcunt.

(b) redde Latīnē:
Simon declared that he would fly.
Nero promised to give him money.
The citizens watched Simon stretching his wings.
Many say that he cannot fly.
They say that no one can fly.
Alas! I hear that he has been killed.

Language

fīō, fīěrī, factus sum, *become, be made, be done, happen.*
This verb serves as the passive voice of **facere.**

INDICATIVE

Present Tense:	fīō	—
	fīs	—
	fit	fiunt
Future Tense:	fīam, fīēs, etc.	
Imperfect Tense:	fīēbam, fīēbās, etc.	
Perfect Tense:	factus sum, es, etc.	
Fut. Perf. Tense:	factus erō, eris, etc.	
Pluperfect Tense:	factus eram, erās, etc.	

INFINITIVE

Present:	fīěrī
Future;	factum īrī
Perfect:	factus-a-um esse

Lesson 6

Exercise 6a

Read the following passage and, with the aid of the notes, try to understand it. Then answer, in English, the questions printed below. Finally, translate the passage into English, using the General Word List if necessary.

A Cure for a Bad Conscience

magnō terrōre Nerō exanimātur; dormīre nōn potest; nam in somniīs effigiēs Britannicī, quem venēnō necāverat, et Octāviae uxōris et Agrippīnae mātris, quās per Anicētum lībertum interfēcerat, semper eum agitant. sēcum saepe reputat: 'ubi tandem remedium terrōris meī invenīrī potest?'

ūnus ex amīcīs Nerōnī 'crēdō,' inquit, 'tē in carminibus solācium inventūrum esse.' Nerō igitur carmina et praecipuē nēniās, quārum erat studiōsus, compōnere coepit. Tigellīnus ōlim eum maximē dēlectāvit quod nūntiāvit ūnam eius nēniārum in balneīs in ōre omnium esse. eō magis cupiēbat in theātrō cantāre et omnium cīvium accipere plausum.

quōdam diē post merīdiem magna multitūdō ad theātrum convēnit. omnēs enim audīverant Nerōnem in scaenā cantātūrum esse. prīmō trepidābat, sed posteā satis bene

Britannicus, son of the Emperor Claudius

praecipuē, especially
nēnia, ditty, popular or folk-song

ōs, ōris, *n.*, the mouth
eō magis, the more (*lit.* by that amount the more)

in scaenā, on the stage
trepidāre, to be excited

cantāvit ad citharam. erant autem in theātrō multī quī iussī erant signō datō plaudere et Nerōnī acclāmāre. hoc fēcērunt ubi Senecam et Burrum vīdērunt togās movēre, et multitūdō eōrum clāmōrem ac plausum excēpit. 'bene, Caesar!' exclāmāvit. 'est tibi vōx sānē dīvīna.' Nerō, gaudiō ēlātus, in omnēs partēs bāsia iactābat.

ad citharam, to the accompaniment of the lyre
signō datō, at a given signal
Seneca, writer and tutor of Nero
Burrus, prefect of the guard, who with Seneca helped to restrain Nero during the first part of his reign
excipere, to take up

Questions

(a) Why was Nero unable to sleep?

(b) What prompted Nero to write songs?

(c) **in balneīs in ōre omnium esse.** Why **in balneīs**? What do you know of **balnea**?
Give the natural English equivalent of: **in ōre omnium esse.**

(d) Why did Nero especially wish to sing in the theatre? Describe a Roman theatre. Name any famous one of which you have heard. Would the size of audience be similar to that of your local theatre?

(e) Who were the cheer leaders and what cue did they give to the people?

(f) How did Nero respond to the applause?

Exercise 6b

What are the direct words?
Example: coquus cēnam parātam esse dīcit.
          direct: cēna parāta est.
flōrēs vernōs pulcherrimōs esse putō.
quis nescit elephantīs memoriam esse tenācissimam?
negō hominem ālīs umquam volātūrum esse.
audīvit prīnceps nūntium pervēnisse.
tibi vōcem esse dīvīnam crēdō.
sōlācium in carminibus inventum īrī crēdimus.
omnēs negāvērunt sē umquam tantum incendium vīdisse.
ignem brevī exstīnctum īrī negāmus.

Exercise 6c

Translate by means of a participle the words printed in italics.
Many came to meet Augustus *as he was about to enter* the city.
He reassured the minds of the citizens *terrified* by rumours of his severity.

The news was given to Nero *as he sat* in his palace.
As he was about to leave (i.e. depart) another messenger reached him.
When he reached the hill, he saw the city *devastated* by the fire.
As he was about to kill Nero the man hesitated.
Ignored (i.e. neglected) by the citizens he retired to his palace.

From Nero to Trajan

Nero is remembered today chiefly by the proverb *to fiddle while Rome burns.* Whatever the truth may be about his conduct during the Great Fire of Rome, we know that during the later years of his rule he behaved as a tyrant and a madman. In the end, condemned to death by the Senate and deserted by the Praetorian Guard, the Emperor's 'Household Troops', he took his own life.

Rome in flames

Nero's reign was a time of peace and prosperity in the far-flung Roman Empire, the frontiers of which were guarded by strong armies under vigorous commanders. These armies now took a hand in the appointment of Nero's successor, and within one year—A.D. 69—four generals in turn were proclaimed emperor.

Vespasian, the choice of the armies of the East, overcame his rivals and became the first of the **Flavian** emperors, so-called from his name, T. Flavius Vespasianus. He was a good ruler and gave stable government to the Empire. No matter how good the emperor was, the populace of Rome still had to be appeased with doles of free bread and oil and free shows in the circus or amphitheatre. The most spectacular monument to Vespasian is the now ruined **Colosseum,** the amphitheatre which he began in A.D. 72 and which was still unfinished when he died in A.D. 79.

The Colosseum

34

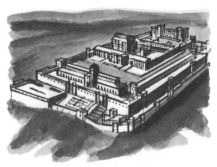

The Temple at Jerusalem

Titus, son of Vespasian, who succeeded his father, was already famous as the conqueror of the Jews, whose temple at Jerusalem he destroyed in A.D. 70. He was an able and popular emperor, but unfortunately died only two years after his accession. The most famous event of his reign was the destruction of Pompeii and Herculaneum by an eruption of Mount Vesuvius in A.D. 79.

81-96 AD

Domitian, who succeeded his brother Titus, enjoyed none of the popularity of his predecessor and his reign is described by the historians as a time of fear and repression. Yet he established good government in the provinces and carried out a programme of road-building in Italy and abroad. He did much rebuilding in Rome itself, where the Temple of Jupiter Capitolinus was his most famous monument. A revolt against him by one of his commanders was the signal for the start of a reign of terror which lasted for eight years until he was murdered in A.D. 96.

Nerva
96-98 AD

Nerva, a good lawyer and a man of peace, was chosen by the Senate to succeed Domitian. Recognising that the Empire needed a strong hand he adopted as his colleague and successor M. Ulpius Traianus—Trajan, the commander of the army in Upper Germany. After two years Nerva died and Trajan, who forms the subject of your next lesson, became emperor.

The Temple of Jupiter Capitolinus

35

Lesson 7

Exercise 7a

The Roman historians have not told us very much about Trajan, emperor from A.D. 98 to 117. Most of our information is derived from the letters of Pliny the Younger, who, while he was governor of the province of Bithynia, kept up a steady correspondence with the emperor, asking his advice on many problems of administration about which he was in doubt, the formation of a fire brigade, for instance, and the treatment and punishment of Christians, as you will learn from the following passages.

C. Plīnius Trāiānō Imp.

dum dīversam partem prōvinciae circumeō, Nīcomēdīae vāstissimum incendium multās prīvātōrum domōs et duo pūblica opera dēlēvit. lātius autem sparsum est, prīmum violentiā ventī, deinde inertiā hominum; oppidānī enim stābant ōtiōsī et immōbilēs neque auxilium dabant;
5 praetereā nūllus erat usquam sīphō, nūlla hama, nūllum īnstrūmentum quō incendia cohibērī possunt. haec tamen omnia, ut iam iussī, parābuntur. ego, domine, collēgium fabrōrum, nōn amplius CL hominum, īnstituī volō, sed prōmittō nēminem nisi fabrum in collēgium receptum īrī. nec erit difficile custōdīre tam paucōs.

Trāiānus Plīniō s.   *especially*

scrībis tē collēgium fabrōrum apud Nicomēdēnsēs instituere velle.
mementō tamen prōvinciam istam et praecipuē eās cīvitātēs ā factiōnibus
eius modī iam vexātās esse. quodcunque nōmen dederimus eīs quī in idem
contractī erunt, hetaeriae fīent. melius igitur erit ea comparārī quibus
ignēs coercērī possunt. dominōs quoque praediōrum monē eōs ipsōs 15
cohibēre ignēs dēbēre. postrēmō, sī rēs postulābit, auxilium eōrum quī
adstābunt advocā.

WORD LIST

*diversus, -a, -um, different
*vāstus, -a, -um, huge, enormous
*prīvātus, -ī, *m.*, private individual
*lātē, widely
*spargō, -ere, -sī, -sum, spread
violentia, -ae, *f.*, violence
inertia, -ae, *f.*, laziness, inactivity
*oppidānī, -ōrum, *m.pl.*, townspeople
immōbilis, -is, -e, motionless, unmoved
*usquam, anywhere
siphō, -ōnis, *m.*, fire-engine
hama, -ae, *f.*, water-bucket
instrūmentum, -ī, *n.*, apparatus
*cohibēre, coercēre, to check, contain, control

*amplius, more
instituō, -ere, -uī, -ūtum, establish, found
recipere, to admit
*iste, -a, -ud, that (of yours)
factiō, -ōnis, *f.*, party, association
*modus, -ī, *m.*, kind, manner
*vexāre, to trouble, plague
contrahō, -ere, -xī, -tractum, collect, assemble
praedium, -iī, *n.*, estate
*moneō, -ēre, -uī, -itum, advise, warn
*postulāre, to demand
advocāre, to summon, call to one's aid

NOTES

1 **Nicomēdiae,** in Nicomedia, the capital of Bithynia.
2 **opera,** buildings.
7 **collēgium,** guild of people engaged in the same trade or profession.
  faber, generally a worker in wood, stone or metal; here a fireman.
11 **apud Nicomēdēnsēs,** among the people of Nicomedia.
12 **mementō,** remember: imperative of **meminī, -isse.**
13 **quodcunque nōmen,** whatever name.
  in idem, for the same purpose.
14 **hetaeriae,** clubs. The Romans were unwilling that conquered peoples should meet together in any great numbers in case they should abuse the privilege given in order to plot against the Roman power.

Language

The Locative case

Nicomēdiae, in *or* at Nicomedia. This is an example of the Locative case which is found with the names of towns and small islands.

How to recognise the Locative case:

Name	Form
1 Place names belonging to the first and second declensions singular, e.g. **Rōma, Corinthus**	same form as genitive —**Rōmae, Corinthī.**
2 Place names having a plural form—any declension—e.g. **Athēnae, -ārum,** *Athens,* **Gādēs, -ium,** *Cadiz*	same form as ablative —**Athēnis, Gādibus.**
3 All other place-names (towns and small islands), e.g. **Carthāgō, -inis,** *Carthage; also* **domus,** *home,* **rūs,** *the country,* **humus,** *the ground*	ending **-ī—Carthāginī, domī, rūrī, humī.**

Exercise 7b

The provincial governor, troubled about the Christians, asks his chief for advice.

C. Plīnius Trāiānō Imp.

soleō, domine, omnia dē quibus dubitō ad tē referre. quis enim potest melius vel cūnctātiōnem meam regere vel īgnōrantiam docēre?

nunc dē Christiānīs magnopere dubitō et saepe mēcum reputō,
5 'dēbetne aliquod discrīmen aetātum esse? dēbetne venia darī eī quī Christiānus fuit sed iam esse dēstitit?' intereā in eīs quī apud mē tamquam Christiānī accūsābantur, hoc fēcī. ipsōs interrogāvī: 'estisne Christiānī?' sī sē esse dīxērunt, iterum iterumque interrogāvī. sī tamen persevērāvērunt, ad supplicium dūcī iussī. neque enim dubitābam eōrum obstinātiōnem
10 dēbēre punīrī.

prōpositus est mihi libellus sine auctōre, multōrum nōmina continēns quī negābant sē aut esse aut fuisse Christiānōs. ubi deōs appellāvērunt et imāginī tuae supplicāvērunt, praetereā maledīxērunt Christō, ego eōs līberārī dēbēre putāvī.

WORD LIST
*referō, -ferre, rettulī, relātum, report, refer to
*cūnctātiō, -ōnis, *f.,* delay, hesitation
ignōrantia, -ae, *f.,* ignorance
*discrīmen, -inis, *n.,* distinction
*aetās, -ātis, *f.,* age
*venia, -ae, *f.,* pardon

persevērāre, to persist
*dēsistō, -ere, dēstitī, cease
obstinātiō, -ōnis, *f.,* stubbornness
prōpōnere, to place before
imāgō, -inis, *f.,* statue, picture
supplicāre, to worship (*with dative*)
maledīcere, to curse, revile (*with dative*)

38

NOTES
2 **soleō,** I am accustomed.
4 **magnopere,** greatly.
5 **aliquod discrīmen,** some distinction.
6 **in eīs,** in the case of those.
tamquam, on the grounds of being.
9 **ad supplicium,** to punishment, death.
11 **libellus sine auctōre,** an anonymous pamphlet or letter.
continēns, containing.

Exercise 7c

More about the Christians.

aliī, ab indice nōminātī, fuisse sē Christiānōs dīxērunt, quīdam ante trēs annōs, quīdam ante plūrēs annōs, sed 'hoc modŏ,' inquiunt, 'commīsimus. quōdam diē ante lūcem convēnimus et carmen Christō quasi deō dīximus et iūrāvimus nōs neque furta commissūrōs esse neque fidem falsūrōs. haec ubi fēcimus, domum discessimus. rursus convēnimus et cibum ūnā 5 cēpimus.'

dē duābus ancillīs, quae ministrae appellābantur, per tormenta quaesīvī. sed nihil invēnī nisi superstitiōnem prāvam. quod rēs mihi vīsa est gravissima, tē cōnsulere festīnāvī.

Trāiānus Plīniō s. 10
bene fēcistī, mī Secunde, quod causās eōrum quī Christiānī esse dīcēbantur, excussistī. nōn omnēs tamen eōdem locō habērī dēbent. illī nōn quaerendī sunt; sī tamen accūsātī sunt, pūniendī sunt. eīs quī negāvērunt sē Christiānōs esse et nostrīs dīs supplicāvērunt, venia est danda. libellī sine auctōre, sī tibi prōpositī sunt, in nullō crīmine locum habēre dēbent. 15

WORD LIST
index, -icis, *m.,* informer
committere, to be guilty of
★**iūrāre,** to swear
★**fūrtum, -ī,** *n.,* theft
★**fidem fallō, -ere, fefellī, falsum,** break one's word
★**ūnā,** together
ancilla, -ae, *f.,* serving maid

superstitiō, -ōnis, *f.,* superstition
prāvus, -a, -um, perverse, wicked, vicious
★**gravis, -is, -e,** important, serious
★**causa, -ae,** *f.,* case
excutiō, -ere, -cussī, -cussum, examine
★**crīmen, -inis,** *n.,* charge, accusation

NOTES
1 **nōminātus, -a, -um,** named.
  ante trēs annōs, three years before.
2 **modŏ,** only.
3 **lūcem,** i.e. **prīmam lūcem,** dawn.
4 **iūrāvimus . . . falsūrōs,** the reference is to the eighth and ninth commandments (Exodus 20: 15, 16).
7 **ministrae,** deaconesses.
  per tormenta quaerere dē, to examine under torture.
12 **locō** here means *category* or *class*.

Language

The Gerundive

Note the forms **quaerendī, pūniendī, danda** used in Trajan's reply to Pliny about the Christians. They are examples of the *gerundive*, a part of the verb which expresses necessity or obligation, e.g.

dandus, -a, -um, *requiring to be given*
exercendus, -a, -um, *requiring to be trained*
quaerendus, -a, -um, *requiring to be sought*
capiendus, -a, -um, *requiring to be captured*
pūniendus, -a, -um, *requiring to be punished*

Thus **illī nōn quaerendī sunt** is to be translated *they must not be, should not be, ought not to be, sought out.*

From Trajan to Marcus Aurelius

Among the monuments which the visitor to Rome will wish to see is **Trajan's Column,** a pillar rising to a height of 38 metres in Trajan's Forum and bearing a sculptured band running round it spirally from base to top which records the events of Trajan's campaigns in Dacia, a state lying to the north of the Danube and corresponding roughly to the modern Romania. This monument reminds us that Trajan, while he was a moderate and wise ruler at home, was also a vigorous commander in the field.

Trajan was succeeded by Hadrian (117–138), who is commemorated by the defensive system which runs across the North of England known as

Trajan's Column

Hadrian's Wall. While the emperors of this period practised none of the extravagances of men like Nero, the populace of Rome remained no less dependent than formerly on free doles of bread, wine and oil. The city itself might be the centre of the Empire, but the real life of that Empire was lived out in the provinces—a fact clearly recognised by Hadrian, who spent more than half of his twenty-one years out of Italy visiting all but the most remote parts of the Empire.

Hadrian, shortly before his death, nominated as his successor T. Aurelius Antoninus, a man more distinguished in the civil than in the military sphere. Unlike Hadrian, he seldom travelled abroad, but gave the Empire more than twenty years of good government. While he never visited Britain in person, his name is commemorated by the **Wall of Antoninus,** built across the Forth-Clyde isthmus in Scotland and constructed for him by Q. Lollius Urbicus in A.D. 142. The senate, in recognition of his devotion to the state, gave him the title **Pius** and he is known to history as Antoninus Pius. Before his death he nominated as his successor his nephew M. Aelius Aurelius, who became known as the emperor Marcus Aurelius. You will gain some impression of this emperor in your next lesson.

41

Lesson 8

Exercise 8a

Marcus Aurelius, who became emperor in A.D. 161, was the fifth in a line of good emperors under whose rule the peoples of the Empire enjoyed prosperity, and, except for the inevitable frontier wars, peace. Marcus Aurelius is remembered as the philosopher emperor, who, if he had not been Roman emperor, would still have won fame by his writings as a philosopher.

facta nōn verba—The Practical Philosopher

fūnambulus

Marcum Aurēlium Antōnīnum ferunt benignitāte fuisse īnsignem et in aliōs beneficia saepe contulisse multīs et mīrīs modīs.

ubi enim fūnambulum quendam, puerum quīndecim annōrum, cecidisse et laesum esse audīvit, culcitās statim iussit omnibus fūnambulīs
5 dehinc subicī.

ōlim māter blandā vōce, 'mī Marce,' inquit, 'sī ōtiōsus es, tēcum paulīsper colloquī volō.' Marcus rīdēns, 'quid est, māter?' inquit, 'nimis sevēra mehercule hodiē esse vidēris.'

'rēs gravissima mihi est in animō, sed tū in studia intentus eam nōn
10 cognōvistī.'

'rem mihi expōne, mea māter, et expōnentem tē attentissimē audiam.'

'nōnne audīvistī brevī sorōrem tuam esse nūptūram sed minimam tum dōtem, ēheu! habitūram. tū autem nōnne iam diū philosophus es

42

inter omnēs virtūte praeclārissimus? nōnne iam didicistī dīvitiās parvī
aestimāre?' 15
   'cur ita mihi blandīris, māter? quid est quod tū ā mē impetrāre vīs?'
   'ōlim, mī fīlī, patrimōnium accēpistī ā patre relictum. vīsne sorōrī
partem dare nūptūrae? sī enim eam accēperit, laeta illa nūbet, tū reliquā
parte fortasse vīvēs contentus.'
   'immō, māter. tōtum eī dabō. sī enim illa laeta patrimōnium accipiet, 20
ego etiam laetior illī trādam.'
   'ō fīlium pium ac benignum! nunc enim tē sciō philosophum nōn
nōmine modŏ sed rēvērā esse.'

WORD LIST

*insignis, -is, -e, famous
*beneficium, -iī, n., act of kindness
*cōnferō, -ferre, -tulī, collātum, bestow
fūnambulus, -ī, m., ropewalker
*laedō, -ere, laesī, laesum, hurt, injure
culcita, -ae, f., mattress
*dehinc, in future
subiciō, -ere, -iēcī, -iectum, put under
blandus, -a, -um, wheedling
*colloquī, to talk, converse
sevērus, -a, -um, serious
intentus, -a, -um, intent (upon)
*studium, -iī, n., study

*expōnō, -ere, -posuī, -positum, explain
*nūbō, -ere, nūpsī, nūptum, wed (see notes)
dōs, dōtis, f., dowry
*aestimāre, to reckon, put a value on
blandīrī, to coax
impetrāre, to gain (a request)
patrimōnium, -iī, n., inheritance
*reliquus, -a, -um, remaining
*contentus, -a, -um, content
*pius, -a, -um, dutiful
*benignus, -a, -um, kind, generous
*rēvērā, in reality

NOTES

1 benignitāte, for, i.e. because of, his liberality.
5 subicī, to be put under: present infin. passive of subicere.
12 nūptūram esse, is about to marry: nūbere is *to marry* when the woman is the subject, dūcere, when the man is the subject.
13 iam diū philosophus es, you have been a philosopher for a long time (and still are).
14 virtūs, here means *virtue*; a commoner meaning is *courage*—the quality of a man (vir).
   parvī, of little account.
16 mihi blandīris, you coax me. blandīrī (followed by dative) is passive in form but has an active meaning.
17 relictum, left.
18 nūptūrae, on her marriage; *lit.*, to your sister, about to marry.
20 immō, on the contrary.
22 fīlium . . . benignum, what a dutiful and generous son!

Exercise 8b

Read the following passage and try to understand it with the aid of the notes. Then answer in English the questions below. Finally, translate it into English, using the General Word List if necessary.

How the Thundering Legion (The Twelfth) got its name

ōlim, dum Marcus Aurēlius contrā Quādōs bellum gerit, eius exercitus ingentī multitūdine barbarōrum cīnctus est. mīlitēs igitur, quoniam neque sē recipere neque prae sitī et calōre pugnāre iam poterant, dē salūte dēspērāre coepērunt. tum ad imperātōrem vēnit praefectus duodecimae legiōnis quae Mytilēnēnsis erat. 'nōnne scīs, imperātor,' inquit, 'mīlitēs legiōnis duodecimae paene omnēs Christiānōs esse? cūr nōn eōs iubēs Deum suum ōrāre? quicquid enim Christiānī precibus petunt, id, ut affirmant, Deus eōrum concēdit.' itaque Marcus, ubi haec audīvit, statim ad Mytilēnēnsēs contendit et eōs auxilium ā Deō petere iussit. 'sī enim ille' inquit 'vōs audīverit et nōbīs tulerit auxilium, maxima ipsī laus tribuētur, glōriam quoque maximam duodecima legiō habēbit.' nūlla mora; mīlitēs Deum ōrant omnēs. ecce! statim caelum nūbibus obscūrātur. simul imber maximus Rōmānīs īnfūsus sitim levāvit; simul barbarī fulmine dē caelō dēiectō perterritī fūgērunt.

Marcus attonitus Christiānōs ēdictō honōrāvit et legiōnī duodecimae nōmen Fulminātam in fūtūrum dedit.

Quādī, a Germanic tribe

quoniam, since
prae (+*abl.*), because of
sitī, abl. of **sitis,** thirst
salūs, -ūtis, *f.*, safety
Mytilēnēnsis, belonging to Mytilene, capital city of Lesbos

quicquid, whatever
precēs, -um, *f.pl.*, prayer

concēdere, to grant

laus, laudis, *f.*, praise

nūbēs, -is, *f.*, cloud
īnfūsus, pouring on
fulmen, -inis, *n.*, flash of lightning, thunderbolt

ēdictō, with a public proclamation

Questions

1 Describe the plight of the Roman army.
2 Why did the Romans not fight their way out?
3 Were the spirits of the Roman soldiers high?
4 Why did the whole army not pray to God?
5 Was Marcus Aurelius himself a Christian?
6 Did he take some time to consider the commander's suggestion? On which Latin word or words do you base your answer?
7 Did the Christian legionaries require time to consider the emperor's request? On which Latin word or words do you base your answer?
8 The Quadi were a German tribe living in a region corresponding to part of the modern Czechoslovakia; Mytilene was the capital of Lesbos, a Greek island in the Aegean Sea. What conclusion would you draw regarding the composition of the Roman army?

Exercise 8c

1 *redde Latinē :*
(a) The soldiers said that they could not fight.
(b) The general believed that the army would be destroyed.
(c) The brigadier (**praefectus**) said that the Christians would pray to God.
(d) 'The army must be saved,' he said, 'with your God's help.'
(e) The Christians promised to pray.
(f) They said that God would hear their prayers.
(g) They soon saw the sky darkened with clouds.
(h) 'In future,' said Marcus, 'the Twelfth will be called the Thundering Legion.'

2 *redde Anglicē :*
(a) Marcus propter benignitātem laudandus est.
(b) praefectus Deum ōrandum esse dīxit.
(c) imperātor legiōnem duodecimam honōrandam esse putāvit.
(d) 'Christiānīs,' inquit, 'grātiae agendae sunt.'
(e) propter eōs enim exercitum servātum esse dīcō.

Lesson 9

Towards the end of the third century A.D. the Roman Empire was governed by four rulers. In 308 Constantine succeeded his father as ruler of Britain and Gaul, but over the next sixteen years he set himself to overcome the other three claimants to imperial power and in 324 he succeeded in becoming sole ruler of the Roman Empire. In 313 he and Licinius, who controlled the East, met at Milan and agreed to grant all their subjects the right to worship as they pleased. Constantine himself, shortly before his death, was baptised as a Christian and from that time Christianity became the official religion of the Roman Empire.

Exercise 9a

Cōnstantius, Cōnstantīnī pater, quī Britanniae et Galliae et Hispāniae praeerat, ad Galērium nūntium mīsit sē fīlium vidēre velle; sē enim aegrōtāre et brevī fortasse ē vītā excessūrum esse. Galērius tamen, quod fraudem timēbat, recūsāvit: dīxit tamen sē dē rē dēlīberātūrum esse.
5 tandem, postquam diū prōcrāstināvit rem, Cōnstantīnum advocāvit et diplōma dedit signātum.

Galērius autem māne solēbat, simul ac rēs pūblicās cōnfēcit, bene cēnāre, neque quisquam eō tempore sinēbātur eum adīre. itaque postrīdiē, ubi eum paenituit Cōnstantīnum dīmīsisse et revocāre voluit, nēmō
10 aderat quī mandāta cōnficeret. ubi tandem cognitum est illum prīdiē post merīdiem ad Galliam discessisse, mīlitēs iussī sunt persequī.

sed nusquam invenīrī potuit; omnium enim equōrum quī erant per viās dispositī, poplitēs succīderat. itaque effūgit atque iter fēcit incolumis ad Portum Itium ubi patrem invēnit bellum contrā Pictōs parantem.
15 Cōnstantius, postquam rem bene gessit, Eborācum rediit atque ibi subitō obiit mortem. statim ab exercitū Cōnstantīnus ūnā vōce appellātus est Augustus.

WORD LIST

*praesum, -esse, -fui, rule, command (*with dative*)
*aegrōtāre, to be ill
*fraus, -dis, *f.,* trickery, deception
recūsāre, to refuse
*dēlīberāre, to consider, weigh carefully

prōcrāstināre, to put off (till tomorrow)
signātus, -a, -um, sealed
*simul ac, as soon as
*sinō, -ere, sīvī, situm, allow
*adīre, to approach (compound of **ire,** to go)

*pridiē, the day before
dispōnō, -ere, -posui, -positum, place
  in different places
poples, -itis, *m.*, knee
succidō, -ere, -cīdī, -cīsum, cut down
  or through

*effugiō, ere, -fūgī, -fugitum, escape
*incolumis, -is, -e, safe, unharmed
*obire mortem, to die

NOTES

2 **Galerius Maximiānus** ruled as Emperor with Constantius from A.D. 305 to 311.
3 **excessūrum esse: excēdere** means *to depart.*
6 **diplōma,** an official letter of recommendation given to people who travelled to the
  provinces; a kind of passport.
7 **Galērius autem,** now Galerius.
8 **neque quisquam,** and no one.
9 **eum paenituit,** it repented him, i.e. he regretted.
10 **qui . . . cōnficeret,** who might carry out, i.e. to carry out.
11 **persequi,** to pursue.
13 **dispositī,** posted at intervals.
   poplitem succīdere, to hamstring.
14 **Portus Itius,** Boulogne.
   Pictī, the Picts, inhabitants of Caledonia.
   parantem, preparing.
15 **Eborācum,** York.

Language

Impersonal verbs

eum paenituit Cōnstantīnum dīmīsisse, lit. *It repented him to have let
Constantine go,* i.e. *He regretted having let Constantine go,* or *He was sorry that
he had let Constantine go.*

paenituit (*pres.* **paenitet**) is an example of an *impersonal verb,* so called
because it does not have a personal subject.

Present Indicative

mē paenitet	*I repent*	**nōs paenitet**	*we repent*
tē paenitet	*you repent*	**vōs paenitet**	*you repent*
eum paenitet	*he repents*	**eōs paenitet**	*they repent*

future: **paenitēbit;** *imperfect:* **paenitēbat;** *perfect:* **paenituit**

Other verbs of the same type are:

mē pudet	*I am ashamed*
mē miseret	*I pity*
mē taedet	*I am weary*

47

Notes

1 Such verbs are followed either by an infinitive as above, or by a noun or pronoun in the genitive case, e.g.

mē pudet errōris, *I am ashamed of my mistake.*

eum miseret nostrī, *He pities us.*

2 In Latin, as in English, impersonal verbs are found referring to the weather and natural happenings, e.g.

pluit, *it is raining.*

advesperāscit, *it is growing dark; evening is drawing on.*

Exercise 9b

The Sign of the Cross

'dum ad Mulvium Pontem contendō cum Maxentiō proelium commissūrus, ecce in caelō et ego et tōtum agmen cōnspeximus crucem coruscam sōlī impositam et haec verba in caelō ipsō īnscrīpta, 'in hōc signō vince!'

proximā nocte mihi in somnō apparuit Christus cum illō signō quod
5 in caelō cōnspexī et mē iussit signum eiusdem fōrmae in proeliō semper ferre.'

haec nārrāvit Cōnstantīnus Eusebiō rērum scrīptōrī et iūre iūrandō cōnfirmāvit.

WORD LIST

*contendō, -ere, -tendī, -tentum, march, hasten
*caelum, -ī, n., sky, heavens
*agmen, -inis, n., column, army (on march)
*crux, -cis, f., cross
coruscus, -a, -um, flashing, glittering
*signum, -ī, n., sign

*vincō, -ere, vīcī, victum, conquer
*proximus, -a, -um, next
*apparēre, to appear, make one's appearance
fōrma, -ae, f., shape, form
iūs iūrandum, iūris iūrandī, n., oath
*cōnfirmāre, to confirm, corroborate

NOTES

1 **Mulvius Pōns,** bridge over the Tiber above Rome on the Via Flaminia.
proelium commissūrus, to join battle.
2 **sōlī impositam,** superimposed upon the sun.
3 **inscrīpta,** inscribed, written upon.
7 **rērum scrīptor,** historian.

Exercise 9c

(a) *redde Anglicē:*
nōs paenitet tibi pecūniam dedisse.
senem vītae taedet.
nōnne vōs miseret pauperum cīvium?
quod pluēbat, in domum festīnābāmus.
discipulōs taedēbit scrībere et numerāre.
nōs pudet male fēcisse.

(b) *redde Latīnē:*
I am weary of sitting at home.
We did not regret having come.
Did Nero pity the citizens?
We were ashamed of our mistake (**error, -ōris,** *m.*).
If it rains tomorrow, we shall be glad.
We help the slaves because we are sorry for them.

11 Disaster in Campania

The present-day visitor to Italy is almost certain to include in his sightseeing tour the ruined cities of Pompeii and Herculaneum, lying near the shore of the Gulf of Naples, which were overwhelmed by an eruption of Mount Vesuvius in the first century A.D. The story of the disaster is briefly told in the next few lessons, but before reading these you should know something about the time and place.

The year was A.D. 79. The Emperor Vespasian had recently died and his son Titus had begun to rule. Italy was a peaceful land, untroubled by the wars which raged on the distant frontiers of the Empire. Pompeii was a provincial town of 30 000 inhabitants, an important port and centre of commerce and industry. Herculaneum, a smaller town of about 4 000 inhabitants, was a fishing port and residential area. A third town, Stabiae, is buried beneath the modern town of Castellamare and is unlikely ever to be uncovered.

The many fine houses as well as public buildings which have been uncovered show that these were rich and prosperous towns. Their citizens were pleasure-loving people, as is proved by the lavish provision for entertainment which has come to light. Pompeii had a large theatre with accommodation for 5 000 people, a smaller one, the Odeon, which could seat 1 200, and an arena or amphitheatre for gladiatorial shows seating 20 000. It also had at least three suites of public baths and a large **palaestra,** a public recreation centre which in addition to a large swimming pool had gymnasia and an outdoor play area where the youths practised the popular ball games. The surrounding country was fertile and the slopes of the hills were no doubt planted with vines and fruit trees as they are today.

Disaster struck without warning. On 24 August A.D. 79 the volcano, which had shown no sign of activity within recorded history, erupted with great violence, burying the towns and country for miles around under a deep layer of volcanic dust and ashes.

Lesson 10

Exercise 10a

A.D. 79 (832 a.u.c.)—A Pompeian Family

Lūcius, puer quattuordecim annōrum, in urbe Pompeiīs habitābat. pater
eius, Marcus Vesōnius Prīmus, homō satis opulentus, in urbe fullōnicam
habēbat. avus (is quoque Marcus appellābātur) ōlim magistrātus fuerat
et ā cīvibus in magnō honōre habēbātur. māter Lūciī, cui nōmen erat
Verānia, fēmina pulchra et benigna, erat fīlia Lūciī Verāniī Hypsaeī, qui   5
et ipse in urbe fullō erat. Lūcius noster ūnum frātrem habēbat, nōmine
Marcum, iam duodēvīgintī annōs nātum, qui, quod fullōnicam discere
nōluerat, apud Aemilium Crēscentem architectūrae operam dabat. eō
tempore tamen is Athēnīs studēbat. sorōrem quoque habēbat ūnam,
nōmine Vesōniam, iam duodecim annōs nātam, quae ā mātre domī   10
ēducābātur. Lūcius ipse apud grammaticum Eudoxum, hominem doctum
sed dūrum et puerīs invīsum, litterīs studēbat.

   M. Vesōnius, cum per urbem ambulābat vel in forō negōtium gerēbat,
ā multīs cīvibus salūtābātur. ipse enim, sīcut pater eius, in magnō honōre
ab omnibus habēbātur. in fullōnicā lībertus Anterus ratiōnēs subdūcēbat   15
et opera omnia cūrābat. M. Vesōnius aliquid novī susceptūrus semper
cōnsulēbat Anterum cui cōnfīdēbat maximē.

WORD LIST

opulentus, -a, -um, wealthy
fullōnica, -ae, *f.*, fuller's shop, laundry
   or the fuller's trade
*avus, -ī, *m.*, grandfather
*magistrātus, -ūs, *m.*, magistrate
*duodēvīgintī, eighteen
architectūra, -ae, *f.*, architecture
*operam dare, to give attention to, study
*ēducāre, to educate, bring up
grammaticus, -ī, *m.*, teacher (high
   school)

*invīsus, -a, -um, unpopular, hateful
*negōtium, -iī, *n.*, business
*sicut, just as
lībertus, -ī, *m.*, freedman
*ratiō, -ōnis, *f.*, account
subdūcere, to draw up
*cūrāre, to attend to
*suscipiō, -ere, -cēpī, -ceptum, to
   undertake
*cōnfīdere (+ *dat.*), to trust

NOTES

2 **fullōnica**, a fuller's shop, equivalent of the modern laundry or dry cleaner's.
4 **cui nōmen erat** . . . , whose name was . . . ; the dative is commonly used to indicate
   possession.
8 **apud** . . . , at the establishment of, or under, Aemilius Crescens.
13 **cum . . . ambulābat vel . . . gerēbat,** whenever he walked or . . . .
16 **aliquid novī**, something (of) new. Compare **quid novī?** what's new?

Exercise 10b

The House

domus Vesōniī, quae prope Viam Stabiānam sita erat, paucōs ante annōs mōtū terrae quassāta, nūper erat refecta, neque lautior ūlla in eā parte urbis domus erat. in vestibulō et ātriō pavīmentum opere tessellātō factum signīs multīs ōrnātum erat. in ātriō tēctum columnīs marmoreīs
5 sustinēbātur; circum erant statuae multae; in mediō impluviō, quod flōribus multīs circumdatum erat, fōns aquam aspergēbat. peristȳlium, quō nūlla pars domūs erat amoenior, porticū cīnctum erat quae umbram grātam sedentibus praebēbat. in mediō flōrēs erant et fruticēs.

in domō decem servī opera omnia efficiēbant. putābant nusquam esse
10 dominum clēmentiōrem quam Vesōnium. ille saepe affirmābat nēminem servōs habēre fidēliōrēs quam sē. omnēs cīvēs Marcum Vesōnium hominem esse fēlīcissimum crēdēbant—nec mīrum.

WORD LIST

*prope, *prep. with acc.,* near
quassāre, to wreck, shatter
*nūper, recently
reficiō, -ere, -fēcī, -fectum, repair
*lautus, -a, -um, elegant
pavīmentum, -ī, *n.,* pavement
*tēctum, -ī, *n.,* roof
*ōrnāre, to adorn, decorate
columna, -ae, *f.,* pillar
marmoreus, -a, -um, of marble
*sustineō, -ēre, -tinuī, -tentum, support

circumdare, to surround
aspergō, -ere, -spersī, -spersum, sprinkle, scatter
*amoenus, -a, -um, lovely, pleasant
porticus, -ūs, *f.,* an arcade
*cīnctus, -a, -um (cingere), surrounded
*praebēre, to afford, offer
frutex, -icis, *m.,* shrub
*efficere, to perform
clēmēns, -tis, kind
*fidēlis, -is, -e, faithful
*fēlīx, -īcis, fortunate

NOTES

2 **mōtū terrae,** by an earthquake. An earthquake devastated Pompeii in A.D. 62.
  neque ūlla domus, and no house . . . .
3 **vestibulum,** the entrance hall and **ātrium,** the main hall, were features of the house of the well-to-do Pompeian.
  opus tessellātum, mosaic.
4 **signīs,** figures, designs.
5 **impluvium,** the basin sunk in the floor of the **ātrium** which received the rain water let in by the space in the roof (**compluvium**).
6 **peristȳlium,** a formal, pillared garden.
7 **quō,** than which.
12 **nec mīrum,** and no wonder!

The peristylium of a Pompeian house.

Language

More about participles

You will find that Latin makes very frequent use of participles; always be careful to translate these into natural (or idiomatic) English.

Examples:
porticus umbram grātam sedentibus praebēbat.
The portico provided welcome shade to those who (or to any who) sat there.

rogantī amīcō Vesōnius respondit sē fīliōs duōs habēre.
In answer to his friend's question Vesonius said that he had two sons.

Vesōnius, aliquid novī susceptūrus, Anterum semper cōnsulēbat.
When Vesonius was about (or intending) to undertake something new, he always consulted Anterus.

domus, paucōs ante annōs quassāta, nūper erat refecta.
The house, damaged a few years earlier, had recently been repaired.
or
The house, which had been damaged . . . .

Vesōnia, ā mātre docta, legere et scrībere sciēbat.
Vesōnia, as a result of her mother's teaching, knew how to read and write.

53

Exercise 10c

A. redde Anglicē :
1 puerī ab Eudoxō docentur in cathedrā sedente.
2 discipulī ab Eudoxō docentur in sellīs sedentēs.
3 puerīs ad forum discessūrīs Verānia pecūniam dedit.
4 rogantibus puerīs Anterus Vesōnium ad balnea discessisse respondit.
5 hortum mūrō cīnctum nēmō intrāre potest.
6 Verāniae in ātrium intrātūrae iānitor epistolam dedit.
7 servōs emptōs Vesōnius domum dūxit.
8 puellīs in peristȳlium ductīs Verānia fābulās nārrat.

B. redde Latīnē :
1 The slaves sing as they work in the garden.
2 The boys hailed Vesonius as he was going to enter the baths.
3 In answer to our questions the doorkeeper said that Verania was in the peristylium.
4 Taking the slaves into the kitchen the cook gave them food.
5 Vesonius slept as he sat under the tree.

cavē canem *(Beware of the dog)*. Design in mosaic on the floor of a Pompeian house.

Lesson 11

Exercise 11a

Publius Lūcium salūtat.

Visitor from Nola, A.D. XII Kal. Sept., 832 a.u.c.

iam fēriae erant. per aestātem, quod sōl calēbat, puerī Pompeiānī nihil
iūcundius esse putābant quam ad lītus dēscendere et in marī natāre vel
in harēnā lūdere. eō diē tamen Lūcius cēterōs puerōs ad mare nōn
comitātus est; Publium enim, cōnsobrīnum Nōlānum, exspectābat quī 5
paucōs diēs Pompeiīs mānsūrus erat. is fīlius erat Publiī Verāniī Hypsaeī,
mercātōris Nōlānī, quī eō annō duovir erat. iam quīndecim annōs nātus,
apud amitam fēriās agere solēbat. Lūcius enim et Publius inter sē
amīcissimī erant.

Lūcius māne domō profectus ad portam Nōlānam festīnāvit, ubi vīdit 10
plaustra multa iam pervēnisse holera et frūctūs et ōva et pullōs ad macellum
portantia. brevī raeda in cōnspectum vēnit et Lūcius mannōs raedāriumque
avunculī agnōvit. ubi ad portam raeda pervēnit et Lūcius īnsiluit, puerī
per viās ad domum Vesōniānam celerrimē vectī sunt. ibi Publius magnō
gaudiō et rīsū ā Verāniā et Vesōniā acceptus et in ātrium ductus est. diū 15
omnēs inter sē colloquēbantur; Verānia dē frātre suō percontāta est, Lūcius
dē lūdō, dē fullōnicā, dē amīcīs suīs multa nārrābat, Publius rogantibus
dē parentibus et frātre suō multa respondēbat. tandem Lūcius, 'nisi
nimis dēfessus es,' inquit, 'Publī, ad balnea festīnābimus; sī enim ante
merīdiem eō pervēnerimus, fortasse meum patrem vidēbimus et domum 20
comitābimur.'

WORD LIST

*iūcundus, -a, -um, pleasant
*harēna, -ae, f., sand
*comitor, -ārī, -ātus sum, accompany
cōnsobrīnus, -ī, m., cousin
*mercātor, -ōris, m., merchant
amita, -ae, f., aunt
*proficīscor, -ī, profectus sum, set out
plaustrum, -ī, n., waggon
holus, -eris, n., vegetable
*frūctus, -ūs, m., fruit
*ōvum, -ī, n., egg
pullus, ī, m., chicken

macellum, -ī, n., market
raeda, -ae, f., carriage
mannus, -ī, m., pony, cob
raedārius, -iī, m., coachman
insiliō, -īre, -uī, jump in
*vehō, -ere, vēxī, vectum, convey, carry
*gaudium, -iī, n., joy
*colloquor, -ī, collocūtus sum, converse, talk
*percontor, -ārī, -ātus sum, enquire

NOTES

1 **A.D. XII Kal. Sept., 832 a.u.c.,** 21st August, A.D. 79.
5 **comitātus est,** accompanied (see Language).
7 **duovir,** a magistrate: the **duovirī** were a court of two magistrates—the highest legal authority in a provincial town.
8 **inter sē,** with one another.
10 **profectus,** having set out or, more naturally in English, setting out (see Language).
16 **colloquēbantur,** they talked.
16 **percontāta est,** (she) asked (see Language).

Language

Deponent verbs

Study these examples from Exercise 11a:

1 Lūcius cēterōs puerōs nōn **comitātus est.**
   Lucius did not accompany the rest of the boys.

2 Lūcius māne **profectus** ad portam Nōlānam festīnāvit.
   Lucius, having set out (setting out) early in the morning, hurried to the Nolan Gate.

3 diū inter sē **colloquēbantur.**
   For a long time they talked with one another.

4 Lūcia dē frātre suō **percontāta est.**
   Lucia asked about her brother.

5 meum patrem domum **comitābimur.**
   We shall accompany my father home.

All the verbs in the above examples which are in heavy type have a passive form, i.e. they look as though they were in the passive voice, but they have an active meaning. Such verbs are known as *deponent verbs*.

Exercise 11b

fur! fur!

puerī domō profectī per multās viās iter fēcerant et iam balnea ingressūrī erant cum hominī ēgredientī occurrērunt quī togam portābat et summā celeritāte fugiēbat. simul duo servī pūblicī ē balneīs cucurrērunt, 'fur! fur!' clāmantēs.

'dī immortālēs!' Lūcius exclāmāvit, 'togam meī patris abstulit.' simul 5 puerī fūrem comprehendere cōnātī sunt—sed frustrā, quod is celerius currere poterat. servī pūblicī, aliquamdiū eum per viās secūtī, tandem dēfessī ad balnea rediērunt. Lūcius et Publius quoque in balnea ingressī Vesōnium salūtāvērunt, quī tamen, quod togam nōn habēbat, eōs domum comitārī nōlēbat. ipsī igitur proficīscuntur, sed, dum caupōnam quandam 10 praetereunt, ecce fūrem vīnum bibentem et togam vendere cōnantem cōnspiciunt. veritī ipsī eum comprehendere servīs pūblicīs vocātīs rem nūntiant. fur comprehenditur et in vincula cōnicitur; toga restituitur Vesōniō, quī puerīs grātiās ēgit et praemia dedit.

WORD LIST

*ingredior, -i, ingressus sum, enter
*ēgredior, -i, ēgressus sum, come out, leave
*occurrō, -ere, occurri (+*dat*.), meet
*celeritās, -ātis, *f*., speed
fur, fūris, *m*., thief
*auferō, -ferre, abstulī, ablātum, take away, steal
*comprehendō, -ere, -prehendī, -prehēnsum, catch, seize
*cōnor, -ārī, cōnātus sum, try
*frustrā, in vain

aliquamdiū, for some time
*sequor, sequī, secūtus sum, follow
*redeō, -īre, -iī, -itum, return
caupōna, -ae, *f*., inn
*praetereō, -īre, -iī, -itum, pass
*bibō, -ere, bibī, drink
*vendō, -ere, -didī, -ditum, sell
*vereor, verērī, veritus sum, fear
*in vincula cōnicere, to throw into prison
restituō, -ere, -uī, -ūtum, restore

NOTES

1 **ingressūrī**, future participle of **ingredī**.
2 **ēgredientī**, present participle of **ēgredī**.
  hominī, dative case because **occurrere**, *to meet*, is accompanied by the dative.
3 **servī pūblicī**, the attendants at the baths, like other municipal workers, were slaves.
12 **servīs pūblicīs vocātīs**, dative case; *lit.* to the summoned attendants they reported . . . Express this in natural English.

Language

More about Deponent verbs

In Exercise 11b you find these examples:

balnea ingressūrī erant.
They were about to enter the baths.

hominī ēgredientī occurrērunt.
They met a man coming out.

fūrem togam vendere cōnantem cōnspiciunt.
They saw the thief trying to sell the toga.

You have already learned that deponent verbs are passive in form but active in meaning; from the above exàmples it is apparent that they have present and future participles which are active in form as well as in meaning.

Exercise 11c

(a) *redde Anglicē:*
1 nōlī verērī, Publī, in flūmine natāre.
  nōn vereor, Lūcī; ad alteram rīpam pervenīre cōnābor.
2 puerī, aliquamdiū inter sē collocūtī, ad balnea profectī sunt.
  puerīs ad balnea profectūrīs Verānia fīcōs dedit.
3 Vesōnium et amīcōs eius in forō colloquentēs vīdērunt.
  diū collocūtī, domum discessērunt.
4 Publius, māne Nōlā profectus, ante merīdiem Pompeiōs pervēnit.
  Verānia, dē frātre suō percontāta, Publium in ātrium dūxit.

(b) *redde Latīnē:*
1 The boys followed the thief through the streets.
2 After following for a long time they saw him in a tavern.
3 He did not see them trying to call the attendants.
4 The boys met Vesonius coming out of the baths.
5 As they were about to enter they heard a shout.
6 Leaving the house in the morning they walked to the forum.

Lesson 12

Exercise 12a

Rūfus fullōnicam custōdit.

a.d. XI, Kal. Sept.
To the Fuller's We Shall Go

postrīdiē Lūcius et Publius prīmō māne ē lectīs surrēxērunt, et manibus
ōribusque lavātīs in tablīnum ad ientāculum vēnērunt. post ientāculum
in peristȳliō paulīsper cessābant, ubi servōs flōrēs cūrantēs spectābant;
deinde Publiō rogantī 'quid hodiē faciēmus?' respondit Lūcius, 'togam
meī patris, quam ā scelestō illō fūre sordidātam esse dīcit, ad fullōnicam 5
ferēmus; cupiō enim vidēre canem nostrum Rūfum quī fullōnicam bene
custōdit. edepol nēmō intrāre audēbit Rūfō vīvō et vigilante.' et Publius,
'euge,' inquit, 'simul enim ego Anterum vidēbō, bonum et hilarem senem
quī semper mē amīcissimē accipit.'

profectī igitur puerī lentē per viās prōgrediuntur; modo ante caupōnam 10
cessant, modo fabrōs labōrantēs spectant; tandem, ubi fullōnica in
cōnspectū erat, Lūcius 'age, Publī,' inquit, 'ego Pompeiānus sum, tū
Nōlānus; cursū certābimus. uter nostrum prior ad fullōnicam perveniet?'
summā vī certāvērunt, sed Publius prior ad fullōnicam pervēnit et iam
intrātūrus erat cum Rūfus ingentī lātrātū exsiluit. territus fūgit Publius. 15
Rūfus tamen catēnā impedītus sequī nōn poterat. accurrit Lūcius et
rīdēns Rūfī caput mulcēre coepit. Anterus ē fullōnicā ēgressus, puerōs
cum gaudiō accēpit et Publium dē parentibus et urbe Nōlā percontātus
est. ipse enim nōnnūllōs amīcōs Nōlānōs habēbat.

WORD LIST

lectus, -ī, *m.*, bed
*surgō, -ere, surrēxi, surrēctum, rise
*ōs, ōris, *n.*, face
*lavō, -āre, lāvī, lavātum, wash
cessō, -āre, -āvī, -ātum, linger
*scelestus, -a, -um, wicked
sordidātus, -a, -um, dirtied
*vīvus, -a, -um, alive
*vigilāre, to be awake
*audeō, -ēre, ausus sum, dare
*simul, at the same time
hilaris, -is, -e, cheerful, merry
*lentē, slowly

*prōgredior, -ī, prōgressus sum, proceed, make one's way
faber, -brī, *m.*, craftsman
cursus, -ūs, *m.*, running, speed of foot
certāre, to compete
*uter? which of two?
lātrātus, -ūs, *m.*, barking
*exsiliō, -īre, -siluī, jump out
catēnā, -ae, *f.*, chain
*impedītus, -a, -um, hindered
accurrere, to run up
mulcēre, to stroke

NOTES

1 **manibus ōribusque lavātīs,** after washing their hands and faces. See Language, p. 61.
7 **edepol,** upon my word!
   Rūfō . . . vigilante, literally, with Rufus alive and awake. Think out other natural English ways of saying this.
10 **modo . . . modo,** at one time . . . at another time.

Language

Semi-deponent verbs

audeō, audēre, ausus sum, *dare,* is one of a small group of *semi-deponent* verbs, i.e. verbs which have a passive form but active meaning in the perfect tense only. Others are **gaudeō, gaudēre, gāvīsus sum,** *rejoice;* **soleō, solēre, solitus sum,** *be accustomed;* **cōnfīdō, -ere, cōnfīsus sum,** *trust.*

Exercise 12b

Tour of Inspection

puerī, in fullōnicam ingressī, paulīsper cum Anterō colloquēbantur. Publius eī rogantī dē Nōlānīs et parentibus suīs multa dīxit, Lūcius, Publiō hortante, dē fūre et togā sordidātā omnia nārrāvit. Anterus rīdēns puerōs fortiter et callidē fēcisse dīxit; togam mox lōtam Vesōniō redditum
5 īrī prōmīsit. deinde puerī, Anterō duce, per fullōnicam errābant, ubi

fullōnēs labōrantes vīdērunt; aliōs in lābrīs vestīmenta sordida alternīs
pedibus occulcantēs, aliōs crētā togās fricantēs spectābant. iūcundum erat
in fullōnicā cessāre sed tandem Lūcius 'dī immortālēs,' exclāmāvit, 'iam
merīdiēs est; tempus est domum redīre ad prandium; famē enim paene
cōnfectus sum.' Anterō igitur et fullōnibus valēre iussīs, currentēs 10
abiērunt.

WORD LIST

*hortārī, to urge, encourage
*callidē, adv., cleverly
lābrum, -ī, n., tub
*vestīmentum, -ī, n., garment
occulcāre, to tread
crēta, -ae, f., fuller's earth, pipeclay

fricāre, to rub
*cōnficiō, -ere, -fēcī, -fectum, exhaust,
finish
*famēs, -is, f., hunger
*valēre iubeō, I bid farewell

NOTES

3 **Publiō hortante,** lit. with Publius urging him. Find as many ways as possible of
expressing this naturally in English.
4 **lōtam,** cleaned (from **lavāre**).
5 **Anterō duce,** lit. with Anterus as guide.
6 **aliōs . . . aliōs,** some . . . others.
alternīs pedibus occulcantēs, demonstrate what the fullers were doing and then
choose a good translation of the words.
10 **Anterō et fullōnibus valēre iussīs,** bidding Anterus and the fullers farewell (see
Language).

Language

Ablative Absolute

1 (a) **Anterō duce** per fullōnicam errābant.
  With Anterus as guide or *Guided by Anterus* or *Under the guidance of
  Anterus, they wandered through the laundry.*
 (b) **Rūfō vīvō** et **vigilante** nēmō intrāre audēbit.
  As long as Rufus is alive and awake, no one will dare to enter. lit. *With
  Rufus alive and being awake* . . . .

In the above examples the phrases in heavy type are simple examples of the
Ablative Absolute construction.

2 (a) **manibus ōribusque lavātīs** in ātrium vēnērunt.
  After washing their hands and faces, they came into the hall. or *When
  they had washed* . . . . (lit. *(with) their hands and faces having been washed*)

(*b*) **Anterō** et **fullōnibus** valēre **iussīs,** abiērunt.
> *After bidding Anterus and the fullers farewell, they went away.* or *When they had bidden* . . . , or simply *Bidding Anterus and the fullers farewell* . . . .
> (lit. (*with*) *Anterus and the fullers having been bidden farewell*)

The above sentences contain typical examples of the Ablative Absolute construction—a noun or pronoun along with a participle, all in the Ablative Case, forming a phrase not attached to the rest of the sentence by any conjunction, hence *ab-solute*, loosened off. There are often several correct methods of translating this construction into English. A literal translation is rarely natural English.

Note
Messālā et **Pīsōne cōnsulibus** coniūrātiō facta est.
A conspiracy took place in the consulship of Messala and Piso.

Since the consuls were elected for one year, the names of the consuls provided a convenient method of identifying the date (year).

Exercise 12c

redde Anglicē:
Lūcius sub arbore sedēns librum legit.
Lūciō sub arbore sedente, Syrus in hortō labōrat.
librum lēctum Lūcius humī dēpōnit.
librō lēctō, Marcus in domum abiit.
canem inventum puerī domum dūxērunt.
cane inventō, puerī domum cucurrērunt.
servīs cessantibus coquus 'festīnāte!' clāmāvit.
servōs cessantēs dominus castīgāvit.
servīs cessantibus, dominus ipse iānuam aperuit.
Rūfō lātrante Publius fullōnicam ingredī verēbātur.

Exercise 12d

redde Latīnē (translate the words in italics by means of the Ablative Absolute construction):
While the cat (**fēlēs, -is,** *f.*) *was sleeping,* the mice were playing.
After attending to the flowers, the slaves lingered in the garden.
When the thief had been caught, the boys returned to the baths.
Since the toga had been restored, Vesonius thanked the boys.
With you as guide, we shall walk through the forum.

Anterus, *having welcomed the boys*, entered the laundry.

Questioned by Anterus (Anterus questioning) Publius told about his father and
mother.

When we had seen Rufus, we went home.

THE FULLONICA

Marcus Vesonius Primus was himself a prosperous man of business and the
industry which he represented—that of the **fullōnēs**—was one of the most
flourishing in the city.

There were two sides to the fuller's craft; in the first place it was a stage in
the preparation of new cloth. The wool was first woven by the weaver,
textor, who then passed it on to the **fullō** who cleaned and processed the
fabric before passing it to the **infector,** dyer, if it was to be dyed; alternatively
it might go straight from the fuller to the clothier, **vestiārius,** such as

Verecundus (Exercise 15a). Since wool weaving was, apparently, the main industry of Pompeii, there was always plenty of work for the **fullōnēs.**

The other side of the fuller's business was a cleaning service. While ordinary domestic washing was, no doubt, done by the household slaves, the cleaning and pressing of the outer garments was then, as it is now, a job for the expert.

A series of wall paintings in one of the **fullōnicae** excavated at Pompeii gives a very full picture of the process. The main equipment was a series of large tanks filled with water, in which the soiled garments were trodden **alternīs pedibus** by the fuller's assistants. Soap powders and detergents were unknown, but a cleansing agent such as **nitrum,** washing soda, was added to the water. After washing, the garment was stretched out to dry in the open air and then brushed to bring up the pile of the cloth. Finally, it was stretched on a beehive-shaped frame and sulphur was burned under it to whiten it. If an extra sheen was desired on the cloth it was rubbed with **crēta,** fuller's earth, to make it shining white (**candida**). A contestant for public office wore his toga **candidāta;** hence our word, *candidate.*

Revision Exercises

A. Revise Deponent Verbs.

redde Anglicē:

domō profectūrus mātrem valēre iussī.
domō proficīscentem soror mē salūtāvit.
māne domō profectus ante merīdiem ad urbem pervēnī.
quod verēbar sōlus īre, duo servī mē comitātī sunt.
in domum ingressum amita mē dē patre meō percontāta est.
ego et Marcus in domō diū collocūtī, in viam ēgressī sumus.
propter multitūdinem difficile erat per viās prōgredī.
diū cōnātī ad forum pervenīre, tandem domum abiimus.

B. Revise Participles, Ablative Absolute.

Translate the words in italics, using participles:

Since the house had been wrecked, Vesonius had gone away.
Later he repaired *the wrecked house.*
Making our way through the city, we saw many wonderful things.
Making our way through the city we came at last to the gate.
Hearing the noise the boys ran to the spot.
Terrified by the noise we closed the door.
The thief was caught *trying to* open the door.
While we were trying to open the door, the thief escaped by the window.
When the toga had been restored, Vesonius sent it to the cleaner's.
When the toga had been restored, Vesonius was satisfied.

C. *redde Latinē:*

With Marcus as guide, Publius walked through the forum.
Vesonius says that he will not go to the baths today.
He has promised to take the boys to the games.
We hope to come home before midday.
I wish to watch the fullers working.
Publius prefers to talk with Anterus.

D. *Test your word power; select the correct meaning.*

interdiū,	*by day, an interval, temporary.*
comes,	*funny, a companion, something for eating.*
volāre,	*to wish, to steal, to fly.*
tēctum,	*a coat, a roof, cloth.*
īnsilīre,	*to live on an island, to leap into, to insult.*
oppidānī,	*students, townsfolk, firemen.*
discrīmen,	*a crime, an illness, a distinction.*
aetās,	*age, summer, a meal.*
īnsignis,	*a sign, a seal, famous.*
avus,	*a bird, a grandfather, a prayer.*
suscipere,	*to undertake, to suspect, to rise.*
fidēlis,	*a musical instrument, a cat, faithful.*

Lesson 13

Exercise 13a

a.d. XI Kal. Sept.
The Sights and Sounds of Pompeii

post prandium, sōle calente, Lūcius et Publius duās hōrās dormiēbant. deinde experrēctus Lūcius, 'expergīscere, Publī!' clāmāvit; 'nōnne dīxistī tē velle forum et tabernās vidēre? festīnēmus igitur in urbem et Forum Pompeiānum īnspiciāmus.' tum Publius ē lectō exsiliēns, 'euge!'
5 exclāmāvit, 'nē mora sit; abeāmus.' puerī statim profectī sunt, sed impedītī multitūdine hominum quī in viīs ambulābant, celeriter prōgredī nōn poterant. tandem autem ad forum pervēnērunt.

in ipsō forō, refectīs aedificiīs quae sēdecim ante annīs mōtū terrae erant quassāta, omnia aspectū praeclāra erant. puerī templa et statuās et
10 porticūs admīrātī mox dēfessī in scālīs templī Iovis cōnsēdērunt. brevī tamen Publius 'nē diutius,' inquit, 'hīc sedeāmus; ecce, prope est macellum; eō dēscendāmus.' dictum factum. ēheu! quantus fuit in macellō strepitus! conclāmābant tabernāriī, servī clāmantēs hūc illūc currēbant, lātrābant canēs, asinī rudēbant, cantābant gallī, īnfantēs plōrā-
15 bant. quibus audītīs Publius, 'dī immortālēs!' exclāmāvit, 'hinc fugiāmus; sī enim hīc manēbimus, sine dubiō surdī erimus.' dum fugiunt, Lūcius, 'age, Publī,' inquit, 'ad pistrīnam Modestī, amīcī nostrī, abeāmus. iūcundum enim est pistōrēs spectāre. sī aderit Modestus ipse, fortasse nōbīs pānem dabit.'

WORD LIST

caleō, -ēre, -uī, be hot
hōra, -ae, f., hour
expergīscor, -ī, experrēctus sum, waken up
*īnspiciō, -ere, -spexī, -spectum, look at, view
*multitūdō, -inis, f., crowd, great number
*aedificium, -iī, n., building
aspectus, -ūs, m., appearance
admīror, -ārī, -ātus sum, admire
scālae, -ārum, f., steps
*strepitus, -ūs, m., noise
*conclāmāre, to shout all together

tabernārius, -iī, m., stall-holder
*hūc . . . illūc, hither and thither
*asinus, -ī, m., ass
rudō, -ere, -īvī, -ītum, bray
gallus, -ī, m., cock
īnfāns, -antis, m., child, infant
plōrāre, to howl, weep
*hinc, hence, from here
*dubius, -a, -um, doubtful; sine dubiō, without doubt
surdus, -a, -um, deaf
pistrīna, -ae, f., bakery
pistor, -ōris, m., baker

NOTES

2 **expergīscere,** imperative singular of **expergīscī.**
3 **festīnēmus,** let us hurry (*for this and other new verb forms, see Language*).
4 **inspiciāmus,** let us look at.
5 **nē mora sit,** let there be no delay; not a minute to lose!
  abeāmus, let's be off.
11 **nē sedeāmus,** let us not sit.
12 **dēscendāmus,** let us go down.
   dictum factum, no sooner said than done.
15 **quibus audītīs,** hearing these.
19 **pānem,** a loaf.

Language

The Present Subjunctive active

In Exercise 13a you met some new verb forms such as the following:

festīnēmus in urbem.	*Let us hurry into the city.*
hīc **sedeāmus.**	*Let us sit here.*
dēscendāmus in macellum.	*Let us go down into the market.*
nē **sit** mora.	*Let there be no delay.*
abeāmus.	*Let us be off.*

These are examples of the present tense active of the *Subjunctive* mood of the verb. See table of forms overleaf. The Subjunctive has many uses which you will learn as they occur; in this exercise the Present Subjunctive is used to indicate a wish, exhortation or command.

N.B. When the Subjunctive is used with these meanings, its negative is not **nōn** but **nē (nē quis, nē quid, nē ūllus, nē umquam).**

Further examples:

hodiē fēlix sim.	*May I be successful today.*
incolumis ad portum perveniās.	*May you come safely to harbour.*
sedeat Lūcia in sellā.	*Let Lucia sit on a chair.*
surgāmus prīmō māne.	*Let us rise very early.*
hodiē fēlīcēs sītis.	*May you be successful today.*
dormiant puerī in lectīs.	*Let the boys sleep in their beds.*
nē umquam dormiant in lūdō.	*Never let them sleep in school.*
nē festīnēmus ad lūdum.	*Let us not hurry to school.*

67

FIRST CONJUGATION **festināre,** *to hurry*
festīn-em, -ēs, -et, -ēmus, -ētis, -ent

SECOND CONJUGATION **sedēre,** *to sit*
sede-am, -ās, -at, -āmus, -ātis, -ant

THIRD CONJUGATION (a) **dēscendere,** *to go down*
dēscend-am, -ās, -at, -āmus, -ātis, -ant

THIRD CONJUGATION (b) **fugere,** *to flee*
fugi-am, -ās, -at, -āmus, -ātis, -ant

FOURTH CONJUGATION **dormīre,** *to sleep*
dormi-am, -ās, -at, -āmus, -ātis, -ant

IRREGULAR

> **esse,** *to be*
> sim, sīs, sit, sīmus, sītis, sint
>
> **posse,** *to be able*
> pos-sim, -sīs, -sit, -sīmus, -sītis, -sint
>
> **velle,** *to wish, to be willing*
> velim, velīs, velit, velīmus, velītis, velint
>
> **īre,** *to go*
> eam, eās, eat, eāmus, eātis, eant

also: nōlim, nōlīs, etc. from **nōlle,** *to refuse, to be unwilling*
mālim, mālīs, etc. from **mālle,** *to prefer*
feram, ferās, etc. from **ferre,** *to carry, bear*
fīam, fīās, etc. from **fierī,** *to become*

Exercise 13b

Read the following passage, and, with the aid of the notes, try to understand it. Then answer the questions on page 70. Finally, translate the passage into English, using the General Word List, if necessary.

ēheu! lanius nimis corpulentus est.

A Visit to the Baker

pistrīna Modestī ā forō nōn procul aberat, sed
puerī lentē eō prōgrediuntur. multa enim
erant īnspicienda. dum ē macellō exeunt, ecce
per viam fugit canis tomācula ōre portāns
quae ē laniēnā quādam fūrātus erat. īrātus
persequitur lanius; ēheu! fugientem cōnsequī
nōn poterat; corpulentus enim erat. haud
procul multitūdō hominum in ūnum locum
convēnerat; quō ubi puerī cucurrērunt, duōs
servōs pugnīs certāre vīdērunt. Lūcius
alterum, alterum Publius hortātur; subitō
dominus alterīus accurrit et ambōs fūste
caedit. fugiunt servī, rīdent eī quī circum-
stābant. inde prōgressī puerī modo sūtōrem
calceōs sarcientem spectant, modo ante
caupōnam morantēs gladiātōrēs quī ibi bibēbant cantantēs audiunt. tandem ad pistrīnam
pervēnērunt. ibi duae molae versābantur;
alteram—gravissima enim erat—asinus versā-
bat, alteram versābant duo servī. quattuor
pistōrēs in mēnsā farīnam subigēbant et pānēs
fōrmābant. Modestus ipse, dum omnia
īnspicit, puerōs vīdit et agnōvit. dē parentibus
percontātus parvum pānem ē furnō extractum
eīs dedit. puerī grātiās eī ēgērunt et laetī
domum festīnāvērunt.

food market —macellum

inspicienda, see p. 40 (Language)

tomāculum, sausage
fūrārī, to steal

pugnus, fist

fūstis, -is, *m.,* cudgel, club

sūtor, -ōris, *m.,* shoemaker
sarciō, -īre, -rsī, -rtum, mend,
  repair
morārī, to delay, linger

mola, -ae, *f.,* millstone, grindstone

mēnsa, -ae, *f.,* table
farīnam subigere, knead the
  dough

furnus, -ī, *m.,* oven

Questions

1 Name three trades, three places of business, and two articles of food mentioned in the passage.
2 Why did the boys not make their way quickly to the bakery? Give two reasons.
3 Were the bystanders anxious to stop the slaves from fighting? Give reasons for your answer.
4 What did the boys find to interest them in the **caupōna**?
5 Name three activities which were going on in the **pistrīna.**
6 Give the principal parts of three deponent verbs (not all of the same conjugation) which occur in the passage.
7 Pick out from the passage two examples of the perfect participle and one example of the present participle of deponent verbs.
8 **persequī,** *to pursue* and **cōnsequī,** *to overtake* are compounds of **sequī,** *to follow*. List four verbs in the passage which are compounds of verbs which you know.

Language

Summary of direct command

PERSON	POSITIVE	NEGATIVE
1st (Exhortation)	*Present Subjunctive* **festīnēmus,** let us hurry	**nē** *with Pres. Subj.* **nē festīnēmus,** let us not hurry
2nd	*Imperative* **festīnā,** hurry (sing.) **festīnāte,** hurry (pl.)	**nōlī, nōlīte** *with Pres. Infin.* **nōlī festīnāre,** do not hurry (sing.) **nōlīte festīnāre,** do not hurry (pl.)
3rd	*Present Subjunctive* **porta aperiātur,** let the door be opened	**nē** *with Pres. Subj.* **nē porta aperiātur,** let not the door be opened

THE PISTRINA

Modestus the Pompeian baker did not guess, when he mixed his dough on 24 August A.D. 79, that he would become one of the most famous bakers in the world. His batch consisted of 81 round loaves, which he put into the oven, as he had done many times before. Normally they would have been taken out after an hour or two, but this time eighteen centuries were to pass before the oven door was opened and the blackened loaves saw the light of day. For no sooner had Modestus closed the door upon the batch than the sky was darkened by the cloud of volcanic dust and ash which engulfed Pompeii. He fled and, we hope, made good his escape. Some of his loaves may be seen, now reduced to charcoal, in the museum at Pompeii. We can still look into the oven of Modestus's bakery, but it is another **pistrina**—that in the **Vicolo Storto**—which tells us most about the process of baking. In fact, the **pistrina** was a combination of flour-mill and bakery where the whole operation from raw material to finished product was carried out. The scene is reconstructed in the picture below.

On the right-hand side of the picture are the mills, operated by donkey-power or slave-power, into which the grain is poured from above and ground by turning the hollow outer millstone over a solid conical inner stone. The flour is collected at the foot of the mill. In the centre, near the oven, two slaves are kneading the dough and making the loaves. Another slave puts loaves into the oven while still another stokes the fire. In the foreground is the shop 'counter' where the master displays his products and serves his customers.

Exercise 13c

redde Latinē:

Don't delay longer, boys; let us go to the forum.
Listen to the noise, Marcus!
Let us not linger here; I cannot bear the noise.
'Catch that dog!' the butcher cries.
Don't run, butcher! You cannot overtake the dog.
Let us watch the bakers, as they knead the dough.
'Let the loaves be drawn from the oven,' shouts Modestus.
May the weather be calm tomorrow.
May you (*sing.*) not be frightened by storms.
May our city never be shaken by an earthquake.

The Forum of Pompeii

Lesson 14

Exercise 14a

a.d. XI Kal. Sept.–a.d. X Kal. Sept.
More Sightseeing

post cēnam Lūcius et Publius paulīsper in peristȳliō sedentēs inter sē
colloquēbantur; deinde Lūcius, 'cum dēfessus sim,' inquit, 'mox cubitum
īre volō; quid crās facere vīs?' Publius autem, 'cum nunc dēfessī sīmus,'
respondit, 'māne dē hāc rē agāmus. et ego enim dormīre cupiō.' statim
igitur cubitum abiērunt.   5

postrīdiē prīmō māne experrēctī in ātrium dēscendērunt. cum tamen
Vesōnius et Verānia nōndum adessent, servī autem in ātriō adhūc
labōrārent, in peristȳlium ēgressī Vesōniam exspectāvērunt. quae ubi
vēnit, Lūcius, 'age,' inquit, 'cum iam trēs adsīmus, dum parentēs
exspectāmus, paulīsper lūdāmus.' dictum factum. modo pilā lūdēbant, 10
modo per lūsum latitābant; tandem autem, Verāniā vocante, in domum
ad ientāculum ingressī sunt.

inter ientāculum Vesōnius 'quid,' inquit, 'puerī, hodiē factūrī estis?'
tum Publius, 'cum paucī modo mihi restent diēs,' respondit, 'iterum in
urbem īre et tabernās īnspicere volō; tabernās enim Pompeiānās meliōrēs 15
esse quam Nōlānās putō.' quod cum Lūciō quoque placēret, puerī post
ientāculum profectī sunt. multa erant in viīs spectanda; hīc complūrēs
canēs pugnant; concurrunt tabernāriī et pugnantēs fūstibus caedunt; illī
ingentī lātrātū aufugiunt; illīc plaustrum, haerentibus in orbitā rotīs,
movērī nōn potest; conclāmant omnēs, plōrat agitātor et mūlōs verberat, 20
sed frustrā. tandem, sublātā parte oneris, mūlī verberantur, multī hominēs
ā tergō trūdunt; ecce movētur plaustrum. rīdentēs abiērunt puerī.

WORD LIST

*cubō, -āre, -uī, -itum, lie down
*cubitum īre, to go to bed
*nōndum, not yet
restāre, to remain, be left
*placēre (dat.), to please; *placet mihi, it pleases me
*complūrēs, several
concurrere, to run together
*aufugere, to flee
illīc, there

*haereō, -ēre, haesī, haesum, stick
orbita, -ae, f., rut
rota, -ae, f., wheel
agitātor, -ōris, m., driver
mūlus, -ī, m., mule
sublātā—perf. part. pass. of tollō, -ere, sustulī, sublātum, remove, raise
*onus, -eris, n., load, burden
trūdō, -ere, trūsī, trūsum, push

NOTES

2 **cum dēfessus sim,** since I am tired. **cum** meaning *since* is followed by the subjunctive mood. Several examples occur in this exercise.
4 **et ego dormīre cupiō,** I also wish to sleep.
6 **cum . . . adessent . . . labōrārent,** since . . . were not yet there . . . were working. **adessent** and **labōrārent** are examples of the Imperfect Subjunctive (see Language).
7 **servī autem . . . ,** and moreover the slaves . . . .
8 **quae ubi vēnit,** (and) when *she* came.
11 **per lūsum latitābant,** they played hide-and-seek, *lit.* they hid in sport.
16 **quod cum Lūciō placēret,** since this pleased Lucius. In natural English this might be 'since Lucius liked this suggestion'.
17 **spectanda,** to be looked at; *more naturally,* to look at.
hīc . . . illīc, here . . . there; in one place . . . in another place.

Language

The Imperfect Subjunctive active

In Exercise 14a you have been introduced to the use of **cum,** meaning *since,* which is followed by the *Subjunctive Mood.*

Examples:
A. 1 **cum dēfessus sim, cubitum īre volō.**
Since I am tired, I wish to go to bed.
2 **cum paucī mihi restent diēs, in urbem īre volō.**
Since few days are left to me, I wish to go into the city.

In the above examples the tense of the Subjunctive is the Present, which is shown in English as the Present Indicative.

B. 1 **cum Vesōnius et Verānia nōndum adessent, puerī Vesōniam exspectāvērunt.**
Since Vesonius and Verania were not yet present, the boys waited for Vesonia.

74

2 **cum servī labōrārent, puerī in peristȳlium ēgressī sunt.**
Since the slaves were working, the boys went out into the peristylium.
3 **quod cum Lūciō placēret, puerī profectī sunt.**
Since this pleased Lucius, the boys set out.

In the above examples the tense of the subjunctive is the *Imperfect* (see table below) and is shown in English as a past tense of the Indicative.

IMPERFECT SUBJUNCTIVE ACTIVE

FIRST CONJUGATION **festināre,** *to hurry*
festīnā-rem, -rēs, -ret, -rēmus, -rētis, -rent

SECOND CONJUGATION **sedēre,** *to sit*
sedē-rem, -rēs, -ret, -rēmus, -rētis, -rent

THIRD CONJUGATION (a) **dēscendere,** *to go down*
dēscende-rem, -rēs, ret, -rēmus, -rētis, -rent

THIRD CONJUGATION (b) **fugere,** *to flee*
fuge-rem, -rēs, -ret, -rēmus, -rētis, -rent

FOURTH CONJUGATION **dormīre,** *to sleep*
dormī-rem, -rēs, -ret, -rēmus, -rētis, -rent

IRREGULAR

esse, *to be*
essem, essēs, esset, essēmus, essētis, essent

posse, *to be able*
possem, possēs, posset, possēmus, possētis, possent

velle, *to wish, to be willing*
vellem, vellēs, vellet, vellēmus, vellētis, vellent

īre, *to go*
īrem, īrēs, īret, īrēmus, īrētis, īrent

also : nōllem, nōllēs, etc. from **nōlle**
mällem, mällēs, etc. from **mälle**
ferrem, ferrēs, etc. from **ferre**
fierem, fierēs, etc. from **fierī**

Note. From the above table you will see how easy it is to recognise the Imperfect Subjunctive, if you know the Present Infinitive.

Exercise 14b

Make each of the following pairs of sentences into a single sentence by using
cum with the appropriate tense of the subjunctive. Then translate your
sentence into English.

Example:

> **pilam habeō. in hortō lūdāmus.**
> **cum pilam habeam, in hortō lūdāmus.**
> *Since I have a ball, let us play in the garden.*

1. servus ōtiōsus stābat. dominus īrātus erat.
2. canēs pugnant. puerī in viam currunt.
3. Vesōniam exspectāmus. in sellā sedēbimus.
4. puerī in ātriō nōn erant. Verānia eōs vocāvit.
5. ōtiōsus esse volō. domī manēbō.
6. sōl calēbat. puerī paulīsper dormiēbant.
7. Publius tabernās īnspicere volēbat. puerī in urbem abiērunt.
8. plaustrum movērī nōn potest. plōrat agitātor.
9. fur celeriter currēbat. puerī eum cōnsequī nōn poterant.
10. clāmōrēs audiēbāmus. ad caupōnam festīnābāmus.

Lesson 15

Exercise 15a

'numquam lectīcam tam lautam vīdī.'

a.d. X Kal. Sept.
Mistress Julia Drives a Hard Bargain

tandem Lūcius et Publius in Viam Longam pervēnērunt. ā sinistrā
Thermae Stabiānae erant, sed cum nōndum hōra quīnta esset, servī
pūblicī ōtiōsī circā iānuam stābant, neque clāmōrēs iuvenum in palaestrā
lūdentium audiēbantur. ā dextrā fullōnicam Stephanī praeteriērunt. dīxit
enim Lūcius, 'cum ipsī fullōnicam habeāmus, hīc nōn morābimur.'   5
    haud procul, ante officīnam Verēcundī vestiāriī octō lecticāriī, dēpositā
lectīcā, humī sedēbant dum dominam exspectābant quae in officīnam
intrāverat. 'numquam, mehercule,' Publius exclāmāvit, 'lectīcam tam
lautam vīdī.' 'nec mīrum,' inquit Lūcius, 'cum lectīca sit Iūliae Fēlīcis,
quae prope amphitheātrum domum habet lautissimam.' simul ex officīnā   10
vōcēs audiuntur Iūliae et Verēcundī.
    'pallam quaerō lāneam quam habēs optimam.'
    'multae et bonae mihi sunt. ecce palla lānā Lūcerīnā texta. nusquam
      pulchriōrem inveniēs.'
    'est vērō pulchra. sed quantī vēnit?'   15
    'minimō vestīmenta vendō. haec sexāgintā modo dēnāriīs vēnit.'
    'sexāgintā! nōn est tantī. vīsne mē spoliāre, sceleste?'
    'immō est plūris. nōnne vidēs eam coccō esse tīnctam?'
    'videō. tantī tamen nōn est. quadrāgintā prō eā dabō.'

20   'ō mē miserum! operam perdidī. minōris quam quīnquāgintā vendere
       nōlō.'
       'quadrāgintā quīnque pro eā dabō. quōs nisi accipere vīs, ego dēnāriōs
       servābō, tibi per mē licēbit pallam servāre.'
       'bene habet, domina; accipiō.'
25   brevī Iūlia ēgressa in lecticam intrāvit et domum lāta est.
       deinde, cum sōl maximē calēret, puerī domum reditūrī erant cum
    Publius, 'quid videō?' clāmāvit. gladiātōrēs enim duo in officīnam Vērī,
    fabrī aerāriī, intrābant. quōs ubi vīdit Lūcius, 'age,' inquit, 'Publī, eō
    festīnēmus. sine dubiō gladiātōrēs galeās aut lōrīcās Vērō reficiendās dant.
30   fortasse licēbit nōbīs eum labōrantem spectāre. interim gladiātōrēs dē
    amphitheātrō percontābimur.'

WORD LIST

*sinister, -tra, -trum, left-hand: **ā sinistrā,** on the left
palaestra, -ae, *f.*, sports area
*dexter, -tra, -trum, right hand; **ā dextrā,** on the right
officīna, -ae, *f.*, workshop
vestiārius, -iī, *m.*, clothier
*lectīca, -ae, *f.*, litter
lecticārius, -iī, *m.*, bearer
*dēpōnō, -ere, -posuī, -positum, set down
domina, -ae, *f.*, mistress
amphitheātrum, -ī, *n.*, arena
*palla, -ae, *f.*, robe
lāneus, -a, -um, woollen
*lāna, -ae, *f.*, wool
*texō, -ere, -uī, textum, weave

*vērō, indeed
*vēneō, -īre, -iī, be sold
quadrāgintā, forty; **quinquāgintā,** fifty; **sexāgintā,** sixty (see page 198)
dēnārius, -iī, *m.*, denarius, a Roman coin worth ten asses
*spoliāre, to rob
coccum, -ī, *n.*, scarlet dye
tinctus, -a, -um, dyed (**tingō, -ere, tīnxī, tīnctum,** dye)
*opera, -ae, *f.*, trouble
*perdō, -ere, -didī, -ditum, waste
*licet, *fut.* **licēbit,** it is permitted
faber aerārius, bronze-smith
*galea, -ae, *f.*, helmet
*lōrica, -ae, *f.*, breastplate

NOTES

2 **thermae,** warm baths; the suites of public baths were known by this name.
  nōndum hōra quīnta would be about 9.30. At the time of our story the Roman day was not divided into hours of a fixed length. Instead it was divided from dawn to dusk into twelve hours which varied in length according to the time of year. The sixth hour always ended at midday; in August the fifth hour would begin between 9.30 and 10.00.
3 **palaestra,** attached to the public baths was a small sports area where the bathers 'warmed up' with ball games or other physical exercises before bathing.
12 **quam habēs optimam,** the best you have.
13 **lānā Lūcerinā,** Lūceria, a town of Apulia in central Italy, was famous for wool of high quality.
15 **quantī vēnit?** what is the price? *Lit.*, for how much is it sold? Do not confuse **vēnīre,** *to be sold*, with **venīre** *to come.*

16 **minimō,** at a very low price.
17 **nōn est tantī,** it is not worth so much.
18 **est plūris,** it is worth more.
20 **minōris vendere nōlō,** I refuse to sell at less . . . . For these expressions of price and value see Language.
22 **prō eā,** for it.
23 **tibi per mē licēbit,** you may, so far as I am concerned; *lit.* it will be permitted to you through me. **licet** is an impersonal verb meaning *it is permitted.*
24 **bene habet,** all right! agreed!
29 **reficiendās,** to be repaired.

Language

Price and Value

In Latin the Ablative Case is used to show *price.*

> **haec palla sexāgintā dēnāriīs vēnit.**
> *This robe is sold for sixty denarii* or *costs sixty denarii.*
> **minimō vestīmenta vendō.**
> *I sell clothes at a very low price.*

The Genitive Case is used to show *value.*

> **hanc pallam magnī aestimō.**
> *I value this robe highly.*

The words **tantī,** so much, **quantī?** how much?, **plūris,** more, **minōris,** less—all genitive—are used for both *price* and *value.*

> **nōn est tantī.** *It is not worth so much*—VALUE.
> **minōris nōn vendam.** *I shall not sell it for less*—PRICE.

79

Gladiators fighting wild beasts.

Exercise 15b

*Read the following passage and, with the aid of the notes, try to understand it.
Then answer in English the questions below. Finally, translate the passage into
English, using the General Word List if necessary.*

ego maximus sum

Lūcius et Publius in officīnam Vērī ingressī
Vērum ipsum et gladiātōrēs salūtāvērunt.
dum Vērus galeam reficit, Lūcius gladiā-
tōribus dīxit, 'vultisne nōbīs aliquid dē rēbus   **rēs gestae,** exploits
gestīs vestrīs nārrāre? gladiātōrēs enim
maximē admīrāmur.' tum tacēbat alter
gladiātor cum Latīnē loquī nōn posset; alter
tamen, cui nōmen erat Anthrax, magnā vōce,
'libenter,' inquit, 'ego dē meīs rēbus gestīs
nārrābō; quis enim mē est audācior? immō   **mē audācior,** bolder than I
cōnstat inter omnēs mē gladiātōrum omnium   (see p. 82)
maximum esse. quis enim mē vel bibendō   **cōnstat inter omnēs,** it is well
vel pugnandō umquam superāvit? audīte,   known
puerī; rem vōbīs nārrābō mīram sed vēram.' '   **vel bibendō vel pugnandō,**
     either at drinking or at fighting

ōlim Rōmae in amphitheātrō vēnātiō cele-brābātur; bēstiae multae et ferōcēs in harēnam immissae cum bēstiāriīs pugnābant et ab eīs occīsae sunt omnēs; periērunt et bēstiāriī multī. tum immissī sunt ingēns leō et ursus quibus nūllae bēstiae maiōrēs et ferōciōrēs umquam vīsae erant. bēstiāriī terribilī aspectū perterritī fūgērunt et ā tergō oppugnātī omnēs ad ūnum occīsī sunt. quantus gemitus per caveam audītus est! tum Caesar—ipse enim aderat—exclāmāvit, 'quis cum hīs bēstiīs pugnāre audēbit? sī superāverit, ingēns pondus aurī habēbit.' tum ego—forte enim aderam—sōlus in harēnam insiluī. statim bēstiae mē petīvērunt. plōrābant spectātōrēs omnēs et dē Anthrace āctum esse dīcēbant. ego tamen—nōnne dīxī mē summā audāciā esse?—alterā manū leōnem, ursum alterā rapuī et capitibus collīsīs mortuōs in terram dēiēcī. magnō gaudiō conclāmāvērunt omnēs et Caesar, 'dī immortālēs,' exclāmāvit, 'hic audāciā superat omnēs. habeat aurum.'

puerī attonitī stābant, sed Vērus rīdēns, 'edepol,' inquit, 'nōn Anthrax appellārī dēbēs, sed Mendax.' rīsit et ipse Anthrax et puerīs dīxit, 'sī crās post merīdiem ad amphi-theātrum vēneritis, Anthracem pugnantem et superantem vidēbitis.' illī, cum eī grātiās ēgissent, laetī domum abiērunt.

post prandium, ut solēbant, paulīsper dormiēbant. deinde, cum propter calōrem, quī eō diē maximus erat, nēmō in urbem īre vellet, puerī cum Vesōniā in peristȳlium ēgressī usque ad vesperum in umbrā lūdēbant.

vēnātiō, -ōnis, *f.*, a fight with wild beasts

gemitus, -ūs, *m.*, groan
cavea, the spectators' seats

petīvērunt, went for me
dē Anthrace āctum est, it's all up with Anthrax

collīdō, -ere, -līsī, -līsum, knock together
mortuus, -a, -um, dead

usque ad, until, right up to
vesper, -i, *m.*, evening

Questions

1 What was Verus doing when the boys entered his workshop?
2 Why did only one gladiator speak?
3 The Latin word **praeclārus** means *glorious;* from Anthrax's description of himself we would describe him not as **praeclārus** but as **glōriōsus.** What do you think this word means?

4 Two types of public entertainer are mentioned in the passage. What were they called and what did they do?
5 Was the type of entertainment described by Anthrax regarded as respectable? Give a reason for your answer.
6 According to his story, was Anthrax popular with the crowd?
7 Using your English dictionary, if necessary, to help you to arrive at the meaning of **Mendax,** suggest an English version of the suggested name.
8 Why did the boys stay at home in the afternoon?

Language

Some uses of the cases

1 *Comparison:*

quis mē est audācior? *Who is bolder than I?*

. . . **quibus nūllae bēstiae maiōrēs et ferōciōrēs umquam vīsae erant.**

. . . *than which no bigger and fiercer beasts had ever been seen.*

(A more natural English translation would be: '*the biggest and fiercest beasts that had ever been seen.*')

When two nouns or pronouns are directly compared by means of an adjective in the comparative degree, the second member of the comparison is often found in the ablative case without **quam,** *than.*

2 *Descriptive phrases:*
   (*a*) gladiātor **magnō corpore** et **ferōci vultū** erat.
   The gladiator was a man of big frame and fierce looks.
   (*b*) vir **summā audāciā** sum.
   or
   vir **summae audāciae** sum.
   I am a man of the greatest boldness.
   (*c*) Lūcius puer **quattuordecim annōrum** erat.
   Lucius was a boy of fourteen years.

When the descriptive phrase (English: *of . . . .*) refers to physical characteristics (Example (*a*)), it is found in the ablative case; when it refers to qualities of mind or character (Example (*b*)) it is in either genitive or ablative case; when it involves any measurement of time, length, height, etc. (Example (*c*)), it is always found in the genitive.

Exercise 15c

1 *redde Anglicē :*

quis fēlīcior est Vesōniō?
Publius celerius currēbat quam Lūcius.
numquam canem vīdī maiōrem Rūfō.
nūllum canem magis timeō quam Rūfum.
Vesōnius homō maximā clēmentiā erat.
iter fēcimus duōrum mīlium passuum.

2 *In three of the following sentences, the ablative case can be used instead of* **quam** . . . . *Rewrite the three, using the ablative case.*

nēmō domum lautiōrem habet quam Vesōnius.
vīdistīne umquam fēminam pulchriōrem quam Verāniam?
ego habeō plūs pecūniae quam tū.
Vesōnia pilam habet minōrem quam Lūcius.
puerī gladiātōrem ferōciōrem quam Anthracem numquam vīderant.
fīcōs dulciōrēs quam hās numquam gustāvī.

In the Street of Abundance, one of the chief shopping areas of Pompeii. Since in most cases the ancient names of Pompeian streets are not known, they are identified by names given to them by the excavators. The Street of Abundance is so called from the number of discoveries made in it.

Lesson 16

Exercise 16a

a.d. IX Kal. Sept.
Earth Tremors and a Troubled Sleep

postrīdiē Lūcius et Publius sērō ē lectīs surrēxērunt; cum enim propter
crēbrōs terrae tremōrēs ad multam noctem vigilāvissent, dēfessī erant.
inter ientāculum, dum Vesōnius et Verānia dē tremōribus loquuntur,
Vesōnia ingressa, 'ō mē miseram,' inquit, 'quam dēfessa sum! propter
5 tonitruum nōn bene dormīvī.' rīdēbant puerī, quamquam et ipsī territī
erant—audācēs enim vidērī volēbant—et Lūcius, 'nōn tonitruō, stulta, sed
terrae tremōribus excitāta es; nōnne intellegis in Campāniā tālia fierī
solēre.' Vesōnius tacēbat sed paulō post, cum in tablīnum sē recēpisset,
ratiōnibus operam dabat. Verānia autem Vesōniam ad sē vocātam in
10 peristӯlium dūxit. 'hodiē,' inquit, 'mea Vesōnia, cum per noctem vigilā-
veris, ōtiōsae erimus. absint librī et cērae et stilus. sī amīcās hodiē invītāre
vīs, bene habet.'
tum Lūcius, 'quid,' inquit, 'mī Publī, nōs ante merīdiem faciēmus?
cum enim nimium diū domī cessāverimus, breve tempus restat. patrem
15 nōs ad lūdōs post merīdiem ductūrum esse spērō. Anthracem enim illum
audācissimum vidēre maximē cupiō.' Publius, 'cupiō et ego,' inquit,
'Anthracem vidēre. interim tamen ad portam Nōlānam eāmus; cum enim
hic diēs fēstus sit, sine dubiō multī Nōlānī hūc venient; fortasse aliquōs
agnōscam.' cum Lūcius adsēnsus esset, puerī ad portam Nōlānam profectī
20 sunt.

WORD LIST

*propter (*with accus.*), because of
*crēber, -bra, -brum, frequent
tremor, -ōris, *m.* (terrae), earth tremor
*loquor, loquī, locūtus sum, talk
*quam! how!
*stultus, -a, -um, silly, foolish
*tālis, -is, -e, such

*tablīnum, -ī, *n.*, private room, study
*sē recipere, to withdraw
invītāre, to invite
*brevis, -is, -e, short
fēstus, -a, -um, festive, festal
adsentior, -īrī, -sēnsus sum, agree

NOTES

1 cum . . . vigilāvissent, since they had lain awake (see Language).
8 cum . . . sē recēpisset, when he had withdrawn.
9 ratiōnibus operam dabat, he devoted his attention to his accounts.
11 absint librī . . . stilus: the literal translation 'let books . . . be absent' is not natural English. Think of a natural translation of the Latin words.
15 Anthracem illum audācissimum—in English, *the bold Anthrax.*

Language

The Perfect and Pluperfect Subjunctive active

1 **cum nōn bene dormīverim, dēfessa sum.**
Since I have not slept well, I am tired.

2 **cum domī cessāverimus, vix duae hōrae restant.**
Since we have lingered at home, scarcely two hours are left.

dormīverim and **cessāverimus** are examples of the perfect subjunctive active.

3 **Vesōnius, cum in tablīnum sē recēpisset, librīs operam dedit.**
When Vesonius had withdrawn to his study, he devoted his attention to his books.

4 **cum ad multam noctem vigilāvissent, dēfessī erant.**
Since they had lain awake far into the night, they were tired.

recēpisset and **vigilāvissent** are examples of the pluperfect subjunctive active.

Note
Observe that in the third of the above examples **cum** means *when.* Followed by the imperfect or pluperfect subjunctive it very often has this meaning.

85

How to recognise perfect and pluperfect subjunctive active:

Principal parts of verb			Perfect Subj.	Pluperf. Subj.
cessō, cessāre	CESSĀV-Ī	cessātum	cessāv-erim	cessāv-issem
maneō, manēre	MĀNS-Ī	mānsum	māns-erim	māns-issem
dūcō, dūcere	DŪX-Ī	ductum	dūx-erim	dūx-issem
dormiō, dormire	DORMĪV-Ī	dormītum	dormīv-erim	dormīv-issem

Table of endings:

Perfect Subjunctive	Pluperfect Subjunctive
dūx-erim	dūx-issem
dūx-eris	dūx-issēs
dūx-erit	dūx-isset
dūx-erimus	dūx-issēmus
dūx-eritis	dūx-issētis
dūx-erint	dūx-issent

Exercise 16b

a.d. IX Kal. Sept.
Feud with Nuceria

dum puerī ad portam Nōlānam lentē ambulant, in vīcō quōdam nōnnūllōs
iuvenēs caupōnam intrātūrōs cōnspiciunt. quōs cum caupō vīdisset, īrātus
'abīte,' clāmāvit, 'hīc Nūcerīnōs nōn accipimus.' simul gladiātōrēs quīdam
quī forte in eā caupōnā bibēbant, ēruptiōne factā iuvenēs in fugam dant.
5 rīsit Lūcius sed Publius attonitus, 'quid agitur?' inquit, 'cūr nōn licet
illīs iuvenibus in caupōnam intrāre?' tum Lūcius ita rem nārrāvit. 'abhinc
annōs vīgintī, cum lūdī gladiātōriī in amphitheātrō Pompeiānō celebrā-
rentur, aderant multī Nūcerīnī. cum autem Pompeiānī gladiātōrī cuīdam
parcere, damnāre eum Nūcerīnī vellent, pugna inter eōs orta est. cum
10 multī vulnerātī, occīsī nōnnūllī essent, rēs Rōmam ad senātum dēlāta est,
et senātūs consultō amphitheātrum Pompeiānum in decem annōs clausum
est. num mīrāris Nūcerīnōs nōbīs invīsōs esse?' simul Lūcius testulā
sublātā in mūrō 'Nūcerīnōs nōn amō' scrīpsit.

tum, quod prope merīdiem erat, puerī, portae Nōlānae et Nōlānōrum
15 immemorēs, domum ad prandium rediērunt.

WORD LIST

*vīcus, -ī, *m.*, street
*caupō, -ōnis, *m.*, innkeeper
ēruptiō, -ōnis, *f.*, sortie
*fuga, -ae, *f.*, flight; **in fugam dare,** to put to flight
*abhinc, ago
*parcō, -ere, pepercī (*with dative*), spare
*pugna, -ae, *f.*, fight
*damnō, -āre, -āvī, -ātum, condemn
*orior, -īrī, ortus sum, arise

*vulnerāre, to wound
dēferō, -ferre, -tulī, -lātum, report
*senātūs cōnsultum, decree of senate
*claudō, -ere, clausī, clausum, close
*miror, -ārī, -ātus sum, wonder, be surprised
testula, -ae, *f.*, fragment of tile
*mūrus, -ī, *m.*, wall
immemor, -oris, forgetful of

NOTES

5 **quid agitur?** What's going on?

10 **rēs Rōmam ad senātum dēlāta est.** *lit.* The affair was reported to Rome to the senate. We would say, to the senate at Rome.

11 **in decem annōs**—for a period of ten years ahead.

12 **num mīrāris?** Are you really surprised? *or* Surely you are not surprised?

testulā sublātā . . . scrīpsit. The writing of slogans on walls was current long before paint sprays were invented. Election slogans and comments on public and private matters scratched on the walls of buildings in Pompeii are a valuable source of information about life in the town.

The amphitheatre at Pompeii

87

Lesson 17

Exercise 17a

a.d. IX Kal. Sept.
Vesuvius erupts

inter prandium Lūcius Vesōniō, 'pater,' inquit, 'cum hodiē lūdī in amphitheātrō celebrentur et amīcus noster Anthrax pugnātūrus sit, vīsne nōs eō dūcere?' cuī pater respondit, 'cum māter tua et soror, ut ipse vidēs, terrae tremōribus perturbātae sint, domī relinquī timent. quae cum ita
5 sint, ego nōlō diū domō abesse. cum tamen videāminī tū et Publius maximē cupere Anthracem istum pugnantem spectāre, ad amphitheātrum vōs comitābor. nōn diū tamen ibi manēbō.'

post prandium Vesōnius, cum in tablīnum sē recēpisset, iterum ratiōnibus sē dedit; cēterī, ut solēbant, paulīsper cubābant. deinde
10 Vesōnius, togā sumptā, cum puerīs profectus est. quanta multitūdō per viās ruēbat! crēderēs Pompeiānōs omnēs amphitheātrum petere. thermae, quō multī cīvēs post merīdiem convenīre solēbant, relictae erant; omnēs enim ad lūdōs abierant. nōnnūllae tabernae iam occlūsae erant; pistōrēs tamen et placentāriī, spē lucrī adductī, lūdōrum immemorēs labōrābant.
15 dum Vesōnius et puerī caupōnam quandam praetereunt, iuvenēs nōn-nūllōs convēnisse vīdērunt et gladiātōrēs quōsdam spectāre quī intus bibēbant; ē quibus ūnus, cum Vesōnium vīdisset, rīdēns 'salvē!' exclāmāvit, 'vir optime, moritūrī tē salūtāmus.' puerī rīdēbant et Lūcius patrī, 'edepol,' inquit, 'vidētur ille gladiātor tē Caesarem esse putāre.'
20 Vesōnius respōnsūrus erat, sed subitō, clāmōre audītō, respexit et 'dī immortālēs,' exclāmāvit, 'quid videō?' surgēbat enim ā summō Monte Vesūviō ātra nūbēs magnitūdine et speciē inūsitātā.

WORD LIST

*perturbāre, to disturb
*timēre, to fear
comitor, -ārī, -ātus sum (*dep.*), accompany
*sūmō, -ere, sūmpsī, sūmptum (togam), put on
ruō, -ere, ruī, rutum, rush
thermae, -ārum, *f.pl.*, public baths
occlūdō, -ere, -clūsi, -clūsum, shut
placentārius, -ii, *m.*, pastry-cook
*spēs, speī, *f.*, hope

lucrum, -ī, *n.*, gain, profit
*addūcō, -ere, -dūxī, -ductum, attract
*intus, within
*moritūrus, -a, -um, about to die
*respiciō, -ere, -spexī, -spectum, look back
āter, -tra, -trum, black
*nūbēs, -is, *f.*, cloud
*magnitūdō, -inis, *f.*, size
*speciēs, -ēī, *f.*, appearance
inūsitātus, -a, -um, unusual

NOTES

4 **quae cum ita sint,** since this is so. Suggest some other ways of saying this in English.

6 **Anthracem istum,** that Anthrax of yours.

11 **crēderēs,** you (or one) would have thought.

18 **vir optime,** sir!

moritūrī tē salūtāmus, we, who are about to die, salute you. These were the words with which the gladiators hailed the emperor when they paraded before him in the arena at Rome before a contest.

22 **magnitūdine et speciē inūsitātā,** of unusual size and shape. (See page 82.)

Mt Vesuvius

89

Exercise 17b

a.d. IX Kal. Sept.
Panic and confusion—the danger grows

paulīsper stant omnēs attonitī; deinde magnus tumultus ortus est cum
simul virī hūc illūc currerent dum cōnantur ad suam quisque domum
pervenīre, simul fēminae et līberī in viās effunderentur virōs patrēsque
vocantēs et deōs lacrimīs implōrantēs.

5   interim nūbēs surgit altius in caelum ingentī et rāmōsae arborī
simillima, modo flammīs candida, modo terrā et cinere sordida. mox sōl
obscūrātur et cinis tamquam imber, prīmō levis, deinde gravior cadere
incipit. tum vērō ingentem tumultum vidērēs. undique tabernāriī,
occlūsīs tabernīs, aut in domibus suīs aut extrā portās urbis salūtem petunt.
10 gladiātōrēs, relictīs in caupōnā armīs et tubīs, ad portam Nōlānam fugiunt.
pistōrēs, pānibus relictīs in fornīs, lucrī immemorēs ad portās urbis
festīnant. cum multa aedificia tremōribus terrae quassāta essent, perīculōsum erat per viās ambulāre. cīvēs igitur multī, nē, dum perīculum
vītant, maiōre perīculō opprimerentur, in domōs suās sē recēpērunt et,
15 iānuīs clausīs, salūtem aut mortem exspectāvērunt. ēheu! multī ita inclūsī
periērunt.

     Vesōnius et puerī, cum multitūdine occurrentium impedīrentur, vix
prōgredī poterant, sed tandem, cum perīcula multa effūgissent, per
cālīginem domum suam cōnspexērunt. iānua clausa erat sed pulsantibus
20 iānitor laetus eam aperuit.

WORD LIST

*tumultus, -ūs, *m.*, confusion
*līberī, -ōrum, *m.*, children
effundō, -ere, -fūdī, -fūsum, pour out;
  effundī (*pass.*), to rush out
*lacrima, -ae, *f.*, tear
*implōrāre, to implore
rāmōsus, -a, -um, spreading, branching
*similis, -is, -e, like
*candidus, -a, -um, bright
cinis, -eris, *m.*, ash
obscūrāre, to darken
tamquam, as if

*imber, -bris, *m.*, shower of rain
*levis, -is, -e, light
*incipiō, -ere, -cēpī, -ceptum, begin
*undique, on all sides, everywhere
tuba, -ae, *f.*, trumpet
*periculōsus, -a, -um, dangerous
*opprimō, -ere, -pressī, -pressum,
  overwhelm
inclūsus, -a, -um (inclūdere), shut in
*vix, scarcely
cālīgō, -inis, *f.*, fog, gloom
pulsāre, to knock at

NOTES

2 **cum simul virī currerent . . . simul fēminae et līberī effunderentur; cum,**
since, applies to both **currerent** and **effunderentur**—imperfect subjunctive passive
of **effundere**; see Language. **effundere** means *to pour something out*; how does the
passive come to mean *rush out*?

12 **cum multa aedificia quassāta essent**, since many buildings had been damaged—
quassāta essent is the pluperfect subjunctive passive of **quassāre**. See Language.

13 **nē opprimerentur**, lest they should be overwhelmed.

17 **occurrentium, pulsantibus**, think out a natural English rendering for these
participles.
cum impedīrentur, since they were hindered.

Language

The Subjunctive, passive voice

1 **cum lūdī hodiē in amphitheātrō celebrentur, vīsne nōs eō dūcere?**
Since games are being celebrated today in the arena, will you take us there?

cum videāminī cupere Anthracem spectāre, vōs comitābor.
Since you seem to be anxious to watch Anthrax, I'll go with you.

celebrentur and **videāminī** are present subjunctive passive of **celebrāre**
and **vidēre** respectively.

2 **cum multitūdine impedīrentur, vix prōgredī poterant.**
Since they were hindered by the crowd, they could scarcely make progress.

nē opprimerentur, in domōs sē recēpērunt.
Lest they should be overwhelmed, they withdrew into their houses.

impedīrentur and **opprimerentur** are imperfect subjunctive passive of
impedīre and **opprimere** respectively.

3 **cum māter tua et soror perturbātae sint, domī relinquī timent.**
Since your mother and sister have been alarmed, they are afraid to be left at home.

perturbātae sint is perfect subjunctive passive of **perturbāre.**

4 **cum multa aedificia quassāta essent, perīculōsum erat per viās ambulāre.**
Since many buildings had been damaged, it was dangerous to walk through the streets.

quassāta essent is pluperfect subjunctive passive of **quassāre.**

SUBJUNCTIVE PASSIVE

FIRST CONJUGATION   **laudāre,** to praise

Present	Imperfect	Perfect	Pluperfect
laud-er	laudā-rer	laudātus sim	laudātus essem
laud-ēris	laudā-rēris	laudātus sīs	laudātus essēs
laud-ētur	laudā-rētur	laudātus sit	laudātus esset
laud-ēmur	laudā-rēmur	laudātī sīmus	laudātī essēmus
laud-ēminī	laudā-rēminī	laudātī sītis	laudātī essētis
laud-entur	laudā-rentur	laudātī sint	laudātī essent

SECOND CONJUGATION   **habēre,** to have, hold

habe-ar	habē-rer	habitus sim	habitus essem

THIRD CONJUGATION   **dūcere,** to lead
                              capere, to take

dūc-ar	dūce-rer	ductus sim	ductus essem
capi-ar	cape-rer	captus sim	captus essem

FOURTH CONJUGATION   **audīre,** to hear

audi-ar	audī-rer	audītus sim	audītus essem

Exercise 17c

Use the most suitable word(s) to fill the blank in each sentence.

1 cum sōl ——, dē viā errāvimus. *calet, vidērāmus, obscūrārētur.*
2 cum terrae tremōribus ——, tē domī nōn relinquam. *erant, perturbāta sīs, audīveris.*
3 Vesōnius, cum clāmōrem ——, respexit. *audīvisset, audiat, audītus erat.*
4 cum ——, tonitruum nōn audīvī. *dormiam, dormīvisset, dormīrem.*
5 cum gladiātōrēs ——, nūllī lūdī erunt. *fūgissent, fūgerint, superābuntur.*
6 cum multitūdine ——, domum nōn perveniēmus. *impediātur, timeāmus, impediāmur.*
7 cum dēfessī esse ——, vōs domī manēre iussī. *vidērēminī, videātis, videāris.*
8 nē —— tabernae; perīculī mox fīnis erit. *claudās, claudantur, claudentur.*

Exercise 17d

respondē Latīnē:

cūr Lūcius et Publius ad lūdōs īre cupiēbant?
cūr māter et Vesōnia domī relinquī nōlēbant?
quid Vesōnius post prandium fēcit?
cūr pistōrēs tabernās nōn clausērunt?
cūr iuvenēs ad caupōnam cōnvēnerant?
cūr Vesōnius, cum respexisset 'dī immortālēs!' exclāmāvit?
cūr tumultus in viīs ortus est?
gladiātōrēsne virtūtis suae memorēs erant?
cūr multī cīvēs in domōs sē recēpērunt?
cūr perīculōsum erat per viās ambulāre?

Lesson 18

Exercise 18a

a.d. IX Kal. Sept.
Night of fear and uncertainty

cum Vesōnius et puerī domum intrāvissent, Verāniam et Vesōniam et
servōs perterritōs in ātriō congregātōs invēnērunt. nūbe enim vīsā et
clāmōribus audītīs perīculum ingēns imminēre sēnserant. Verānia igitur,
ut Vesōnium domum revocāret, Lucriōnem, servum fidēlem, ad Amphi-
5 theātrum mīserat quī eum quaereret. is tamen nōndum redierat.

iam cinis per compluvium incidēns terrōrem omnium augēbat, sed
Vesōnius, quamquam ipse perturbātus erat, 'agite,' inquit, 'cōnsīdāmus
ut paulisper quiēscāmus. posteā dē salūte nostrā dēlīberābimus. ecce cinis
iam levior esse mihi vidētur.' cum cōnsēdissent, aliī alia dīcēbant, cum
10 subitō Lūcius 'ēheu,' exclāmāvit, 'Rūfī canis meī oblītus eram. sine mē,
pater, ad fullōnicam īre ut Rūfum solvam nē catēnā impedītus pereat.'
sed Vesōnius 'minimē vērō,' inquit, 'mī fīlī, hīc manēbis nōbīscum nē
propter turbam dē viā errēs et pereās ipse. crēdō Anterum Rūfum
cūrātūrum esse.'

15 iam hōra octāva erat, sed crēderēs sōlem iam occidisse; tam dēnsa
cālīgō lūcem abstulerat. tum coquus, ut animōs omnium cōnfirmāret,
hilariter, 'ēheu!' exclāmāvit, 'cēnae immemorēs hīc sedēmus. ego in
culīnam festīnābō ut cēnam parem. Acanthiō et Paegnium mēcum
veniant.'

20 Traniō autem, cui Vesōnius maximē cōnfīdēbat, 'domine,' inquit,
vīsne mē sinere ēgredī in viās ut Lucriōnem quaeram? est enim amīcissimus
mihi, tibi fidēlissimus. fortasse propter tenebrās dē viā errāvit.' sed
Vesōnius, 'ego quoque,' respondit, 'dē Lucriōne sollicitus sum; sī tamen
adhūc superest, sine dubiō domum redībit; sīn periit, tū nūllō modō eum
25 adiuvāre poteris. hīc igitur manēbis ut vīvōs adiuvēs.'

mox modica cēna appōnitur sed, cum propter timōrem cibum minimē
appeterent, brevī cubitum abiērunt omnēs praeter ipsum Vesōnium, quī
cum Phaniscō, servō ā manū, in tablīnum sē recēpit ut tabulās suās et
aurum argentumque in ūnum locum colligeret. posteā is quoque in
30 cubiculum sē cōntulit; brevis tamen et inquiētus somnus.

WORD LIST

imminēre, to threaten, be imminent
*****sentiō, -īre, sēnsī, sēnsum,** realise
*****ut,** in order that
incĭdō, -ere, -cĭdī, -cāsum, fall (into)
*****augeō, -ēre, auxī, auctum,** increase
*****cōnsidō, -ere, -sēdī, -sessum,** sit down
*****quiēscō, -ere, quiēvī, quiētum,** rest
*****oblitus eram (oblivīscī),** I had forgotten
*****solvō, -ere, solvī, solūtum,** loosen, release
*****nē,** lest
*****turba, -ae,** *f.,* crowd, confusion
occĭdō, -ere, -cĭdī, -cāsum, (of the sun) set
cōnfirmāre, to strengthen
hilariter, gaily

*****tenebrae, -ārum,** *f.pl.,* darkness
*****sollicitus, -a, -um,** troubled, anxious
*****adhūc,** still, even now
*****supersum, -esse, -fuī,** survive
sīn, but if
modicus, -a, -um, modest, sparse
appōnō, -ere, -posuī, -positum, set down (a meal)
*****timor, -ōris,** *m.,* fear
appetō, -ere, -īvī, -ītum, desire, have an appetite for
*****praeter** (*with acc.*), except
tabulae, -ārum, *f.pl.,* account books
*****argentum, -ī,** *n.,* silver
*****colligō, -ere, -lēgī, -lēctum,** collect, gather

NOTES

2 **congregātōs,** huddled, gathered (perfect participle of **congregārī,** to gather together).

4 **ut Vesōnium revocāret,** literally, 'in order that she might recall Vesonius'; the natural English translation would be 'to recall Vesonius'.

5 **quī eum quaereret,** literally 'who might look for him'. What is the natural way of saying this in English?

10 **canis meī oblītus eram,** the verbs **oblivīscī,** *to forget* and **meminisse,** *to remember,* are regularly followed by the genitive case.
   sine mē; sine, the imperative of **sinere,** *to allow,* must not be confused with **sine,** the preposition meaning *without.*

28 **servus ā manū,** secretary.

30 **sē contulit,** went off, took himself off to (**cōnferre**).

Language

Purpose

1 **cōnsidāmus ut paulisper quiēscāmus.**
Let us sit down so that we may rest for a little.

2 **sine mē īre ut Rūfum solvam.**
Allow me to go to release Rufus.

95

3 Verānia, ut Vesōnium revocāret. Lucriōnem ad Amphitheātrum mīserat.
Verania, in order to recall Vesonius, (or so as to . . . ,) had sent Lucrio to the Amphitheatre.

4 coquus, ut animōs omnium cōnfirmāret, hilariter exclāmāvit . . . .
The cook, to cheer everyone up, exclaimed gaily . . . .

In Latin *purpose* is expressed by **ut,** *in order that, so that,* followed by the present or imperfect subjunctive; this is often called a Final or Purpose Clause. The natural way of translating such purpose clauses into English is often the present infinitive. See examples 2 and 4 above.

Note

I hīc manēbis nē dē viā errēs et pereās ipse.
You will stay here lest you lose your way and perish yourself.

When the purpose is negative—in order not to do something—**nē,** *lest,* takes the place of **ut.**

2 Verānia servum mīserat quī Vesōnium quaereret.
Verania had sent a slave to look for Vesonius.—literally, *who should look for Vesonius.*

The relative pronoun, followed by the present or imperfect subjunctive, often indicates purpose.

Poor Rufus! Cast of the body of Vesonius's dog, found in the ruins of the fullonica.

Exercise 18b

a.d. VIII Kal. Sept.
Preparations for departure: destination Nola

Vesōnius, cum per noctem propter magnōs et assiduōs imbrēs ventōsque
turbulentōs vigilāvisset, paulō ante lūcem ē lectō surrēxit. nōndum diēs
erat sed ignēs quī ā Monte Vesūviō fulgēbant lūmen lūridum et terribile
praebēbant. quō visō Vesōnius uxōrem suam et līberōs et familiam omnem
excitāvit et statim in ātrium congregārī iussit. 5

cum convēnissent, Vesōnius 'mihi pareant omnēs,' clāmāvit; 'hinc
statim discēdendum est. Cariō (is coquus fuit) cibum ē culīnā ferat;
Phaniscus saccum nummōrum portet. cētera omnia relinquenda sunt.
Portam Nōlānam petēmus ut inde, sī nōbīs dī favēbunt, in agrōs effugiāmus.
posteā fortasse Nōlam ad domum Verāniī pervenīre poterimus. agmine 10
factō per viās prōgrediēmur. antecēdent Thespriō et Olympiō ut nōbīs
iter patefaciant. nōbīscum in mediō Cariō cibum, nummōs Phaniscus
portābit; ancillae Verāniam et Vesōniam comitābuntur. ā tergō cēterī
agmen cōgent nē multitūdine sequentium obterāmur.' haec dum dīcit,
iānitor exclāmāvit, 'nisi festīnāveritis, hīc inclūsī perībimus omnēs. iam 15
enim iānua cumulō cineris obstructa vix aperīrī potest.' tum vērō trepi-
dātiōnem magnam vidērēs. omnēs in viam effūsī sunt.

quantus ibi terror fuit! viae aliae ruīnā domōrum obstructae erant,
aliae multitūdine fugientium complēbantur. propter cinerem quī pumicibus
mixtus iam dēnsissimus incidēbat, vix prōgredī vel etiam stāre poterant. 20
terrōrem augēbant clāmōrēs virōrum, fēminārum ululātūs, quirītātūs
īnfantium. Vesōnius, ut animōs omnium cōnfirmāret, saepe 'bonō este
animō,' clāmāvit, 'crēdō prope esse portam Nōlānam.' saepe, nē quis dē
viā errāret, ūnum quemque nōmine vocāvit. tandem ad portam pervēnērunt
et aegrē in agrōs effūgērunt. 25

WORD LIST

assiduus, -a, -um, incessant
turbulentus, -a, -um, stormy
fulgeō, -ēre, fulsī, fulsum, shine
*lūmen, -inis, *n.*, light
lūridus, -a, -um, pale
*pareō, -ēre, -uī (*dat.*), obey
saccus, -ī, *m.*, bag
nummī, -ōrum, *m.pl.*, coins, money
*faveō, -ēre, fāvī, fautum (*dat.*), favour
*antecēdō, -ere, -cessī, -cessum, go
ahead

*patefaciō, -ere, -fēcī, -factum, open
up
ancilla, -ae, *f.*, female servant
obterō, -ere, -trīvī, -trītum, crush
cumulus, -ī, *m.*, heap
obstructus, -a, -um (obstruere),
blocked
ruina, -ae, *f.*, collapse
trepidātiō, -ōnis, *f.*, alarm
*compleō, -ēre, -plēvī, -plētum, fill

pūmex, -icis, *m.*, pumice stone;
  pūmicēs, pebbles, *lapilli*
***mixtus, -a, -um (miscēre),** mixed

ululātus, -ūs, *m.*, wailing
quirītātus, -ūs, *m.*, shriek
***aegrē,** with difficulty

NOTES

4 **familia:** this does not mean 'family' in our sense of the word, but rather the household slaves—the staff or establishment.

6 **hinc discēdendum est,** we must leave this place.

8 **cētera omnia relinquenda sunt,** everything else must be left behind.

14 **agmen cōgere,** to bring up the rear; literally, to close the column. You have already met **cōgere** meaning *to compel*. Its other main meaning is *to gather up, compress into one place,* hence, *close.*

19 **pūmicēs: pūmex,** pumice, is a light volcanic stone, fragments of which, in great quantity, rained on Pompeii, mingled with dust and ashes. Nowadays they are usually referred to as *lapilli*.

22 **bonō este animō,** cheer up!

23 **nē quis dē viā errāret,** lest anyone (or, so that no one) should lose his way. **quis** (*neut.* **quid**) after **nē** means anyone.

24 **ūnum quemque,** each one; **quisque,** of which **quemque** is the accusative case, means *each.*

Exercise 18c

redde Anglicē:

per viās festīnāmus ut quam celerrimē domum perveniāmus.

Vesōnius domum festīnāvit ut uxōrem et fīliam servāret.

lentē prōgrediar nē dē viā errem.

cōnsēdimus nē dēfessī essēmus.

coquus cibum parābit nē omnēs famē pereant.

iānitor iānuam aperuit ut omnēs ēgrederentur.

Traniō domī manēbit ut nōs adiuvet.

Lūcius exīre volēbat ut Rūfum servāret.

coquus cibum sēcum portāvit, nē in itinere famē perīrent.

Vesōnius servōs mīsit quī viam patefacerent.

Revision Exercises

A. *From each of the following pairs of sentences form a single sentence, using* **cum.**

Example:

    pecūniam habeō. pānem emam.—cum pecūniam habeam, pānem emam.

(*a*) hīc manēre nōn possumus. in viam ēgrediāmur.
(*b*) sōl nōn fulgēbat. dē viā errāvimus.
(*c*) omnēs ad lūdōs abierant. multae tabernae dēsertae erant.
(*d*) pistrīna occlūsa erat. pānem emere nōn poterāmus.
(*e*) tū domum vēnistī. nihil timēmus.
(*f*) lūdī celebrābantur. ingēns multitūdō aderat.
(*g*) tū loquēris. ego tacēbō.
(*h*) puerī ē lectīs surrēxērunt. ad ientāculum dēscendēmus.

B. Revise *commands, wishes.*

    redde Anglicē:

nē hīc cessēmus; celeriter per viās prōgrediāmur.
abīte, scelestī! nē Nūcerīnus ūllus in meam caupōnam veniat.
Vesōnius mox domum veniat; vereor enim hīc sōla manēre.
nē quis ē domō exeat; omnēs nōbīscum maneant.
nōlīte cessāre; portae aperiantur.
dī nōbīs faveant; in agrōs effugiāmus.
omnēs mē sequantur; nē quis dē viā erret.
nē umquam urbs nostra tantā clāde opprimātur.

C. Revise *purpose.*

    1 *redde Anglicē:*

puerī ad lūdōs īre volunt ut Anthracem videant.
servum mittam quī ā fullōnicā togam recipiat.
dormīte paulīsper nē dēfessī sītis.
agmine factō prōgressī sumus nē multitūdine obtererēmur.
Vesōnius duōs servōs praemīsit quī viam patefacerent.
ut incolumēs ad portam veniātis, omnēs mihi pāreant.

2 *redde Latīnē:*

Let us buy a dog to guard the house.
Rufus guards the laundry by night so that no one may enter.
Verania sent two slaves to buy bread.
The boys hurried from the market lest they might be deafened (become deaf).
They lingered at the inn to hear the gladiators singing.
Then they went off to the Via Longa to see the shops.

D. Revise **ferre** and **fierī**.

Identify:

fer	ferte
ferrī	fīēmus
fierī	ferēmur
fertis	fierent
fierētis	ferent

E. *Test your word-power. Distinguish between the following pairs of words:*

ōvum	ovis
interim	interdiū
hīc	hinc
fāma	famēs
occĭdere	occīdere
avus	avis
parāre	parēre
prope	propter
sōl	sōlus
vĕnīre	vēnīre

Lesson 19

Exercise 19a

Perilous Journey

in agrōs ēgressī aliquamdiū prōgressī erant, cum Vesōnia dēfessa, 'māter', exclāmāvit, 'longius ambulāre nōn possum. hīc cōnsīdāmus ut paulīsper quiēscam.' Verānia—fīliae enim miserēbātur—cōnsīdere volēbat, sed Vesōnius 'stulta!' exclāmāvit, 'nōnne vidēs ubīque prōstrāta corpora virōrum et fēminārum et līberōrum, quī dēfessī cōnsēdērunt neque posteā 5 surgere potuērunt. sī Vesōnia ambulāre nōn potest, Traniōnem rogābō ut eam umerīs portet.' simul 'Traniō!' magnā vōce clāmat. sed quamquam iterum iterumque Traniōnem vocāvit, ille nōn respondit. tum Vesōnius 'ēheu!' exclāmāvit, 'periit Traniō, quō servum fidēliōrem numquam habuī.' tum Olympiō, lacrimīs Vesōniae mōtus, 'vīsne,' inquit, 'mihi 10 permittere ut eam portem? libenter id faciam. fuit enim semper mihi amīcissima.' cum Vesōnius sē velle dīxisset, Vesōnia laeta in umerōs Olympiōnis sublāta est.

mox, cum relūxisset paulum, gaudēbant omnēs quod diēs adesse vidēbātur. ēheu! nōn diēī sed adventantis ignis indicium erat. et ignis 15 quidem ad eōs nōn pervēnit sed cinis multus et gravis incidēbat. tum vērō, cum lassitūdine cōnfectī essent, Vesōnius omnibus permīsit ut paulīsper cōnsīderent; monuit tamen ut surgerent saepe ut cinerem excuterent nē opertī perīrent.

tandem illa cālīgō tenuāta quasi in fūmum vel nebulam discessit. 20 mox vērus diēs erat et sōl etiam effulsit, lūridus tamen, quālis solet esse cum dēficit. tum vērō magnum plōrātum audīrēs; ubi enim urbs Pompeiī fuerat, ingēns plānitiēs, altō cinere tamquam nive operta oculīs occursābat.

WORD LIST

*longius, farther
misereor, -ērī, miseritus sum (*with gen.*), pity
*ubīque, everywhere
prōstrātus, -a, -um, stretched out
*umerus, -ī, *m.*, shoulder
*permittō, -ere, -mīsī, -missum (*with dat.*), allow
relūxit, it grew lighter
adventāns, -antis (adventāre), approaching
*indicium, -iī, *n.*, sign
*quidem, indeed

lassitūdō, -inis, *f.*, weariness
excutiō, -ere, -cussī, -cussum, shake off
opertus (operīre), covered
tenuātus, -a, -um, thinned out
nebula, -ae, *f.*, mist
effulgeō, -ēre, -fulsī, shine out
*quālis, -is, -e, such as
dēficit, it is eclipsed
plōrātus, -ūs, *m.*, wailing
plānitiēs, -ēī, *f.*, level expanse
*nix, nivis, *f.*, snow
*oculus, -ī, *m.*, eye
occursāre (*dat.*), to meet

NOTES

6 **Traniōnem rogābō ut** . . . , simply, I shall ask Tranio to . . . . What is the literal translation?

9 **quō servum fidēliōrem numquam habuī,** the literal translation—than whom I never had a more faithful slave—is clumsy. Think of a better one.

10 **vīsne mihi permittere ut** . . . ? See note on line 6 above.

14 **cum relūxisset paulum,** when it had grown a little lighter. As in English, so in Latin impersonal expressions are used to describe the weather and natural phenomena, e.g. **pluit,** *it rains,* **tonat,** *there is thunder*; so, **relūcēscit,** *it grows light again.*

18 **monuit ut surgerent,** see note on line 6 above.

21 **quālis solet esse,** such as it is accustomed to be.

22 **cum dēficit,** during an eclipse.

Exercise 19b

Uncle Veranius to the Rescue

interim Nōlae apud Verānium trepidātiō erat maxima. Caecilia, uxor eius, prae dolōre nūllum cōnsilium capere poterat; Verānius ipse, dē fīliō sollicitus, servīs imperāvit ut raedam mannōsque parārent. simul ā vīcīnīs duōbus petīvit ut raedās mannōsque sibi commodārent, et Caeciliam
5 monuit ut servōs iubēret cibum et lectōs parāre. 'sī enim,' inquit, 'Vesōnius cum Verāniā et līberīs et familiā ex urbe effūgit, sine dubiō Nōlam petet. sī eōs in itinere invēnerimus, hūc eōs vehēmus.' ipse, quō celerius Pompeiōs pervenīret, cisiō profectus est, iussīs raedāriīs quam celerrimē sē sequī.
10   Vesōnius interim, cum Traniōnem quaesīvisset neque potuisset invenīre, ad suōs regressus Cariōnī imperāvit ut cibum omnibus distribueret. quem cum ēdissent, eōs monuit nē diūtius morārentur. 'sī enim,' inquit 'nōs ante noctem Nōlam perventūrōs esse spērāmus, festīnandum est.' cum igitur Olympiōnem rogāvisset ut iterum Vesōniam in umerōs tolleret,
15 omnēs agmine factō profectī sunt.

cum vix duo mīlia passuum prōgressī essent, Publius, multō pulvere procul vīsō, 'ecce,' exclāmāvit, 'nescioquis ā Nōlā appropinquat,' et statim, cisiō patris agnitō, 'dīs grātiās!' exclāmāvit. 'meus pater est; salvī sumus.' mox Verānius ad eōs pervēnit et, cum ē cisiō dēsiluisset, maximō cum
20 gaudiō ab eīs acceptus est. cum autem eōs lassitūdine paene cōnfectōs

esse vīdisset, 'bonō este animō,' exclāmāvit, 'raedae adsunt quibus celerrimē
Nōlam vehēminī.' neque multō post eae pervēnērunt.

    maximō gaudiō Nōlae apud Verānium acceptī sunt, praecipuē ā
Caeciliā quae dē salūte fīliī suī dēspērāverat. posteā, ubi corpora cūrāvērunt, dē exitiō urbis et cāsibus suīs omnia nārrāvērunt.   25

WORD LIST

prae dolōre, for grief
*imperō, -āre, -āvī, -ātum (*dat.*), order,
  command
vīcīnus, -ī, *m.*, neighbour
commodāre, to lend
*hūc, (to) here, hither
cisium, -iī, *n.*, light carriage
distribuō, -ere, -uī, -ūtum, distribute
*edō, -ere, ēdī, ēsum, eat

*duo mīlia passuum, two miles
pulvis, -eris, *m.*, dust
*appropinquāre, to approach
salvus, -a, -um, saved
*dēsiliō, -īre, -uī, -sultum, jump down
*dēspērāre, to despair
*exitium, -iī, *n.*, destruction
*cāsus, -ūs, *m.*, adventure

NOTES

7 **quō celerius Pompeiōs pervenīret,** so as to reach Pompeii more quickly. **quō** takes the place of **ut** when the clause of purpose contains an adjective or adverb in the comparative degree.

8 **cisium,** the cisium was a light 'run-about' two-wheeled carriage, used for rapid travel; the **raeda** was a heavier four-wheeled 'saloon' coach.

18 **dīs grātiās,** thanks be to the gods!

24 **ubi corpora cūrāvērunt,** when they had refreshed themselves. **corpora cūrāre** means to attend to one's bodily needs of food, drink, refreshment.

Language

Indirect Command

Exercises 19a and 19b contain several examples like the following:

Traniōnem rogābō ut eam portet.
I shall ask Tranio to carry her.

Verānius servīs imperāvit ut raedam parārent.
Veranius ordered the slaves to prepare the coach.

Vesōnius omnibus permīsit ut cōnsīderent.
Vesonius allowed all to sit down.

eōs monuit nē diūtius morārentur.
He warned them not to delay longer.

You will see from the above examples that verbs meaning *to command, to request, to allow, to warn* are followed in Latin by **ut** or **nē** and the present or imperfect subjunctive, as in purpose clauses. As in the above examples, this type of clause is often translated into English by the present infinitive, 'to . . .'

Notes

1 **Verānius raedāriōs iussit sē sequī.**
Veranius ordered the coachmen to follow him.

sine mē Verāniam portāre.
Allow me to carry Verania.

iubēre, to order (negative **vetāre,** to forbid) and **sinere,** to allow, are followed by the present infinitive in Latin as in English.

2 **Vesōnius imperāvit ut cibus omnibus darētur.**
Vesonius ordered that food should be given to all.

Sometimes the clause of purpose after a verb of commanding etc. must be translated quite literally.

Exercise 19c

1 *Below are a number of indirect commands; change them to the direct form, i.e. state the actual words spoken, and translate each pair into English.*

> *Example:* Indirect: **Lūcius ā patre petīvit ut sēcum ad lūdōs venīret.**
> *Lucius asked his father to come with him to the games.*

> Direct: **Pater, mēcum ad lūdōs venī.**
> *Father, come with me to the games.*

(*a*) tē moneō ut cibum et lectōs parēs.
(*b*) Vesōnius Phaniscō imperat ut saccum nummōrum portet.
(*c*) Verānius servōs iussit raedās quam celerrimē parāre.
(*d*) Vesōnius omnibus imperāvit ne Traniōnem exspectārent.
(*e*) Vesōnius omnēs sedēre sīvit.

2 *Change from direct to indirect form, using the words provided, and translate each example into English.*

> *Example:* Direct: **Olympiō! Vesōniam portā** (Vesōnius rogāvit).
> *Olympio, carry Vesonia.*

> Indirect: **Vesōnius Olympiōnem rogāvit ut Vesōniam portāret.**
> *Vesonius asked Olympio to carry Vesonia.*

(*a*) cōnsīdite paulīsper ut quiēscātis (Vesōnius nōbīs permittit).
(*b*) festīnent omnēs ad portam Nōlānam (Vesōnius iussit).
(*c*) nōlī exīre, Traniō! (Vesōnius nōn permīsit).
(*d*) manēte domī, fēminae! (Vesōnius monuit).
(*e*) nōlīte cōnsīdere, uxor mea et fīlia! (Vesōnius imperat).

The Disaster and After

A model of the ruins of Pompeii.

The pleasant life of ancient Pompeii ended abruptly on the afternoon of 24 August A.D. 79, when Mount Vesuvius erupted, and a hail of volcanic ash, cinders and small stones (*lapilli*) fell on the town, burying it to a depth of six metres. Many of the inhabitants escaped to the open country, but many others perished, some caught in the streets while trying to escape, others entombed in their houses where they probably died quickly, asphyxiated by the poisonous gases which accompanied the eruption. At the same time a torrent of volcanic mud engulfed low-lying Herculaneum to a depth of twenty metres. This mud gradually hardened into a concrete mass from which the town has still been only partly excavated.

After the eruption the survivors of the Pompeians returned, and by digging and tunnelling contrived to rescue many valuables from the houses and public buildings. However, no attempt was made to rebuild the town, and for centuries the site was forgotten. It was rediscovered in the early eighteenth century when a prince of Naples, who was building a new palace, was anxious to find a source of marble. His attention was drawn, first to Herculaneum, then to Pompeii, where excavation was much easier. Before long the importance of the site, not as a marble quarry, but as an archaeological find, was recognised and systematic excavation, begun in 1763, has been going on ever since, with the encouragement of successive governments.

As a result of these excavations, and particularly the scientific ones of recent years, it is possible to reconstruct a detailed picture of the life of an Italian town in the first century of our era. We can walk again in the streets and squares where Marcus Vesonius Primus and his fellow-merchants walked, inspect the oven where Modestus baked his bread, admire the shop-sign of Verecundus, examine the tools of Verus, sit in the tavern where the last gladiators of Pompeii were drinking on that August day of A.D. 79, and look down on the arena where men fought to the death to make a Pompeian holiday.

Lesson 20

Beasts, Birds and Bees

Most of what we know about the lost city of Pompeii is gleaned from the actual ruins; but we do get a vivid impression of the eruption from two letters of Pliny the Younger who was at Misenum with his uncle, Pliny the Elder, when the disaster occurred. He tells how his uncle, a man of keen scientific curiosity, as soon as he saw the strange cloud over Vesuvius, set out in a naval cutter (he was admiral of the fleet) to investigate the phenomenon. He stayed to help some of the distressed inhabitants of the area, but delaying too long in the danger zone, perished himself.

The best-known of the many books of the older Pliny is the *Natural History*, a work in which he brings together a great volume of knowledge from many sources. It is not science or natural history in our sense, but rather the fruits of his wide reading on many subjects.

This lesson includes three passages based on his *Natural History*.

Exercise 20a

A Famous Hound

Alexandrō Magnō, dum Indiam petit, rēx Albāniae dōnō dedit inūsitātae magnitūdinis canem. eius speciē dēlectātus iussit ursōs, mox aprōs et deinde dammās ēmittī, sed adeō eōs canis contempsit ut iacēret immōtus. sēgnitiā tantī corporis offēnsus, imperātor occīdī eum iussit. nūntiātum
5 est hoc rēgī; itaque alterum mittēns addidit mandāta nē in parvīs animālibus experīrī vellet, sed in leōne elephantōve; dīxit duōs sibi fuisse; hōc occīsō praetereā nūllum fore. nūlla mora fuit; Alexander leōnem frāctum prōtinus vīdit. posteā elephantum iussit indūcī. statim horrēbant villī canis per tōtum corpus; prīmum ingentī lātrātū intonuit, mox summā arte
10 oppugnāvit, nunc adsultāns, nunc recēdēns, dōnec elephantus assiduē rotātus magnō fragōre ad humum concidit.

WORD LIST

aper, -prī, *m.*, wild boar
damma, -ae, *f.*, deer
***contemnō, -ere, -tempsī, -temptum,**
  scorn, despise
***iaceō, -ēre, -iacuī,** lie
***immōtus, -a, -um,** motionless
sēgnitia, -ae, *f.*, inactivity
offēnsus, -a, -um, disgusted
***addō, -ere, -didī, -ditum,** add
***experīrī,** to test
***frangō, -ere, frēgī, frāctum,** break,
  tear to pieces

prōtinus, immediately
horreō, -ēre, -uī, bristle
villus, -ī, *m.*, hair
intonō, -āre, -uī, thunder
adsultāre, to dash up to
recēdere, to retreat
***dōnec,** until
***assiduē,** continuously
rotāre, to spin round
concidō, -ere, -cidī, collapse

NOTES

1 **dōnō dedit,** gave as a gift. **dōnō** is the dative case of **dōnum**—literally for a gift.
3 **adeō . . . ut,** to such an extent . . . that. See Language.
7 **fore,** alternative to **futūrum esse,** future infinitive of **esse.**

Exercise 20b

The Sad Tale of a Raven

Tiberiō prīncipe, ē templō Castŏris et Pollūcis corvus in sūtrīnam
proximam dēvolāvit. is tam celeriter sermōnī adsuēfactus est ut cottīdiē
māne ēvolāret in forum et Tiberium, deinde Germānicum et Drūsum
Caesarēs nōminātim, mox trānseuntem populum Rōmānum salūtāret.

5 posteā ad tabernam redībat. hoc per paucōs annōs avis fēcit ita ut omnibus
nōta esset. hanc manceps proximae sūtrīnae occīdit, sīve īrā sīve invidiā
adductus; sed tanta erat plēbis cōnsternātiō ut prīmō pulsus ex eā regiōne,
mox interfectus sit. fūnus autem avis celebrātum est; super Aethiopum
duōrum umerōs lectus ferēbātur; praecēdēbat tībīcen et corōnae omnium
10 generum usque ad rogum, quī dextrā Viae Appiae ad secundum lapidem
cōnstrūctus erat.

WORD LIST

sūtrīna, -ae, *f.*, shoemaker's stall
dēvolāre, to fly down
adsuēfactus, -a, -um, accustomed
*****sermō, -ōnis,** *m.*, conversation, human
speech
nōminātim, by name
*****nōtus, -a, um,** well-known
manceps, -ipis (sūtrīnae), *m.*, stall-
holder
*****invidia, -ae,** *f.*, envy
*****plēbs, -is,** *f.*, common people
cōnsternātiō, -ōnis, *f.*, dismay

*****pellō, -ere, pepulī, pulsum,** drive
fūnus, -eris, *n.*, funeral
*****avis, -is,** *f.*, bird
lectus, -ī, *m.*, bier
praecēdere, to go in front
tībīcen, -inis, *m.*, flute-player
*****genus, -eris,** *n.*, sort, kind
rogus, -ī, *m.*, funeral pyre, pile
*****lapis, -idis,** *m.*, milestone
*****cōnstruō, -ere, -strūxī, structum,**
build, raise

NOTES

2 **tam celeriter . . . ut,** so quickly that . . . . See Language.
4 **Caesarēs,** members of the imperial family.
populum Rōmānum trānseuntem, the Roman people as they passed.
5 **fēcit ita ut,** did this with the result that . . . . See Language.
6 **sīve . . . sīve (seu . . . seu),** whether . . . or, either . . . or, perhaps . . . perhaps.
8 **Aethiopum,** Aethiops was not necessarily an Ethiopian, but was a name applied to
any member of the Negro race.

Language

Result—Consecutive Clauses

Note sentences like the following:

1 **adeō eōs canis contempsit ut iacēret immōtus.**
The dog so despised them that it lay motionless.

2 **tanta erat plēbis cōnsternātiō ut . . . interfectus sit.**
Such (so great) was the indignation of the people that he was (actually) killed.

The above examples show how *result* is expressed in Latin; a word meaning *so, such* in the principal clause is followed by a clause introduced by **ut,** *that,* having its verb in the subjunctive mood. Such clauses are known as Consecutive Clauses. Note that the subjunctive of a Consecutive Clause is translated into English by the indicative.

Notes

1 **adeō,** *so, to such an extent,* is found with verbs, adjectives or adverbs.
  tam, *so,* is found only with adjectives and adverbs.
  ita, *so, in such a way,* is found only with verbs.

2 (*a*) **avis tam callida est ut omnēs dēlectet.**
     The bird is so clever that it amuses everyone.
  (*b*) **avis tam callida est ut omnēs dēlectāverit.**
     The bird is so clever that it has amused everyone.
  (*c*) **avis tam callida erat ut omnēs dēlectāret.**
     The bird was so clever that it amused everyone.
  (*d*) **manceps tam invidus erat ut avem occīderit.**
     The stallholder was so jealous that he actually killed the bird.

   Unlike clauses of purpose, which use only the present or imperfect subjunctive, consecutive clauses use any tense of the subjunctive which the meaning requires. Note however that, as in example (*d*) above, the use of the perfect subjunctive after a past tense in the principal clause emphasises the fact that the result actually happened.

3 **adeō canis parva animālia contempsit ut nōn surgeret.**
   The dog so despised small animals that it did not rise.

   Unlike clauses of purpose, which have negative **nē,** any negative (**nōn, numquam, nēmō, nūllus**) is found after **ut** in consecutive clauses.

Exercise 20c

The wonderful world of the bees

apēs opera mīrē dīvidunt; statiō ad portās castrōrum; quiēscunt in
mātūtīnum dōnec ūna cēterōs bombō excitet; tunc ūniversae prōvolant,
sī diēs mītis futūrus est; praedīvīnant enim ventōs imbrēsque et tum sē
continent tēctīs.
   cum agmen ad opera prōcessit, aliae flōrēs gerunt pedibus, aliae   5
aquam ōre. eae quibus est adulēscentia ad opera exeunt, seniōrēs intus

operantur. eae quae flōrēs comportant priōribus pedibus fĕmina onerant. excipiunt eās ternae vel quaternae quae exonerant; officia enim intus quoque dīvīsa sunt—aliae struunt, aliae poliunt, aliae suggerunt, aliae
10 cibum comparant; neque enim sēparātim vescuntur nē inaequālitās operis et cibī et temporis fīat.

WORD LIST

*apis, -is, f., bee
statiō, -ōnis, f., picket
bombus, -ī, m., a buzzing
*ūniversae, in a body
praedīvināre, to forecast
*continēre, to hold
*tēcta, -ōrum, n.pl., house
*adulēscentia, -ae, f., youth
*senior, -ōris, older
operārī, to work

fĕmur, fĕminis, n., thigh
excipere, to receive
*officium, -iī, n., duty
struō, -ere, strūxī, strūctum, build
poliō, -īre, -īvī, -ītum, smooth, polish
suggerō, -ere, -gessī, -gestum, heap up
*sēparātim, separately
*vescor, vescī, feed
inaequālitās, -ātis, f., inequality

NOTES

1 statiō ad portās, understand est.
2 in mātūtīnum, into the morning; in tells us that they sleep on until the alarm wakens them.
   prōvolant; in Exercise 20b you found dēvolāre and ēvolāre. What, then, does prōvolāre mean?
7 fĕmina, accusative plural of fĕmur; not to be confused with fēmina, a woman.
8 ternae vel quaternae, groups of three or four.
   exonerant: if onerāre means to load, what does exonerāre mean? And what does exonerate mean in English?

Exercise 20d

redde Latīnē:

Vesonius is such a man that all the citizens praise him.
So great was the crowd that it was difficult to walk.
The fog was so dense that we could not see.
The danger is so great that we are afraid.
The city has been so destroyed that we can never return there (thither).
The bird was so clever that it greeted Caesar by name.
The man was so jealous that he (actually) killed the bird.
So great was the anger of the citizens that the man fled.

III   A glimpse of Roman Life

In Lesson 20 you learned something about Pliny the Elder who was clearly a very learned man and a notable writer. However, when we speak nowadays of Pliny we usually mean his nephew, the Younger Pliny, who was born at Como in A.D. 61. From the ten books of letters which he has left we learn a great deal about him and the times in which he lived. As a youth he was of a studious nature—a fact which probably saved his life in A.D. 79 when he declined his uncle's invitation to go with him to investigate the eruption of Vesuvius because he preferred to continue his study of Livy. In later life he was a conscientious provincial governor in Bithynia in Asia Minor under the emperor Trajan, with whom he conducted an interesting correspondence on a variety of subjects, including the formation of a fire brigade and the treatment of the Christians (see Lesson 7). In Exercise 21a we find him helping to found a school for the youth of his native Como, and in the following lessons we learn something about his attitude to youth and to sport—still burning questions nineteen centuries later.

A view of Como, the birthplace of Pliny.

Lesson 21

Exercise 21 a

Education in Como

Pliny the Younger tells how he founded a school in his native Como.

nūper cum in patriā meā fuī, vēnit ut mē salūtāret fīlius amīcī praetextātus
et mihi rogantī num studēret respondit 'etiam'. 'ubi?' inquam. 'Mediōlānī.'
'cūr nōn hīc?' et pater eius (erat enim ūnā atque etiam ipse addūxerat
puerum) 'quia nūllōs hīc magistrōs habēmus.' 'quārē nūllōs? nam maximē
5 intererat vestrā quī patrēs estis (et forte complūrēs patrēs audiēbant) ut
līberī vestrī hīc potissimum discerent. dīcite enim, quaesō, ubi iūcundius
morārī possint quam in patriā aut pudīcius ēducārī quam sub oculīs
parentum aut minōre sūmptū quam domī. aestimāvistisne quantulum sit,
pecūniā collātā, condūcere magistrōs et quod nunc in habitātiōnēs et
10 viātica impendātis, adicere mercēdibus? atque ego, quī nōndum līberōs
habeō, parātus sum tertiam partem eius quod cōnferre vōbīs placēbit dare.
nihil honestius praestāre līberīs, nihil grātius patriae potestis. ēducentur
hīc quī hīc nāscuntur statimque ab īnfantiā nātāle solum amāre et
frequentāre cōnsuēscant.'

WORD LIST

*studeō, -ēre, -uī, be a student, go to
school
*quia, because
*quārē? why, wherefore?
complūrēs, -plūra, several
pudīcus, -a, -um, virtuous
*sūmptus, -ūs, *m.*, expense
quantulum, how little
*condūcō, -ere, -xī, -ctum, hire
habitātiō, -ōnis, *f.*, lodging
viāticum, -ī, *n.*, travelling expenses
impendō, -ere, -dī, -sum, spend

*adiciō, -ere, -iēcī, -iectum, add
*mercēs, -ēdis, *f.*, fee, salary
cōnferre, to contribute
*honestus, -a, -um, honourable
*praestō, -āre, -stitī, provide
*nāscor, nāscī, nātus sum, be born
infantia, -ae, *f.*, infancy
solum, -ī, *n.*, soil, land
frequentāre, to people, fill with people
*cōnsuēscō, -ere, -suēvī, -suētum,
grow accustomed

NOTES

1 **patria,** native town.
  praetextātus, young; he had not reached the age of 16 when he would assume the
  toga virīlis.

2 **rogantī num studēret,** when I asked if he went to school. See Language.
etiam, yes.
Mediōlānī, at Milan; locative case of **Mediōlānum.**
3 **ūnā,** along with him.
5 **intererat vestrā,** it would have been to your advantage.
6 **hīc potissimum,** here in preference to all other places.
8 **aestimāvistisne quantulum sit?** Have you reckoned how small a thing it is? See
Language.
11 **eius quod cōnferre vōbīs placēbit,** *lit.* of what it will please you to contribute, i.e.
of what you choose or decide to contribute.

Language

Indirect Questions

Examples:

mihi rogantī num studēret respondit 'etiam.'
When I asked if (or whether) he went to school, he replied 'yes'.
The speaker's direct question: **studēsne?**

dīcite ubi iūcundius morārī possint.
Tell me where they can stay more pleasantly.
Direct question: **ubi iūcundius morārī possunt?**

aestimāvistisne quantulum sit . . . ?
Have you reckoned how small a thing it is?
Direct question: **quantulum est?**

rogāvī nōnne puerī domī studērent.
I asked if the boys did not go to school in their home town.
Direct question: **nōnne puerī domī student?**

dīc mihi utrum iūcundius sit hīc morārī an Mediōlānī.
Tell me whether it is more pleasant to stay here or at Milan.
Direct question: **utrum iūcundius est hīc morārī an Mediōlānī?**

rogāvī utrum domī morārī vellent necne.
I asked whether they wished to stay at home or not.
Direct question: **utrum domī morārī vultis annōn?**

By studying the above examples you will understand what is meant by an
Indirect Question.

Note:
1 that its verb is in the Subjunctive Mood. This is translated into English
by the Indicative.

2 that it follows a verb meaning to *ask*, *say*, *think*, e.g. **rogāre, dīcere, aestimāre.**

3 that it is introduced by an interrogative word such as **num,** *if, whether*; **utrum ... an,** *whether ... or*; **utrum ... necne,** *whether ... or not*; **quis, quid,** *who, what*; **cūr,** *why*; **quandō,** *when*; **ubi,** *where*; **unde,** *where from*; **quō,** *where to*.

Exercise 21 b

Write down the direct form of each of the following indirect questions. Then translate both indirect and direct forms into English.

Example: **dīc mihi quid factūrī sītis.** *Tell me what you will do or are going to do.*

> **quid faciētis** *or* **factūrī estis?** *What will you do? or What are you going to do?*

1 puerum rogāvī num legere et scrībere scīret.
2 dīcite mihi utrum hīc studēre velītis necne.
3 nesciēbam cūr puerī Mediōlānum abiissent.
4 nunc intellegō cūr domī nōn mānserītis.
5 rogō quandō magistrōs conductūrī sītis.
6 'dīcite mihi,' inquam, 'quid fēcerītis.'
7 patrēs rogāvī nōnne magistrōs condūcere cōnātī essent.
8 mē rogāvērunt unde magistrōs condūcere possent.
9 vidēbitis quam dīligenter puerī studeant.
10 puerī mīrantur quālēs magistrōs habitūrī sint.

Exercise 21 c

The Schoolmaster's Neighbour complains

The following conversation is based on a short poem by the poet Martial (a contemporary of Pliny) who came from Spain and settled in Rome in A.D. 64. There he established a reputation as a writer of epigrams—short and pithy poems— on many subjects of public and personal interest. He seems to have taken a special ill-will to his neighbour, a noisy schoolmaster, who forms the subject of his best-known poems.

MARTIAL: quid est, Dama? quis tantum tumultum tam māne concitat?

DAMA: est ille lūdī magister quem bene nōvistī, ille quī turbulentōs discipulōs semper castīgat summā vōce.

MARTIAL: quota hōra est? caput enim mihi dolet neque diū dormīvī noctū. ei mihi, nimis vīnī sūmpsī, et cibī quoque nimis.   5

DAMA: sunt adhūc tenebrae. nōndum cristātī rūpēre silentia gallī.

MARTIAL: ō mē miserum! in crucem magistrī lūdōrum et omnēs gallī cristātī! nēmō causidicus tantā vōce clāmat. nēmō faber incūdem tantā vī tundit. cum illum audīvī, venit mihi in mentem amphitheātrum et turba victōrī magnō clāmōre   10 faventium.

DAMA: īram cohibē, domine, sī sapis; sī minus, in morbum incidēs.

MARTIAL: tacē, sceleste! statim abī ad illum magistrum!

DAMA: quid, quaesō, eī dīcam, cum convēnerō?

MARTIAL: eum rogā quantam operae mercēdem accipiat. et sī volet   15 discipulōs dīmittere, prōmitte mē eī bis tantum datūrum esse.

WORD LIST

*tumultus, -ūs, *m.*, disturbance
concitāre, to stir up
turbulentus, -a, -um, troublesome
*dolēre, to ache, to grieve
*noctū, during the night
ei mihi, pity me!
adhūc, still
cristātus, -a, -um, crested
gallus, -ī, *m.*, cock
causidicus, -ī, *m.*, advocate

incūs, -ūdis, *f.*, anvil
tundere, to beat, hammer
cohibēre, to restrain
sapiō, -ere, -iī, be wise
*morbus, -ī, *m.*, sickness, disease
incidere, to fall into
*convenire, to meet, come face to face with
*opera, -ae, *f.*, trouble

NOTES

4 **quota hōra est?** what time is it? **quot?** means how many? and **quotus** bears the same relation to **quot** as, for example, **tertius** does to **trēs.**

6 **rūpēre** = **rūpērunt,** 3rd person plural, perfect indicative active of **rumpō, -ere, rūpī, ruptum,** to break.

7 **in crucem,** to the cross with, i.e. a curse upon; crucifixion, the punishment reserved for slaves and low criminals who were not Roman citizens, was regarded as a shameful or accursed form of death.

9 **cum illum audīvī,** whenever I hear him. **cum** used with the perfect and pluperfect indicative has the meaning *whenever.*

10 **turba ... faventium;** take **turba faventium** together—the crowd of those who support . . . .

Lesson 22

Exercise 22a

(1) Father and Son

abhinc paucōs diēs mē praesente castīgābat pater quīdam fīlium suum,
quod nimis pecūniae expenderet in equīs canibusque emendīs. simul ac
fīlius discessit, patrī cum rīsū 'heus tū,' inquam, 'numquamne fēcistī
quod ā patre culpārī posset? nōn modo fēcistī, sed etiam adhūc id facis

5 quod fīlius tuus, sī repentě pater ille fīat, tū fīlius, parī gravitāte castīget.
omnēs enim hominēs aliquō errōre dūcuntur. aliī in aliīs rēbus sibi
indulgent.

hōc tantae sevēritātis exemplō admonitus, haec tibi scrīpsī nē quandō
tū quoque fīlium tuum dūrius tractārēs. mementō, quaesō, et tē esse

10 hominem et hominis patrem.'

WORD LIST

*expendō, -ere, -dī, -sum, spend
*repente, suddenly
*pār, paris, equal
*gravitās, -ātis, f., seriousness
*error, -ōris, m., mistake
indulgeō, -ēre, -sī (dat.), indulge

sevēritās, -ātis, f., strictness, severity
*exemplum, -ī, n., example
admonitus, -a, -um (admonēre),
  warned
*tractāre, to treat

NOTES

1 mē praesente, in my presence. What construction is this?
2 in equīs canibusque emendīs, on buying horses and dogs.
5 sī fīat . . . castīget, if he were to become . . . would rebuke.
8 nē quandō . . . lest at any time . . . .

(2) A scholar in the hunting field

cum audīveris, mī amīce, quid mihi hodiē ēvēnerit, rīdēbis; nec mīrum;
quam cupidus enim sim vēnātiōnis, bene scīs. ego, Plīnius ille quem
nōvistī, trēs aprōs pulcherrimōs çēpī! 'ipse?' inquis. ipse; neque tamen
inertiam meam et quiētem omīsī.

5   ad rētia sedēbam; nōn vēnābulum aut lanceam habēbam, sed stilum et
cērās. aliquid scrībēbam ut, sī manūs vacuās, plēnās tamen cērās
reportārem. nōn est contemnendum hoc studiī genus; mīrum enim est

quōmodo animus agitātiōne mōtūque corporis excitētur; iam undique
silvae et sōlitūdō et illud silentium quod vēnātiōnī datur, cōgitātiōnem
maximē incitant. itaque, sī cōnsilium meum probābis, cum vēnāberis, 10
nōn modo pānem ac vīnum, sed etiam cērās tēcum ferēs. sīc enim
cognōscēs nōn Diānam magis quam Minervam in montibus errāre.

WORD LIST
*ēvenīre, to happen
*cupidus, -a, -um, fond of
vēnātiō, -ōnis, f., hunting
inertia, -ae, f., inactivity
*quiēs, -ētis, f., rest
*omittō, -ere, -mīsī, -missum, give up
vēnābulum, -ī, n., hunting spear
lancea, -ae, f., lance
*vacuus, -a, -um, empty
*plēnus, -a, -um, full

*contemnō, -ere, -tempsī, -temptum,
  despise
agitātiō, -ōnis, f., activity, agitation
*mōtus, -ūs, m., movement
sōlitūdō, -inis, f., loneliness, solitude
*cōgitātiō, -ōnis, f., thought
*incitāre, to rouse, induce
probāre, to approve of
*vēnor, -ārī, -ātus sum, hunt

NOTES
 7 nōn est contemnendum, is not to be despised.
 8 iam, moreover, furthermore.
12 Diāna, goddess of hunting.
   Minerva, goddess of learning.

Language

More about Indirect Questions

Examples:

quam cupidus sim vēnātiōnis bene scīs.
You know well how keen I am on hunting. or *You are well aware of my passion for hunting.*

nesciēbāmus quam altum flūmen esset.
We did not know how deep the river was, or *. . . the depth of the river.*

dic mihi unde hoc cognōveris.
Tell me (from) where you have learned this. or *Tell me the source of your information.*

An Indirect Question may often be translated into English by using nouns like *depth, source, time, destination* (abstract nouns).

Exercise 22b

This imaginary conversation is based on a view of the popular sport of chariot-racing expressed by Pliny in one of his letters.

	IULIA:	īrātus esse vidēris, mī Sexte. quis quidve tē vexāvit?
	SEXTUS:	fīlius tuus.
	IULIA:	meus? numquam meum appellās Marcum nisi tē irrītāvit. [*ridēns*]
		quid tantum commeruit fīlius noster? num tam grave est ut eī
5		ignōscere nōn possīs?
	SEXTUS:	cūr semper domī sedeat in librīs tōtus, ego nōn possum intel-
		legere. nōn est puerī sānī semper studēre, praesertim cum fulget
		sōl et omnēs ad circum conveniunt.
	IULIA:	et tū quoque, ut opīnor.
10	SEXTUS:	ita vērō; sīc enim vīvitur ab omnibus virīs Rōmānīs.
	IULIA:	quālis Rōmānus est Marcus?
	SEXTUS:	mollis et librīs tam dēditus ut numquam ipse corpus exerceat
		neque aliōs spectet sē exercentēs.
	IULIA:	quot puerī, tot sententiae. quid tibi respondit rogantī ut tēcum
15		ad lūdōs venīret?
	SEXTUS:	ōrātiōnem mehercule habuit quam inānēs sint lūdī.
		[*Marcī vōcem imitātur*]
		nihil novum est in lūdīs. satis est eōs semel spectāvisse. mīror

tot mīlia virōrum tam stultē identidem cupere equōs currentēs, hominēs curribus īnsistentēs vidēre. neque vēlōcitāte equōrum 20 neque hominum arte dēlectantur, sed pannō. pannum amant. sī tamen in mediō cursū colōrēs hūc illūc trānsferantur, quid faciant? statim favor quoque trānseat et agitātōrēs illōs, equōs illōs, quōrum clāmitant nōmina, relinquant.

et multa eius modī ——; quae mē Rōmānum pudēbat audīre. 25 abeō ad lūdōs.

IULIA: valē. vincat factiō prasina! [*discēdēns* SEXTUS *frontem contrahit; factiōnī enim venetae ipse favet.*]

WORD LIST

irrītāre, to annoy
commereō, -ēre, -uī, -itum, be guilty of
*ignōscō, -ere, -nōvī, -nōtum (+*dat.*), forgive
*sānus, -a, -um, healthy
*praesertim, especially
opīnor, -ārī, -ātus sum, suppose
*mollis, -is, -e, soft, spineless
dēditus, -a, -um, devoted
*sententia, -ae, *f.*, opinion
*inānis, -is, -e, foolish, worthless
*semel, once

*imitārī, to imitate
identidem, again and again
*currus, -ūs, *m.*, chariot
insistō, -ere, -stitī, stand on
vēlōcitās, -ātis, *f.*, speed
pannus, -ī, *m.*, piece of cloth (see note)
favor, -ōris, *m.*, support, favour
agitātor, -ōris, *m.*, driver
clāmitāre, to keep on shouting
prasinus, -a, -um, green
frontem contrahere, to frown
venetus, -a, -um, blue

NOTES

1 **quidve; -ve** added to a word means *or* just as **-que** means *and*, e.g. **terrā marīque,** by land and sea.

4 **num tam grave est,** is it really so serious *or* you don't mean to say it is so serious.

6 **in librīs tōtus,** absorbed in his books.

7 **nōn est sānī puerī,** it is not (the mark) of a healthy boy.

cum sōl fulget, at a time when the sun is shining. What would be the meaning of **cum sōl fulgeat?**

10 **sīc vīvitur,** thus life is lived. This is an example of an impersonal verb. Compare **pugnātum est,** a battle was fought.

14 **quot puerī tot sententiae.** This is an adaptation of a Latin proverb—**quot hominēs tot sententiae.** It means that everyone is entitled to his own opinion.

16 **ōrātiōnem habuit quam inānēs sint.** Stated in its simplest form this is just **'dīxit quam inānēs sint lūdī'**—an indirect question

21 **pannus,** the 'colour', i.e. the coloured garment worn by the charioteer to show the team to which he belonged.

sī colōrēs trānsferantur, quid faciant? If the colours were to be changed, what would they do? See Language.

25 **mē pudēbat,** I was ashamed, *lit.* it shamed me (see page 47).

Language

Conditional Sentences

A conditional sentence is one which contains a clause introduced by **sī,** *if*, or **nisi,** *unless.*

Type 1

sī ōtiōsus es, tēcum colloquī volō.
If you are at leisure, I wish to speak to you.

sī superāverit, ingēns pondus aurī habēbit.
If he wins, he will receive a great weight of gold.

sī pluēbat, domī manēbāmus.
If it rained, we stayed at home.

nisi dēfessus es, ad balnea ībimus.
Unless you are tired, we shall go to the baths.

When the verb is in the indicative mood, the condition is of the type—'If *a* is (was, will be) true, then *b* is (was, will be) true,' and is known as a *simple* condition.

Type 2

sī pater ille fīat, tē castīget.
If he were to become the father, he would scold you.

sī colōrēs trānsferantur, quid faciant?
If the colours were changed over, what would they do?

When the verb in both the **sī**-clause and the principal clause is in the present subjunctive, the condition is of the type—'If (or Suppose) *a* were to come true, *b* would be true', and is known as an *improbable* condition.

Exercise 22c

(*a*) *redde Anglicē:*
1 sī fīlius patrem castīget, ego rīdeam.
2 sī audiam Plīnium aprum cēpisse, nōn crēdam.
3 sī tē aprum cēpisse dīcis, tibi crēdō.
4 sī magister puerōs dīmittat, ego gaudeam.
5 sī magistrōs condūxeritis, fīliī vestrī domī ēducābuntur.
6 sī ad lūdōs eam, nihil novum videam.

(*b*) *redde Latīnē:*
1 If you are my friend, you will help me.
2 If a boar were to come, I should run away.
3 If the boys arrive at school late, the master will scold them.
4 If my son were to become a merchant, he would be rich.
5 If we were to lose our way (**dē viā errāre**), we would shout out.
6 If Lucrio has perished, we cannot help him.

(*c*) It was the practice among Roman writers of the Empire to hire a hall and invite their friends to come and listen to their latest compositions. The following passage tells of a comic incident at one such **recitātiō**.

redde Anglicē:
rem mīram nūper audīvī dē recitātiōne Passēnī Paulī. ille enim, cum recitāret, ita coepit dīcere, 'Prīsce, iubēs.' ad hoc Iavolēnus Prīscus (aderat enim quod Paulō amīcissimus erat), 'ego vērō nōn iubeō.' cogitā quī rīsus hominum, quī iocī inde ortī sint. Prīscus tamen est homō omnīnō (*altogether*) dubiae sānitātis. eī igitur quī sunt recitātūrī cūrāre dēbent nōn modo ut ipsī sint sānī sed etiam ut sānōs invītent.

Lesson 23

Slaves and Masters

The story of slavery in any age and in any country is not a pretty one; Roman writers give us many hints about the harsh conditions in which slaves lived and worked, and the cruel treatment which they received. It is pleasant to find that there was another side to the story and that faithful slaves were, on occasions, prepared to sacrifice their lives for kind (and sometimes not so kind) masters.

Exercise 23a

(1)

cum ā triumvirīs prōscrīptus C. Plōtius Plancus in regiōne Salernitānā latēret, eī quī miserum persequēbantur latebrās odōrātī sunt. servī tamen ab eīs comprehēnsī multumque ac diū tortī, negābant sē scīre ubi dominus esset. nōn sustinuit deinde Plancus tam fidēlēs tamque ēgregiōs servōs
5 ulterius cruciārī: prōcessit igitur in medium iugulumque gladiīs mīlitum obiēcit. est difficile dīnōscī utrum dignior fuerit dominus an servī. ille enim cōnstantem servōrum fidem experiēbātur, hī iūstā dominī misericordiā quaestiōnis saevitiā līberātī sunt.

WORD LIST

prōscrībō, -ere, -scrīpsī, -scrīptum, proscribe, outlaw
*lateō, -ēre, -uī, lie hid
latebrae, -ārum, *f.pl.*, hiding place
odōror, -ārī, -ātus sum, smell out, scent, detect
*torqueō, -ēre, -torsī, -tortum, torture, twist
*ēgregius, -a, -um, excellent, admirable
*ulterius, further, longer
cruciāre, to torture

iugulum, -ī, *n.*, throat
ōbiciō, -ere, -iēcī, -iectum, offer, present
dīnōscō, -ere, distinguish, discern
cōnstāns, -antis, steadfast, faithful
*fidēs, -eī, *f.*, loyalty
*misericordia, -ae, *f.*, compassion, pity
quaestiō, -ōnis, *f.*, examination, investigation with torture
*saevitia, -ae, *f.*, cruelty, severity

NOTES

1 **triumvirī,** after the death of Julius Caesar the Roman state was ruled for a time by three men—Octavianus (later Augustus), Marcus Antonius (Mark Antony, the friend of Caesar) and Lepidus. Their rule was marred by proscriptions, lists of citizens who

were outlawed, who might be killed with impunity and whose property was forfeit.

regiō Salernitāna, the district of Salernum—the modern Salerno in the Gulf of Naples.

4 **sustinuit,** he could not endure that they should be tortured further.

6 **dīnōscī,** present infinitive passive; the natural English translation is 'It is difficult to decide . . . .'

(2)

Antius Restiō, prōscrīptus ā triumvirīs, cum omnēs domesticōs circā rapīnam ac praedam occupātōs vidēret, dissimulātā fugā sē domō intempestā nocte subdūxit. ēgressum tamen fūrtīvum servus, quī ab eō pūnītus ac inexpiābilī litterārum notā inustus erat, animadvertit, et vestīgia hūc atque illūc errantia secūtus, comitem voluntārium sē dominō 5
addidit. posteā ubi sēnsit cupidōs sanguinis mīlitēs adesse, mīrā arte dominum servāvit. nam illō cēlātō rogum exstruxit eīque senem pauperem ā sē comprehēnsum et occīsum superiēcit. interrogantibus deinde mīlitibus ubi esset Antius, respondit, 'sī adesset ille tam scelestus homō, libenter eum vōbīs trāderem. sī autem paulō ante pervēnissētis, eum invēnissētis 10
vīvum. nunc tamen mihi crūdēlitātis poenās dat. Antius enim in illō rogō ūritur.'

WORD LIST

domesticus, -ī, *m.*, a member of a household

rapīna, -ae, *f.*, plunder

***praeda, -ae,** *f.*, booty

***occupātus, -a, -um,** busy, engaged

***dissimulāre,** to conceal, hide

sē subdūcere, to withdraw

fūrtīvus, -a, -um, secret, stealthy

ēgressus, -ūs, *m.*, departure

inexpiābilis, -is, -e, unforgivable

nota, -ae, *f.*, mark, brand

inūrō, -ere, -ussī, -ustum, burn in, brand (compound of **ūrere,** to burn)

***animadvertō, -ere, -vertī, -versum,** notice, observe

***vestīgium, -iī,** *n.*, track, footprint

voluntārius, -a, -um, voluntary, of free will

***cupidus, -a, -um,** eager, desirous

***sanguis, -inis,** *m.*, blood

superiaciō, -ere, -iēci, -iectum, throw upon

***crūdēlitās, -ātis,** *f.*, cruelty

***poenās dare,** to pay the penalty, be punished

NOTES

1 **circā rapīnam ac praedam occupātōs,** busied about plunder and booty

2 **intempestā nocte,** at dead of night.

4 **inexpiābilī litterārum notā,** an unforgivable brand. Branding was one of the severest punishments inflicted on slaves. Letters once burned on the forehead were there for life.

9 **sī adesset . . . , sī pervēnissētis,** see Language.

Language

More about Conditional Sentences

Type 3

(*a*) **sī adesset, libenter eum vōbīs trāderem.**

If he were here (but he is not), I should gladly hand him over to you.

When the verb in both clauses is in the imperfect subjunctive, the condition is of the type, 'If *a* were true (but it is not), *b* would be true (but it is not).'

(*b*) **sī paulō ante pervēnissētis, eum invēnissētis vīvum.**

If you had come a little earlier (but you did not), you would have found him alive (but you did not).

When the verb in both clauses is in the Pluperfect Subjunctive, the condition is of the type 'If *a* had been true (but it was not), *b* would have been true (but it was not).'

(*c*) **nisi dominum cēlāvissem, nōn iam vīveret.**

If I had not concealed my master (but I did), he would not now be alive (but he is).

When the verb of the *if*-clause is in the pluperfect subjunctive and that of the principal clause in the imperfect, the condition is of the type 'If *a* had been true (but it was not), *b* would now be true (but it is not).'

In such sentences the condition is not fulfilled, and they are known as *unfulfilled* conditions.

Exercise 23b

(*a*) *redde Anglicē:*

1 sī dominus meus inventus erit, occīdētur.
2 sī dominus meus inveniātur, occīdātur.
3 sī dominus meus adesset, in magnō perīculō esset.
4 nisi dominum cēlāverō, mīlitēs eum invenient.
5 nisi dominum cēlāvissem, mīlitēs eum invēnissent.
6 sī dominum mīlitibus trādidissem, iam līber essem.

(*b*) *Translate the following sentences into English, and, since each contains an unfulfilled condition, show this by 'but . . . .'*

Example: sī fīlius meī similis esset, lūdōs amāret.

If my son were like me, he would love the games—but he is not like me.

1 nisi in librīs tōtus essem, tēcum īrem.
2 sī vērus Rōmānus fuissēs, amphitheātrum amāvissēs.
3 sī colōrēs trānslātī essent, favor quoque trānsiisset.
4 sī vēnātiōnis cupidus essem, vēnābulum mēcum portārem.
5 sī cērae plēnae essent, libenter domum abīrem.
6 sī meum cōnsilium probārēs, cērās, nōn vēnābulum in montēs ferrēs.

Exercise 23c

Master and Slaves—the Dark Side

rem atrōcem Larcius Macedo ā servīs suīs passus est. superbus erat
dominus et saevus et quī patrem suum fuisse servum meminisse nōllet.
lavābātur in vīllā Formiānā cum repente eum servī cinxērunt. alius faucēs
invādit, alius ōs verberat, alius pectus et ventrem contundit, et cum esse
exanimem putārent, abiciunt eum in fervēns pavīmentum ut experīrentur   5
num vīveret. ille, sīve quia nōn sentiēbat, sīve quia sē nōn sentīre simulābat,
mortem obiisse vidēbātur. tandem effertur, excipiunt servī fidēliōrēs.
eōrum vōcibus excitātus et recreātus locī frīgore, sublātīs oculīs agitātōque
corpore, vīvere sē dēmōnstrat. diffugiunt servī; quōrum magna pars
capta est, cēterī quaeruntur. ipse paucīs diēbus aegrē fōcilātus nōn sine   10
ultiōnis sōlāciō ē vītā dēcessit.

WORD LIST

*atrōx, -ōcis, terrible, savage, violent
*patior, patī, passus sum, suffer,
  endure, undergo
*superbus, -a, -um, proud, arrogant,
  tyrannical
*saevus, -a, -um, cruel
*meminī, -isse, remember
faucēs, -ium, *f.pl.,* throat
*invādō, -ere, -vāsī, -vāsum, attack,
  set upon
venter, -tris, *m.,* belly, stomach
contundō, -ere, tudī, -tū(n)sum,
  bruise
exanimis, -is, -e, lifeless

fervēns, -entis, burning, hot
*sentīre, to be conscious
*simulāre, to pretend
efferō, -ferre, extulī, ēlātum, carry out
  for burial
excipiō, -ere, -cēpī, -ceptum, receive,
  take up
*recreāre, to revive, restore
*dēmōnstrāre, to show, indicate
diffugere, to flee in different directions,
  disperse
fōcilāre, to restore to life
ultiō, -ōnis, *f.,* revenge

NOTES

2 **et quī . . . nōllet,** and one who was unwilling to forget. The subjunctive implies
that he was the kind of man who was unwilling to forget.

Lesson 24

Exercise 24a

effigiēs scrībentis capitī catēnīs īnsonābat.

A Ghost Story (1)

erat Athēnīs domus magna sed īnfāmis. per silentium noctis strepitus
vinculōrum longius prīmō, deinde ē proximō audiēbātur: mox appārēbat
effigiēs, senex quī crūribus compedēs, manibus catēnās gerēbat quatiē-
batque. inde eī quī habitābant per metum vigilābant noctēs trīstēs:
5   vigiliam morbus et posteā mors sequēbātur. dēserta igitur est domus et
tōta illī mōnstrō relicta; prōscrībēbātur tamen, seu quis emere seu quis
condūcere vellet.

venit Athēnās philosophus, legit titulum, audītōque pretiō, cum omnia
interrogāvisset, domum condūcit. ubi nox aderat, ā servīs petīvit cērās,
10   stilum, lūmen: deinde suōs omnēs dīmittit: ipse ad scrībendum animum,
oculōs, manum intendit nē vacua mēns inānēs sibi metūs fingeret.

WORD LIST

infāmis, -is, -e, disreputable, having a
  bad reputation
effigiēs, -ēī, f., ghost
crūs, crūris, n., leg
compēs, -edis, f., fetter, shackle
*gerere, to bear, wear, carry
quatiō, -ere, quassī, quassum, shake
*trīstis, -is, -e, grim, sad, melancholy
*metus, -ūs, m., fear

*dēserō, -ere, -seruī, -sertum, abandon
mōnstrum, -ī, n., monster, supernatural
  being
titulus, -ī, m., notice, placard
intendō, -ere, -tendī, -tentum, direct,
  concentrate
*mēns, mentis, f., mind
*inānis, -is, -e, vain, groundless, empty
*fingō, -ere, fīnxī, fictum, invent, devise

2 **ē proximō,** from very close at hand.
4 **inde,** as a result.
5 **vigiliam,** sleeplessness.
6 **prōscrībēbātur,** it was advertised.
   seu quis emere . . . vellet, to see if anyone should wish. **seu . . . seu** is another form of **sīve . . . sīve.**
10 **ad scrībendum animum intendit,** he concentrated his attention on writing.

Exercise 24b

A Ghost Story (2)

initiō silentium noctis: deinde quatiēbātur ferrum, vincula movēbantur. ille nōn tollēbat oculōs, nōn remittēbat stilum, sed offirmābat animum. tum crēbrēscēbat fragor et iam intrā līmen audiēbātur. respicit, videt agnōscitque nārrātam sibi effigiem. stābat illa innuēbatque digitō. hic contrā ut paulum exspectāret manū significat rūrsusque cērīs et stilō 5 incumbit. illa scrībentis capitī catēnīs īnsonābat. sine morā tollit lūmen et sequitur. ībat illa lentō gradū quasi gravis vinculīs. postquam dēflexit in āream, subitō ē cōnspectū discessit et dēserit comitem. quī dēsertus folia collēgit quō melius locum indicāret. postrīdiē adit magistrātūs, monet ut illum locum effodī iubeant. inveniuntur ossa quae collēcta pūblicē 10 sepeliuntur. domus posteā rīte conditīs mānibus līberāta est.

WORD LIST

*initium, -iī, *n.,* beginning
*ferrum, -ī, *n.,* iron, chains
remittere, to relax grip on, let go
offirmāre, to make firm, resolute
crēbrēscō, -ere, crēbruī, become frequent, increase
*intrā (*prep. with acc.*), within, inside
*līmen, -inis, *n.,* threshold
innuō, -ere, -uī, give a sign
*digitus, -ī, *m.,* finger
*significāre, to indicate, make known
incumbere, to devote oneself to
īnsonāre, to make a noise

*lentus, -a, -um, slow
*gradus, -ūs, *m.,* step
dēflectō, -ere, -flexī, -flexum, turn aside
*ārea, -ae, *f.,* courtyard
*folium, -iī, *n.,* leaf
indicāre, to show, point out
effodiō, -ere, -fōdī, -fossum, dig up or out
*ŏs, ŏssis, *n.,* bone
pūblicē, at the state's expense
*sepeliō, -īre, -pelīvī, -pultum, bury

NOTES

4 **nārrātam sibi effigiem,** the ghost he had been told about.
   innuēbat digitō, made a sign with his finger. Can you think of one English word which means to make a sign with the finger?
5 **contrā,** on the other hand.
9 **quō melius locum indicāret,** to mark the place better (see page 96).
11 **rīte conditīs mānibus,** when the ghost had been duly laid (**mānēs,** the spirits of the dead).

Lesson 25

Exercise 25a

The Werewolf (1)

cum adhūc servus essem, habitābāmus in Vīcō Angustō; nunc Gavillae
domus est. ibi, sīcut dī volunt, amāre coepī uxōrem Terentiī caupōnis,
Melissam. quam benigna fuit! sī quid ab illā petiī, numquam mihi
negātum est; sī fēcit assem, sēmissem habuī; sī sēmissem habuī, illī
5　mandāvī nec unquam falsus sum.

　　huius contubernālis ad vīllam suprēmum diem obiit. itaque per
scūtum per ocream ēgī quemadmodum ad illam pervenīrem: mīrum
autem est nī in rēbus angustīs amīcī appārent. forte dominus Capuam
abierat. nactus ego occāsiōnem persuādeō hospitī nostrō ut mēcum ad
10　quīntum mīliārium veniat. erat autem mīles, fortis tamquam Orcus.
proficīscimur nōs circā gallicinia. lūna lūcēbat tamquam merīdiē. vēnimus
intrā monumenta. subitō homō meus exuit sē et omnia vestīmenta
secundum viam posuit. mihi anima in nāsō erat; stābam tamquam mortuus.
repente lupus factus ululāre coepit et in silvās fūgit. ego prīmō nesciēbam
15　ubi essem; deinde accessī ut vestīmenta eius tollerem: illa autem lapidea
facta sunt.

WORD LIST

*coepī, -isse, began
*negāre, to refuse
sēmis, -issis, *m.*, half an as
*fallō, -ere, fefellī, falsum, deceive
contubernālis, -is, *m. or f.*, mate
*nancīscor, -ī, nactus sum, obtain, get
*occāsiō, -ōnis, *f.*, chance, opportunity
*hospes, -itis, *m.*, guest, friend
mīliārium, -iī, *n.*, milestone
*lūna, -ae, *f.*, moon
*lūceō, -ēre, -xī, shine, be bright

*monumentum, -ī, *n.*, memorial, monu-
　ment
exuō, -ere, -uī, -ūtum, strip, unclothe
secundum (*prep. with acc.*), along, beside
*pōnō, -ere, posuī, positum, lay, place
*lupus, -ī, *m.*, wolf
ululāre, to howl
*accēdō, -ere, -cessī, -cessum,
　approach
lapideus, -a, -um, of stone

NOTES

6　**suprēmum diem obiit**, met his last day, i.e. died. **obīre** alone is found meaning
　to die. In English what is an obituary notice?
7　**per scūtum per ocream ēgī**, by hook or by crook I contrived . . . .
8　**nī** = **nisi**.
　in rēbus angustīs, in straits, i.e. in time of trouble.

11 **circā gallicinia,** about cock-crow, dawn.
12 **intrā monumenta,** to the place where the tombstones began. Main roads (e.g. the Via Appia) outside cities were often lined with tombs.
13 **anima in nāsō erat,** 'my breath was in my nose'. What is the equivalent English expression which indicates extreme fright?

Exercise 25b

The Werewolf (2)

ego perterritus sum: gladium tamen strīnxī et in tōtā viā umbrās cecīdī dōnec ad vīllam amīcae meae pervenīrem. ubi intrāvī, paene mē animus relīquit; sūdor mihi per artūs fluēbat; oculī mortuī; vix tandem refectus sum. Melissa mea mīrārī coepit quod tam sērō ambulārem, et 'sī ante' inquit 'vēnissēs, saltem nōs adiūvissēs; lupus enim vīllam intrāvit et 5 sanguinem tamquam lanius omnibus pecoribus mīsit. nec tamen nōs dērīsit, etiamsī fūgit: servus enim noster lanceā collum eius trāiēcit.'

haec ut audīvī, operīre oculōs amplius nōn potuī, sed prīmā lūce Gāī nostrī domum fūgī, et postquam vēnī in illum locum in quō lapidea vestīmenta erant facta, nihil invēnī nisi sanguinem. ut vērō domum vēnī, 10 iacēbat mīles meus in lectulō tamquam bōs et collum eius medicus cūrābat. intellēxī illum versipellem esse, nec posteā cum illō pānem gustāre potuī, nōn sī mē occīdissēs.

WORD LIST

*stringō, -ere, strīnxī, strictum, draw, unsheath
*caedō, -ere, cecīdī, caesum, cut, strike, kill
*dōnec, until
sūdor, -ōris, *m.,* sweat
artus, -ūs, *m.,* limb
*fluō, -ere, -ūxī, flow
saltem, at least

*pecus, -oris, *n.,* cattle, herd, flock
*collum, -ī, *n.,* neck
*trāiciō, -ere, -iēcī, -iectum, pierce
operiō, -īre, -uī, opertum, close
lectulus, -ī, *m.,* couch
*medicus, -ī, *m.,* doctor
versipellis, -is, *m.,* werewolf, one who can change himself into a wolf
gustāre, to taste

NOTES

2 **mē animus relīquit,** I fainted.
3 **vix tandem refectus sum: reficere** means to restore to a former condition. *A literal translation is:* I was scarcely at length restored to my former condition; *translate* I could scarcely get over it.
6 **sanguinem . . . pecoribus mīsit,** bled all the cattle like a butcher.
nec tamen nōs dērīsit, he did not make fools of us; we had the last laugh.
8 **ut audīvī,** when I heard. The same meaning of **ut** occurs below—**ut vēnī.**
12 **nec posteā . . . occīdissēs,** after that I could not have tasted bread with him—not if you had killed me.

Exercise 25c

Read the following passage and try to understand it with the aid of the notes. Then answer in English the questions below. Finally, translate the passage into English, using the General Word List, if necessary.

Of Stories Weird and Wonderful

cum ē Graeciā in Ītaliam redīrēmus, Brundisiī in terram ē nāvī ēgressī sumus. dum in illō portū ambulāmus, fascēs librōrum vēnālium expositōs subitō cōnspeximus. quōs ego cōnspectōs cupidissimē statim petīvī. erant autem istī omnēs librī Graecī mīrāculōrum fābulārumque plēnī. quamquam ipsa volūmina squālēbant et aspectū erant taetrō, tamen appropinquāvī et pretium percontātus sum. mīrā vīlitāte adductus librōs plūrimōs minimō emō eōsque omnēs duābus proximīs noctibus percurrō.

squālēre, to be dirty
taeter, -tra, -trum, foul, shocking
vīlitās, -ātis, *f.*, cheapness

erant in illīs librīs scrīpta huius modī: Scythās illōs quī sub ipsīs septentriōnibus vītam agunt, corporibus hominum vescī; item ibi habitāre hominēs ūnum oculum in frontis mediō habentēs.

Scythae, Scythians, a nomadic tribe
septentriōnēs, -um, *m.pl.,* seven stars of the Great or Little Bear
item, likewise

id etiam in īsdem librīs scrīptum invēnimus: in terrā Āfricā esse quōsdam hominēs quī vōce atque linguā effascinent. sī enim illī forte nimis laudāverint pulchrās arborēs, segetēs laetiōrēs, īnfantēs amoeniōrēs, ēgregiōs equōs, bovēs optimōs, perīre repente haec omnia.

effascināre, to bewitch

seges, -etis, *f.*, crop

Questions

1 What do you gather about the interests of the writer? Quote the Latin word(s) on which you base your answer.
2 Did he get a bargain of the books? Give a reason for your answer.
3 Give one English word which, if the writer's story is true, would describe the Scythians.
4 What direction is indicated by **sub septentriōnibus**?

5 There is a famous ancient story of a man with one eye; what was he called?
6 According to the story, would the people in Africa be said to practise 'the evil eye'?
7 What did the objects of their bewitchment have in common?
8 What is the usual meaning of **laetus**?
Give a good translation of it as applied to **segetēs**.
9 What is the difference between **duābus proximīs noctibus** and **duās proximās noctēs**?
10 On page 200 you will find a summary of the uses of the ablative case. See how many of these you can identify in this passage.

Exercise 25d

The Psylli declare war on the South Wind, but the South Wind deals the last blow.

ōlim in terrā Āfricā—ita enim Herodotus nārrat—habitābant Psyllī quōrum fīnēs ventus Auster identidem vexābat, sed quōdam tempore flābat tam diū tantāque vī ut agrōs quōs colēbant omnēs siccāverit. Psyllī igitur, cum hanc tantam iniūriam molestē ferrent, dēcrētum (*a decree*) fēcērunt ut armīs sūmptīs ad Austrum quasi ad hostem rēs repetītum (*to demand redress*) proficīscerentur. atque ita profectīs Auster magnō spīritūs agmine vēnit obviam eōsque ūniversōs cum omnibus cōpiīs armīsque cumulīs montibusque harēnārum supervectīs (**supervehere**, *to carry over*) operuit.

Lesson 26

Dreams

Everyone has dreams. Nowadays we do not attach a great deal of importance to them, since we know that they are often the result of some quite natural cause, such as an overtaxed digestive system. To the Romans, however, the interpretation of dreams was a matter of great importance.

Exercise 26a

The following light-hearted conversation is, of course, imaginary, but gives an impression of the way in which conduct could be influenced by a dream.

[PUBLIUS QUĪNTUM *offendit incautum prope amphitheātrum. prīmō neuter neutrum agnōscit.*]

PUBLIUS: cavē, imprūdēns! paene mē praecipitem dedistī in pulverem!

QUĪNTUS: et tū, brūte! quantā mē vī pepulistī! prōspice quō eās!

5 PUBLIUS: [QUĪNTUM *tum prīmum agnōscit*]. ō Quīnte, quam laetus tē videō. nōn tē anteā agnōvī. quō festīnās tantō cursū?

QUĪNTUS: Titum quaerō. prōmīsī mē ad templum Veneris eum conventūrum esse quārtā hōrā, sed sērō pervēnī. rēbus domesticīs dētinēbar.

10 PUBLIUS: [*manū indicāns*]: ecce Titum! quam lentē ambulat et quam pallidō est vultū! aeger esse mihi vidētur.

QUĪNTUS: salvē, Tite! quid est? esne aeger? num febrem tertiānam habēs quae nunc per urbem pervādit?

TITUS: minimē, sed tēcum īre ad amphitheātrum nōlō.

15 QUĪNTUS: sed Flammus ille, mehercule, omnium gladiātōrum facile prīnceps, hodiē pugnat.

TITUS: ego tē comitārī nōn possum. sī tamen tū mēcum vēneris in sēcrētum, cūr nōlim tibi dīcam.

PUBLIUS: tuā pāce, Quīnte, discēdam. cupidissimus sum Flammī videndī.

20 valēte, Quīnte et Tite!

QUĪNTUS   } valē, Publī!
TITUS   }

[TITUS QUĪNTUM *in sēcrētum dūcit*.]

QUĪNTUS: mihi omnia nārrā, Tite. attentissimē audiam.

TITUS: hesternā nocte cubitum īvī. in somnō mihi vīsus sum abdūcī
         et in lūdum gladiātōrium āscrībī. statim in arēnam prōgressus   25
         cum rētiāriō contendī, Thrāce ferōcissimō, quō nēminem
         unquam vīdī ferōciōrem.

QUĪNTUS: quid posteā?

TITUS: subitō mē cēpit rētī et mihi ōrantī et obsecrantī ut dīmitterer,
         populus negāvit. 'iugulā!' clāmāvit et pollice versō omnēs mē   30
         dēstināvērunt ad mortem. cum autem mē rētiārius esset gladiō
         interfectūrus, ē somnō excitātus sum ā frātre parvulō mē
         gladiō ligneō percutiente et magnā vōce clāmante. 'surge, Tite!
         tē occīsūrus salūtō.'

         numquam posteā ad lūdōs ībō. nam quō animō gladiātor   35
         mortem exspectet superātus, nunc dēmum intellegō.

WORD LIST

offendō, -ere, dī, -sum, meet with
***incautus, -a, -um,** unawares, off guard
***imprūdēns, -entis,** careless
praeceps, -cipitis, headlong
brūtus, -a, -um, stupid
***pellō, -ere, pepulī, pulsum,** knock against
rēs domesticae, private affairs
***dētineō, -ēre, -tinuī, -tentum,** hold back, detain
***pallidus, -a, -um,** pale
***vultus, -ūs,** *m.,* face

***aeger, -gra, -grum,** sick, ill
pervādō, -ere, -vāsī, -vāsum, spread through
āscrībō, -ere, -scrīpsī, -scrīptum, enrol
***contendere,** to fight, compete
dīmittere, to let go
iugulāre, to cut the throat
pollex, -icis, *m.,* thumb
dēstināre, to doom
percutiō, -ere, -cussī, -cussum, strike

NOTES

1 **offendere** means to knock against, hence to meet unexpectedly; compare our
   colloquial expression *to bump into.*
2 **neuter neutrum agnōscit,** neither recognised the other.
12 **febrem tertiānam,** tertian fever, a fever which occurred in spasms every third
   day.
17 **in sēcrētum venīre,** to come aside.
19 **tuā pāce,** by your leave.
24 **hesternā nocte,** last night (**hesternus,** adjective from **herī**).
29 **ōrantī et obsecrantī,** earnestly begging.
36 **nunc dēmum,** now at last. The meaning is that now I realise if I never did so
   before.

Exercise 26b

bubulcum ad portam exspectat.

Warned in a Dream

illa duo somnia saepissimē commemorantur ā Stōicīs. ūnum dē Simōnide:
is ōlim īgnōtum quendam prōiectum mortuum vīdit eumque humāvit;
deinde in nāvem cōnscēnsūrus ab eō quem sepelīverat ita monērī vīsus
est: 'nōlī id facere; sī enim nāvigāveris, perībis naufragiō.' itaque Simōnides
5 rediit, periērunt cēterī quī tum nāvigāvērunt.

    alterum ita trāditum est: ōlim duo amīcī iter ūnā faciēbant et, cum
Megaram vēnissent, alter ad caupōnem dēvertit, ad hospitem alter. dum
post cēnam dormiunt, mediā nocte in somnīs eī quī in hospitiō erat,
amīcus vīsus est ōrāre ut subvenīret, quod sibi mors ā caupōne parārētur.
10 prīmō perterritus somniō surrēxit, deinde, cum sē collēgisset, recubuit.
tum eī dormientī īdem ille vīsus est rogāre ut, quoniam sibi vīvō nōn
subvēnisset, mortem suam inultam esse nē paterētur. dīxit sē interfectum
in plaustrum ā caupōne esse cōniectum et suprā iniectum faenum. petēbat
ut māne ad portam adesset priusquam plaustrum ex oppidō exīret. hōc
15 somniō commōtus māne bubulcum ad portam exspectāvit et rogāvit quid
esset in plaustrō. ille perterritus fūgit; mortuus ērutus est; caupō, rē
patefactā, poenās dedit.

WORD LIST

*somnium, -iī, n., dream
*commemorāre, to relate, mention
*ignōtus, -a, -um, unknown
humāre, to bury
*cōnscendere (nāvem), to embark
naufragium, -iī, n., shipwreck
dēvertō, -ere, -rtī, -rsum, lodge, put up at
*hospes, -itis, m., host, guest, friend
hospitium, -iī, n., hospitality, lodging
*ōrāre, to beg, entreat
*subveniō, -īre, -vēnī, -ventum (dat.), help, come to the help of
recumbō, -ere, -cubuī, lie down
quoniam, since

inultus, -a, -um, unavenged
*patior, -patī, -passus sum, suffer, allow
*suprā (adv.), above, on top
faenum, -ī, n., hay
*priusquam, before
*oppidum, -ī, n., town
*commoveō, -ēre, -mōvī, -mōtum, disturb, agitate
bubulcus, -ī, m., ox-driver, one who ploughs with oxen
ēruō, -ere, -ruī, -rutum, dig out, search out
*patefacere, to disclose, reveal, expose

NOTES

2 prōiectum, stretched out; we would say simply *lying dead*.
6 ūnā, together.
9 quod sibi mors parārētur. He said quod mihi mors parātur.
10 cum sē collēgisset, when he had pulled himself together, recovered his calm.

Exercise 26c

Telling and asking

redde Latīnē:

My friend tells me that he will not go to the games.
Tell me why you do not wish to hunt.
Tell your friend to bring his pen and tablets.
Tell him not to arrive late.
Tell me the story which you heard.

Ask your friend to stay for a few days.
Ask him if he intends to go away tomorrow.
Ask him whether he intends to go away or to stay.
Ask him whether he intends to go away or not.
Why did you not ask for (petere ā) money from your father?

IV On the Northern Front

Before the invasions of Julius Caesar in 55 and 54 B.C., the Romans had little first-hand knowledge of Britain and its inhabitants. No doubt Roman traders had made occasional journeys there, but any information that they had been able to pass on was limited and concerned mainly the coastal towns of the southeast corner.

It is not surprising, therefore, that the Romans thought of the Britons as a barbarous people living at the end of the world and that Caesar himself judged them uncivilised and lacking in culture. In this he was mistaken, but perhaps he was deceived by their appearance, especially in battle, when the woad with which they stained their faces and the long hair they affected must have made them look unusually savage.

In fact, the tribes who inhabited the southern and south-eastern parts of the island had made considerable progress towards civilisation. This was largely due to the influence of successive waves of invaders from Europe, particularly the Belgae, who had brought with them from Gaul their native arts and skills. The tribes who lived farther from the south coast, although they spoke the same language—Celtic—followed a more primitive way of life than their southern neighbours. They lived in hut villages or lake settlements and practised an elementary form of agriculture.

When Caesar made his raids on their shores the Britons were already using a gold coinage and conducting an extensive trade with Europe. The chief exports from Britain were corn and cattle, but others of importance were gold, silver, iron, hides, slaves and hunting dogs. There were also many imports, including wine, silver tableware, fine pottery, ivory, jewellery and glass.

The Britons also used the heavy wheeled plough in agriculture and the chariot in warfare—further evidence of the progress they had made. Celtic art appears to have flourished even in those early days, for it is known that the Britons were skilful in adorning wooden bowls and tankards with bronze and in inlaying bronze with enamel.

Lesson 27

Exercise 27a

(1)

The sight of the resolute Britons somewhat dismayed even the seasoned Roman soldiers on their first visit to Britain, and only the brave example of the standard-bearer of the tenth legion saved the day.

atque nostrīs mīlitibus cūnctantibus, maximē propter altitūdinem maris, is quī decimae legiōnis aquilam ferēbat, contestātus deōs, ut ea rēs legiōnī fēlīciter ēvenīret, 'dēsilīte', inquit, 'mīlitēs, nisi vultis aquilam hostibus prōdere: ego certē meum reī pūblicae atque imperātōrī officium praestiterō.' hoc cum vōce magnā dīxisset, sē ex nāvī prōiēcit atque in hostēs aquilam   5
ferre coepit. tum nostrī cohortātī inter sē, nē tantum dēdecus admitterētur, ūniversī ex nāvī dēsiluērunt. quōs cum mīlitēs quī erant in proximīs nāvibus cōnspexissent, subsecūtī hostibus appropinquārunt.

WORD LIST

*cūnctor, -ārī, -ātus sum, hesitate
*altitūdō, -inis, *f.*, depth, height
*aquila, -ae, *f.*, the eagle, the standard of the legion
contestor, -ārī, -ātus sum, pray, call to witness
*prōdō, -ere, -didī, -ditum, betray

*certē, at least, at any rate
*praestō, -stāre, -stitī, fulfil
*cohortor, -ārī, -ātus sum, urge
*dēdecus, -oris, *n.*, disgraceful act
admittere, to commit
*subsequor, -ī, subsecūtus sum, follow up

139

NOTES

2 **is qui aquilam ferēbat**—the aquilifer, standard-bearer.
4 **praestiterō**, I shall have fulfilled, i.e. it will be on record that I have fulfilled.
6 **cohortātī inter sē**, urging one another.
7 **ūniversī**, all together, in a body.
8 **appropinquārunt**, a shortened form of **appropinquāvērunt**.

Exercise 27b

The Romans, however, had more than the warlike Britons to contend with, for unusually high tides, so different from those of the Mediterranean Sea, upset their plans, and stormy weather played havoc with their ships.

The following passage refers to the night of 31 August, 55 B.C.

eādem nocte accidit ut esset lūna plēna. hic diēs maritimōs aestūs maximōs in Ōceanō efficere cōnsuēvit, sed id nostrīs erat incognitum. ita ūnō tempore nāvēs longās, quibus Caesar exercitum trānsportāverat quāsque in āridum subdūxerat, aestus complēverat, et nāvēs onerāriās, quae ad
5 ancorās erant dēligātae, tempestās afflīctābat. complūribus nāvibus frāctīs, cum cēterae fūnibus ancorīs reliquīsque armāmentīs āmissīs, ad nāvigandum inūtilēs essent, magna totīus exercitūs perturbātiō facta est. neque enim nāvēs erant aliae quibus mīlitēs reportārī possent, et omnia dēerant quae ad reficiendās nāvēs erant ūsuī. praetereā, quod omnēs
10 putābant sē hiemāre in Galliā dēbēre, frūmentum hīs in locīs in hiemem prōvīsum nōn erat.

WORD LIST

*maritimus, -a, -um, of the sea
*aestus, -ūs, *m.*, tide
*efficiō, -ere, -fēci, -fectum, cause
*cōnsuēscō, -ere, -suēvī, -suētum, become accustomed
*incognitus, -a, -um, unknown
āridum, -ī, *n.*, dry land
subdūcere, to draw up, beach
*ancora, -ae, *f.*, anchor
dēligāre, to tie up, moor
afflīctāre, to batter

*frangō, -ere, frēgī, frāctum, wreck, break
fūnis, -is, *m.*, rope, cable
armāmenta, -ōrum, *n.pl.*, tackle
*āmittō, -ere, -mīsī, -missum, lose
*inūtilis, -is, -e, useless
*perturbātiō, -ōnis, *f.*, confusion
dēerant, (dēesse), were lacking
*ūsuī, of use (see note)
hiemāre, to pass the winter
*prōvideō, -ēre, -vidī, -vīsum, provide

NOTES

1 **accidit ut,** it happened that . . . .
2 **Ōceanus,** the great sea which was believed to encircle the earth.
   incognitum, the Romans, accustomed to the Mediterranean where there is little tidal movement, were taken by surprise by the high tides of the English Channel.
3 **nāvēs longās . . . nāvēs onerāriās; nāvēs longās** is the object of **complēverat, nāvēs onerāriās** of **afflictābat.** The **nāvēs longae** were the sleek warships, built for speed; the **onerāriae** were the broad, slower transports.
6 **ad nāvigandum,** for sailing.
9 **ad reficiendās nāvēs,** for repairing the ships.
   ūsui, of use; **ūsui** is, of course, dative case and literally means *for use.*

Language

The gerund and gerundive

1 **ad nāvigandum,** *for (the purpose of) sailing.*
   nāvigandum is an example of the *gerund,* a verbal noun found only in the accusative, genitive, dative *and* ablative cases, singular.

Examples:

acc. **ad nāvigandum,** *for (the purpose of) sailing.*
gen. **nāvigandī causā,** *for the purpose of sailing.*
dat. **nāvigandō operam dare,** *to pay attention to sailing.*
abl. **nāvigandō nocte nāvēs servābimus.** *By sailing by night we shall save the ships.*

How to recognise the gerund:
1st conjugation,   **nāvig-andum**
2nd conjugation,   **doc-endum**
3rd conjugation, (*a*) **dūc-endum**
                 (*b*) **capi-endum**
4th conjugation,   **audi-endum**

2 **ad nāvēs reficiendās,** *for (the purpose of) repairing the ships.* **reficiendās** is an example of the *gerundive* (see page 40). You already know this part of the verb, meaning *requiring to be* . . . . This meaning applies only to the nominative case (and the accusative in indirect statement.)
   In the other cases it is used in place of the gerund when the verb has an object. Thus, instead of **ad reficiendum nāvēs,** Latin says **ad nāvēs reficiendās,** for the purpose of the ships being repaired, i.e. of repairing the ships.

Exercise 27c

redde Anglicē:

Plīnius studiōsus erat legendī et scrībendī.
ad scrībendās epistulās stilum portābat.
nāvēs aptae (*fit*) sunt ad nāvigandum.
puerī discunt legendō.
itaque librīs legendīs operam dent.
pecūniae petendae causā vēnī.
pecūniā dandā maximē mē adiuvābis.
studendō animum intendam.

Exercise 27d

Roman and Briton. An imaginary interrogation of a British prisoner-of-war.

CAESAR: centuriō, dūc ad mē captīvum; multa eum rogāre cupiō. [*intrat iuvenis Britannus, vitrō īnfectus sed gestū tam superbō ut in Caesarem dēfigat oculōs neque umquam dēmittat.*]

5   dīc mihi, quaesō, quā rē adductī Britannī pāce petītā contrā nōs coniūrāverint.

CAPTĪVUS: Britannī, ubi Rōmānōs nāvibus frāctīs esse magnopere perturbātōs vīdērunt, rebelliōnem facere cōnstituērunt ut Rōmānōs frūmentō prohibērent bellumque in hiemem prōdūcerent. spērābant enim, sī Rōmānī aut superātī aut reditū interclūsī

10 essent, nēminem posteā in Britanniam bellī causā trānsitūrum esse.

CAESAR: et quō iam Britannī, virī fortissimī, sē recēpērunt? nusquam enim eōs nunc videō.

CAPTĪVUS: ad locum ita nātūrā et arte mūnītum ut neque adīrī neque capī

15 ā Caesare possit. inde ōlim impetū factō Rōmānōs in mare repellent.

CAESAR: ad Britannōs redī et eīs persuādē nūllō modō eōs arma Rōmānōrum sustinēre posse. sī prūdentēs erunt, pācem statim petent. Rōmānī enim vēnērunt nōn ut agrōs eōrum vāstent et

20 omnia bona dīripiant, sed ut multa in eōs cōnferant beneficia. nōbīs adiuvantibus viās meliōrēs, fundōs fēcundiōrēs habēbunt, et mōribus lēgibusque Rōmānīs ūtentur.

CAPTĪVUS: redībō, Caesar, sed hoc certō tibi affirmō, nūllā rē Britannōs adductum īrī ut lībertātem quam accēperint ā maiōribus trādant.

WORD LIST

vitrum, -ī, *n.,* woad
infectus, -a, -um, stained
gestus, -ūs, *m.,* bearing
***dēfīgō, -ere, -fīxī, -fīxum,** fix
***dēmittō, -ere, -mīsī, -missum,** let drop
***coniūrāre,** to conspire
***addūcō, -ere, -dūxī, -ductum,** induce, persuade
rebelliō, -ōnis, *f.,* revolt
***prohibeō, -ēre, -uī, -itum,** keep back
prōdūcere, to prolong
***reditus, -ūs,** *m.,* return

interclūdō, -ere, -clūsī, -clūsum, cut off
***adeō, -īre, -iī,** approach
repellō, -ere, reppulī, repulsum, drive back
***sustineō, -ēre, -uī, -tentum,** withstand
***vāstāre,** to lay waste
***dīripiō, -ere, -uī, -reptum,** plunder
cōnferre, to confer, bestow
***beneficium, -iī,** *n.,* kindness
fēcundus, -a, -um, fertile
***ūtor, ūtī, ūsus sum** *(abl.),* enjoy
***maiōrēs, -um,** *m.pl.,* ancestors

NOTES

4 **pāce petītā,** after asking for peace. What construction?
10 **bellī causā,** *literally* for the sake of war. Try to give a more idiomatic translation.
14 **ita nātūrā et arte mūnitum,** *literally* 'so fortified by nature and by (human) skill'. Try to improve on this.
22 **ūtentur,** will enjoy.

'quā rē adductī contrā nōs coniūrāvistis?'

143

Revision Exercises

A

Revise participles, deponent verbs, ablative absolute.

redde Latinē:
Following the leader we came at last to the gate.
With the children following, Vesonius made his way through the streets.
When I had found Rufus, I took him home.
When I had found Rufus, I was glad.
Hearing a shout, we looked back.
The storm damaged the ships which had been moored.
When the ships had been moored, the soldiers pitched camp.
When the Romans have been overcome, no one will come to Britain.
After speaking with the prisoner, Caesar sent him away.
When Augustus was emperor, the Roman citizens were fortunate.

B

Revise *purpose* and *result*.

redde Latinē:
The fog was so dense that we could not see the road.
Come with us so that you may not lose the way.
Rufus guards the house so that no one may enter.
Rufus guards the house so well that no one can enter.
The philosopher brought books to read. (i.e. which he might read).
He was so intent on reading that he heard nothing.
Caesar sent a centurion to bring the prisoner to him.
'Bring the prisoner to me,' he said, 'so that I may speak with him.'

C

Revise the 'three indirects'—statement, question, command.

Translate the following sentences into English and then state in Latin the actual words spoken.

Example:

ā dominō petīvī ut domum mihi venderet.
I asked the owner to sell me the house—**domum mihi vende.**

persuādē Britannīs ut pācem petant.
eīs persuādē Rōmānōs ā barbarīs vincī nōn posse.
dīcite mihi cūr rebelliōnem fēceritis.
spērābāmus vōs reditū interclūsōs superātum īrī.
nōn intellegimus cūr nāvēs aestū complētae sint.
aquilifer mīlitēs cohortātus est nē cūnctārentur.
rogābant omnēs nōnne in Galliā hiemātūrī essent.
imperātor negāvit Rōmānōs vēnisse ut agrōs Britannōrum vāstārent.

D

Revise *subjunctive*: select the proper word.

cum lūna plēna ——, aestūs maximī erant.	*erat, fuit, esset.*
nāvēs —— nē tempestāte afflīctentur	*subductae sint, subdūcāmus, subdūcēmur.*
nē umquam posthāc tantam tempestātem ——.	*sit, videam, vīdī.*
cum ——, magnam nūbem vīdimus.	*respeximus, respiciāmus, respexissēmus.*
—— in viam; nē quis in domō ——.	*ēgrediāmur, ēgrederentur; cessābit, cesset.*
cum Larcius ——, ā servīs cīnctus est.	*lavābat, lavet, lavārētur.*
cum domus īnfāmis ——, nēmō eam emere volēbat.	*fuit, esset, fuerat.*
ad scrībendum saepe animum ——.	*intendātur, intendāris, intendās.*

Lesson 28

Almost a hundred years were to elapse before the next Roman invasion of Britain took place. In A.D. 43 during the reign of the Emperor Claudius, an attack was launched with four legions, the Second Augusta, the Ninth Hispana, the Fourteenth Gemina and the Twentieth Valeria Victrix. The Romans landed in Kent and, despite resistance from British forces under Togodumnus and Caratacus, advanced steadily, crossing the Thames and reaching Camulodunum (Colchester). Many tribes offered no resistance and submitted voluntarily.

The early English historian, the Venerable Bede, who was born in 672, writes thus of Claudius' invasion.

Exercise 28a

Claudius imperātor, cupiēns sē ūtilem reīpūblicae ostentāre prīncipem, bellum quaesīvit. itaque expedītiōnem in Britanniam mōvit, quae excitāta esse in tumultum propter nōn redditōs trānsfugās vidēbātur. trānsvectus in īnsulam est quam neque ante Iūlium Caesarem neque post eum quisquam
5 adīre ausus fuerat, ibique sine ūllō proeliō ac sanguine intrā paucissimōs diēs plūrimam īnsulae partem in dēditiōnem recēpit. Orcadas etiam īnsulās ultrā Britanniam in Ōceanō positās Rōmānō adiēcit imperiō, ac sextō quam profectus erat mēnse Rōmam rediit, fīliōque suō Britannicī nōmen imposuit.

WORD LIST
*ūtilis, -is, -e, useful
ostentāre, to show
*tumultus, -ūs, m., rebellion
trānsfuga, -ae, m., deserter
trānsvehor, -vehī, -vectus sum, cross

*in dēditiōnem recipere, to receive in surrender
*ultrā (prep. with acc.), beyond
*adiciō, -ere, -iēcī, -iectum, add
*impōnō, -ere, -posuī, -positum, give (as a title)

NOTES
6 **Orcades insulae,** the islands of Orkney.
8 **sextō quam profectus erat mēnse,** in the sixth month after he had set out. **quam** is here equivalent to **postquam.**

Exercise 28b

Pomponius Mela, who lived during the reigns of Claudius and Nero, was one of the first Roman writers to deal systematically with the geography of the ancient world. He has left us a manual of geography known as the 'Chorographia', in which he describes places, peoples and the customs they observed.

Here is part of his description of Britain and its inhabitants.

Britanniam tam diū clausam aperit ecce prīncipum maximus, nōn indomitārum modo ante sē vērum īgnōtārum quoque gentium victor.

   Britannia est triquetra et Siciliae maximē similis, plāna, ingēns, fēcunda, vērum iis quae pecora quam hominēs benignius alant.

   fert nemora saltūsque ac praegrandia flūmina, alternīs mōtibus modo   5
in pelagus, modo retrō fluentia et quaedam gemmās margarītāsque generantia.

   fert populōs rēgēsque populōrum, sed sunt incultī omnēs, atque ut longius ā continentī absunt, ita magis aliārum opum īgnārī, tantum pecore ac fīnibus dītēs.   10

   pugnant nōn equitātū modo aut peditātū, vērum et bīgīs et curribus gallicē armātī: covinnōs vocant, quōrum falcātīs axibus ūtuntur.

WORD LIST

indomitus, -a, -um, unconquered	**gemma, -ae,** *f.*, precious stone
vērum, but	**margarīta, -ae,** *f.*, pearl
triquetrus, -a, -um, triangular	**generāre,** to produce
plānus, -a, -um, level	**incultus, -a, -um,** uncivilised
*****benignē,** kindly, favourably (see note)	**continēns, -entis,** *f.*, continent
*****alō, -ere, aluī, altum,** support	*****opēs, -um,** *f.pl.*, wealth
nemus, -oris, *n.*, forest	*****īgnārus, -a, -um,** ignorant
saltus, -ūs, *m.*, mountain pasture	*****fīnēs, -ium,** *m.pl.*, territory, land
praegrandis, -is, -e, very large	**bīgae, -ārum,** *f. pl.*, two-horsed chariot
*****mōtus, -ūs,** *m.*, movement, tide	**armātus, -a, -um,** armed
*****retrō,** backwards	**falcātus, -a, -um,** armed with scythes
pelagus, -ī, *n.*, the open sea	**axis, -is,** *m.*, axle
*****fluō, -ere, fluxī, fluxum,** flow	

NOTES

1 **clausam,** closed to foreigners.

4 **iis quae . . . alant** to be taken with **fēcunda**—productive of those things which are more favourable to the support of cattle than of men.

5 **fert,** it has, contains; in line 8 **fert** may be translated 'it supports'.

  alternīs mōtibus . . . fluentia, a reference to tidal estuaries such as those of Thames, Humber, Severn.

8 **ut . . . ita,** in proportion as . . . so; the farther they are from the continent, the more ignorant they are of the outside world.
9 **tantum,** only.
10 **ditēs = divitēs.**
11 **equitātū** means *with cavalry*; what do you think **peditātū** means?
12 **gallicē,** in the Gallic fashion.

INSCRIPTIONS

Inscriptions on stone or metal left behind by the Romans tell us much about the occupying forces and about everyday life in the province. More than 2 000 of these have been discovered in Britain, on buildings, altars, milestones, tombstones, roof-tiles, even domestic utensils, which were stamped with the number of a legion in much the same way as a modern hotel will stamp its name on its cutlery to discourage pilfering.

Here is an inscription found in Sussex, which introduces us to Cogidubnus, of whom you will read more in Lesson 29:

```
N]EPTVNO · ET · MINERVAE
        TEMPLUM
PRO · SALVTE · DOM[VS] · DIVINAE
EX ·] AVCTORITA[TE · TI ·] CLAVD ·
CO]GIDVBNI · R · LEGAT · AVG · IN · BRIT ·
COLLEGIVM · FABRORVM · ET · QVI · IN · EO
SVNT · D · S · D · DONANTE · AREAM
CLEM]ENTE · PVDENTINI · FIL ·
```

'To Neptune and Minerva this temple is dedicated (with prayers) for the health of the divine (i.e. the emperor's) house with the support of Tiberius Claudius Cogidubnus, King and Representative of Augustus in Britain by the Metalworkers' Guild and its members at their own expense, the site being gifted by Clemens, son of Pudentinus.'

Consider how much we learn from this inscription:

1 Although it was recorded only a few years after the invasions the formal Roman religion was already established in South Britain.

2 A British tribe (the Regnenses) that accepted Roman rule was received into friendly partnership, and its king, Cogidubnus, was not only allowed to retain his title and his local authority but was honoured with the additional title of Legatus Augusti.

3 Metal-working was not only a well-established industry, but those engaged in it were organised in a **collēgium** or *guild*.

Lesson 29

One of the first British kings to make his peace with the invaders was Cogidubnus whose capital was Noviomagus (Chichester). His association with the Romans was very profitable, for a part of his palace, recently discovered and excavated, clearly reveals the extent of his wealth; and his unusual double title of 'King of the Regnenses and Legate of Augustus in Britain' indicates how unique his relationship with the Romans was.

Exercise 29a

[calidissimō quōdam diē Septembrī nāvis onerāria Noviomagum appropinquat. nautās et magistrum ē nāve ēgredientēs praefectus portūs ita salūtat.]

PRAEFECTUS: salvēte, nautae! salvē, magister! unde vēnistis?

MAGISTER: Massiliā.

PRAEFECTUS: quem quidve petitis?

MAGISTER: Cogidubnum, rēgem Regnēnsium et lēgātum Rōmānum.

PRAEFECTUS: spērō mehercule vōs rēs importāre īnsolitās. nihil enim, nisi īnsolitum, illum dēlectābit.

MAGISTER [*graviter*]: pretiōsissima importāmus, vitrum caeruleum ex Aegyptō, Massiliā vīnum dulcissimum et unguenta suāvissima; [*iocōsē*] quae cum rēx olfēcerit, tōtus esse nāsus volet.

PRAEFECTUS [*rīdēns*]: sī vēra dīcis, laetus sānē vōs accipiet. etiam Rōmānōs ipsōs superat luxuriā.

MAGISTER: ubi, quaesō, est rēgia Cogidubnī? eō statim festīnāre velim, longā nāvigātiōne dēfessus.

PRAEFECTUS: vidēsne, magister, illa balnea marmorea prope portum sita?

MAGISTER: videō.

PRAEFECTUS: post illa rēgiam inveniētis, quā nihil est splendidius, nē Rōmae quidem.

MAGISTER: ō praefectum glōriōsum! num splendidior est Prīncipis ipsīus domō?

25 PRAEFECTUS: est profectō. et cum eam vīderis, omnibus rēbus īnstructam, *furnished* columnīs marmoreīs ōrnātam, prātīs, flōribus, arboribus *adorned* distīnctam, tum dēmum intellegēs cūr ita glōrier. est enim tam pulchra tamque magna ut animō concipī nōn possit.

MAGISTER: tibi grātiās agō. hanc tam mīrābilem rēgiam rēctā petēmus.

30 PRAEFECTUS: fēlīciter tibi!

WORD LIST

*calidus, -a, -um, warm
praefectus portūs, harbour-master
*īnsolitus, -a, -um, unusual
*pretiōsus, -a, -um, valuable
caeruleus, -a, -um, blue
*dulcis, -is, -e, sweet
unguentum, -ī, n., perfume
suāvis, -is, -e, sweet, delightful
olfaciō, -ere, -fēcī, -factum, smell
*nāsus, -ī, m., nose
luxuria, -ae, f., extravagance

*rēgia, -ae, f., palace
*nāvigātiō, -ōnis, f., sailing, voyage
glōriōsus, -a, -um, boastful
splendidus, -a, -um, magnificent
*nē . . . quidem, not even
īnstructus, -a, -um, furnished
prātum, -ī, n., park, lawn
distīnctus, -a, -um (distinguere), adorned
glōriārī, to boast
animō concipere, to imagine

NOTES

5 **Massilia,** Marseilles.
10 **vitrum** here means glass. It also means woad (Exercise 27d).
14 **sānē,** surely, doubtless.
15 **superat,** he outdoes.
16 **velim,** I should like.
20 **quā,** than which—ablative of comparison.
25 **est profectō,** it is, I can assure you.
29 **rēctā (viā),** straight.
30 **fēliciter tibi,** good luck to you!

Exercise 29b

rēgiae appropinquat magister nāvis cum duōbus servīs quī cistam inter sē
portant gravissimam. magnōs cachinnōs audiunt; brevī post in cōnspectum
venit rēx (vir corpore rōbustō, fuscō vultū, longīs capillīs), trēs hospitēs
comitātus. quibus dīmissīs, in rēgiam revertitur. subitō dispēnsātor manū
significat ut magister et servī sē sequantur. ad rēgem dūcuntur.

RĒX: salvē, magister. opportūnē vēnistī. nihil enim novī ex Āfricā
neque ē Galliā comparāvī hīs tribus mēnsibus et magnō
studiō emendī nunc moveor. quid nōbīs potes ostendere?

MAGISTER: ecce, ō rēx Cogidubne, exempla optima vitrī caeruleī et vīnī
dulcissimī et unguentī suāvissimī. quae sī comparāveris, 5
omnēs tibi invidēbunt: in ōre enim omnium et Britannōrum
et Rōmānōrum tū et rēgia tua et epulae tuae sine dubiō erunt.

RĒX: est tibi vōx blandissima, magister! sed quid prō illīs, quaesō,
tū petis?

MAGISTER: nihil, ō rex, nisi iūs commerciī cum Regnēnsibus. in portum 10
enim intrantēs, frūmentum vīdimus optimum. laetus multōs
illīus modiōs Noviomagō reportem.

RĒX: et laetus tibi dem, sed frūmentum nōndum est mātūrum
neque erit intrā vīgintī diēs. [cōgitat.] cōnsilium excōgitāvī
bonum. dum frūmentum mātūrēscat, hīc habitābis; hospes 15
meus eris. interdiū tibi licēbit omnēs urbis partēs vīsere,
portum, hortōs, balnea, agrōs; post cēnam dē frūmentō
aliīsque rēbus inter nōs dēlīberābimus. sīc trānsībit glōria
Cogidubnī in Ītaliam et Aegyptum et Āsiam!

WORD LIST

cista, -ae, *f.*, box, chest
cachinnus, -ī, *m.*, guffaw, loud laughter
*rōbustus, -a, -um, strong
fuscus, -a, -um, dark, swarthy
*capillī, -ōrum, *m.pl.*, hair
revertor, -ī, -versus sum, return
dispēnsātor, -ōris, *m.*, steward
*opportūnē, at the right time
*studium, -iī, *n.*, passion, desire

*invideō, -ēre, -vīdī, -vīsum (*dat.*), envy
*epulae, -ārum, *f.pl.*, banquet
blandus, -a, -um, flattering
iūs commerciī, the right to trade
modius, -iī, *m.*, measure (of corn)
*mātūrus, -a, -um, ripe
*excōgitāre, to think out
*mātūrēscō, -ere, mātūruī, ripen

NOTES

11 **laetus reportem,** I should gladly take back.
15 **dum frūmentum mātūrēscat,** until such time as the corn is ripe.

Exercise 29c

Saying 'when' in Latin.

cum, *when* is followed by present, future, future perfect indicative and by imperfect or pluperfect subjunctive.

ubi, *when, as soon as*
postquam, *after*
simul ac, *as soon as*
ut, *when, as*

are followed by the indicative mood, usually perfect (past definite) tense.

redde Anglicē :

postquam nāvis in portum vēnit, nautae ēgressī sunt.
praefectus, ut nautās ēgredientēs vīdit, eōs salūtāvit.
simul ac in portum vēnimus, frūmentum vīdimus optimum.
cum mercātōrēs hūc veniunt, rēs pretiōsissimās portant.
nautae, cum rēgiam vīdissent, stābant attonitī.
ubi rēx unguenta olfēcit, maximē gaudēbat.
cum vitrum caeruleum vīderit, emere volet.
ubi frūmentum mātūruit, nautae discessērunt.
postquam dē Cogidubnō cognōvī, rēgiam eius īnspicere volēbam.
ut eam vīdī, praefectum vēra dīxisse intellēxī.

Lesson 30

Under successive governors the legions advanced, the Ninth Hispana proceeding up the east side of Britain and establishing its headquarters, first at Lindum (Lincoln) and later at Eboracum (York). The Second Legion moved westwards and after much fighting established itself at Isca Silurum (Caerleon in S. Wales). The Twentieth fought its way towards the N.W. and finally made Deva (Chester) its headquarters. The Fourteenth Legion in the year 67 was withdrawn from Britain by the Emperor Nero during a time of peace.

Progress was not always easy. The tribes of Wales in particular were difficult to conquer and sometimes peoples like the Iceni, who had already been defeated, rose in revolt, either because of wrongs inflicted upon them by the Romans or because of oppressive taxation. In A.D. 61, while Suetonius Paulinus, the governor at that time, was waging war in N. Wales and preparing to attack the island of Anglesey, which was a stronghold of the Druids, Boudicca, the queen of the Iceni, resenting the cruelty of certain Roman officers to herself and her daughters, rebelled against Roman rule and marched against Camulodunum (Colchester).

Exercise 30a

Dio Cassius, who wrote a history of Rome in Greek, attributes the following sentiments to Boudicca when she addressed her people and incited them to rebel against the Romans.

quantum differat lībertās ā servitūte, omnēs ūsū didicistis. quās enim
contumēliās iniūriāsque nōn accēpimus quō ex tempore illī ad Britanniam
pervēnērunt? quae ōlim habēbāmus, eīs iam sumus prīvātī, et sī quid
superest nōbis, eī impōnitur vectīgal. melius fuit sub corōnā vēnīre quam
5 illud ināne nōmen lībertātis retinēre. quis tamen nōbis haec attulit mala?
ipsī, inquam, attulimus. Rōmānōs enim expellere dēbuimus in patriam
intrantēs, ut ōlim maiōrēs nostrī C. Iūlium Caesarem expulērunt.

vōs tamen admoneō nē Rōmānōs timeātis quī neque numerō neque
virtūte sunt nōbīs superiōrēs. et haec loca, nōbīs nōtissima, illīs īgnōta
10 sunt atque īnfesta. dēmōnstrāte igitur illōs, quī nihil nisi leporēs ac vulpēs
sunt, canibus lupīsque imperāre velle.

WORD LIST

*differō, -ferre, distulī, dīlātum, differ
servitūs, -ūtis, *f*., slavery
*ūsus, -ūs, *m*., experience
contumēlia, -ae, *f*., insult
*iniūria, -ae, *f*., wrong
prīvāre (+*abl*.), to deprive of
*superesse, to remain, be left over
*impōnō, -ere, -posuī, -positum, impose

vectīgal, -ālis, *n*., tax
*retinēre, to retain
afferō, -ferre, attulī, allātum, bring to
*malum, -ī, *n*., evil, calamity
*admonēre, to warn
*superior, -ius, superior
*īnfestus, -a, -um, unsafe, dangerous
lepus, -oris, *m*., hare
vulpēs, -is, *f*., fox

NOTES

4 **melius fuit,** it would have been better.
sub corōnā vēnīre, to be sold into slavery.
6 **expellere dēbuimus,** we ought to have driven out.

Exercise 30b

Tacitus, the Roman historian, refers to the revolt of the Iceni thus in his 'Agricola'.

Boudiccā generis rēgiī fēminā duce, sūmpsērunt ūniversī bellum; ac
sparsōs per castella mīlitēs cōnsectātī, expugnātīs praesidiīs, ipsam
colōniam invāsērunt ut sēdem servitūtis, neque ūllum in barbarīs saevitiae

genus omīsērunt īrātī et victōrēs. et nisi Paulīnus, cognitō prōvinciae
mōtū, properē subvēnisset, āmissā Britanniā esset: illam tamen ūnīus 5
proeliī fortūna veterī patientiae restituit.

WORD LIST

*genus, -eris, *n*., birth, family, kind
*rēgius, -a, -um, royal
*spargō, -ere, sparsī, sparsum, scatter
castellum, -ī, *n*., fort
consector, -ārī, -ātus sum, hunt down
expugnāre, to take by storm, capture
*praesidium, -iī, *n*., garrison, post

*colōnia, -ae, *f*., colony
*sēdēs, -is, *f*., seat, home
omittere, to leave out, disregard
properē, quickly, hastily
*fortūna, -ae, *f*., luck, successful outcome
patientia, -ae, *f*., submission

NOTES

1 **sūmpsērunt bellum,** this means the same as **sūmpsērunt arma.**
3 **ut sēdem,** as being the seat . . . .
  ūllum in barbarīs saevitiae genus, any kind of savagery found among barbarians.
5 **mōtus** here means *uprising* or *rebellion.*
6 **veterī; vetus** here means *former* (lit. *old*).

Exercise 30c

In A.D. 78 Julius Agricola was appointed governor of Britain. After campaign-
ing against the Ordovices of North Wales, who had recently rebelled, he began to
turn his eyes towards Scotland. Soon the Roman legions were pressing forward
from Chester and York and within two years had reached the isthmus between the
Clyde and Forth, where a line of forts was built. During the next three years
Agricola advanced through Perthshire and Strathmore to the north of Scotland,
where in 84 he challenged the united forces of the Caledonian tribesmen in the
decisive battle of Mons Graupius.

In a speech which he is said to have delivered before the battle, Calgacus tried
to inspire his men by pointing out what other tribes had done and by belittling the
Romans and the composition of their army.

'ita sublātā spē veniae, tandem sūmite animum. Brigantēs fēminā duce
exussērunt colōniam, expugnāvērunt castra ac, nisi fēlīcitās in socordiam
vertisset, exuere iugum potuērunt. nōs integrī et indomitī prīmō statim
congressū ostendāmus quālēs sibi Calēdonia virōs sēposuerit.

exercitus Rōmānus est ex dīversissimīs gentibus contractus; nunc eum 5
secundae rēs tenent, mox adversae solvent. omnia victōriae incitāmenta

prō nōbīs sunt. nūllae Rōmānōs coniugēs accendunt; nūllī parentēs fugam exprobrātūrī sunt; nūlla plērīsque patria est. paucōs numerō, trepidōs īgnōrantiā, caelum ipsum ac mare, īgnōta omnia, circumspectantēs
10 dī nōbīs trādidērunt. īte igitur in aciem et maiōrēs vestrōs et posterōs cōgitāte.'

WORD LIST

*tollō, -ere, sustulī, sublātum, remove, take away

exūrō, -ere, -ussī, -ustum, burn out or up

*fēlicitās, -ātis, f., good fortune, success

socordia, -ae, f., indolence, stupidity

exuere, to shake off

iugum, -ī, n., yoke

integer, -gra, -grum, whole, untouched, fresh

congressus, -ūs, m., encounter, meeting

*ostendō, -ere, -ndī, -ntum, show

sēpōnō, -ere, -posuī, -positum, set apart

*gēns, gentis, f., race

*solvō, -ere, solvī, solūtum, loosen, break up

incitāmentum, -ī, n., inducement, incentive

*coniūnx, -iugis, f., wife

accendere, to inflame, rouse, stir

exprobrāre, to reproach with, blame for

*plērīque, most, the majority

trepidus, -a, -um, alarmed, anxious

circumspectāre, to look around

*trādō, -ere, trādidī, trāditum, hand over

*aciēs, -ēī, f., line of battle, battle

posterī, -ōrum, m.pl., descendants, posterity

*cōgitāre, to think of

NOTES

1 **sūmite animum,** exactly our expression 'take heart'.
5 **contractus,** made up of, *lit.* drawn together from.
6 **rēs secundae,** success; **rēs adversae,** failure.
7 **prō nōbīs,** on our side.

Exercise 30d

redde Anglicē:

dum frūmentum mātūrēscēbat, nāvis in portū manēbat.

dum mīlitēs morantur, aquilifer in mare dēsiluit.

mīlitēs propter timōrem morātī sunt dōnec aquilifer in mare dēsiluit.

Britannī in silvīs sē cēlābant dum Rōmānī abīrent.

nautae exspectant dum magister ā rēgiā redeat.

dum magister rēgiam īnspectābat, nautae in marī natābant.

Lesson 31

THE WALL

In less than twenty years from the victory of Mons Graupius the forts north of the Tyne-Solway line had been abandoned and the Roman garrisons had fallen back. This may have been caused by greater pressure from the northern tribes or by a reduction in the number of Roman troops in Britain.

When the Emperor Hadrian visited Britain in 122, he caused the wall which bears his name to be built from the Tyne to the Solway Firth, a distance of eighty Roman miles. The eastern portion was made of concrete faced with stone, the western of turf. Varying in height from four to five metres and reinforced along its course by forts, milecastles and turrets, and protected further on its northern side by a broad ditch and rampart, it must have presented a formidable barrier to hostile tribesmen.

The wall was built by legionary soldiers, who have left us many inscriptions telling us of the portions the various detachments of men erected, but the garrison itself consisted of auxiliary forces drawn from different parts of the world.

Exercise 31a

The lesson which follows imagines the thoughts and experiences of Titus Vitellius Tancinus, a new recruit from sunny Spain, who is despondent at the prospect of soldiering in the more rigorous climate of North Britain.

Interlude on the Wall (1)

TITUS: quam frīgida est tempestās Britannica! semper flant ventī! ex
omnibus partibus simul! semper nūbilum est caelum! semper
tergum, genua, corpus horrent! dēsunt ignēs; dēest cibus; dēest
voluptās! quantō teneor dēsīderiō Hispāniae patriae, ubi sōl
semper calet neque ūllō labōre corpus unquam fatīgātur! [*Hears* 5
something.] quid est? putō . . . mē cantum audīre. ecce! mīlitēs in
castra revertentēs cantant. dē quō? dē quā rē? ha, ha, he. dē
centuriōne cantant. nunc verba audiō.

    'centuri-uri-ōnem
    habēmus ūnicum.   10
    quis enim pūgiōnem
    portat in proelium
    Pictīs īnfēnsiōrem?

quam frīgida est tempestās!

quis fābulam nārrat
15   in diēs longiōrem,
cum inde remeat?
Marcus, Marcus, Marcus nōnae centuriae,
semper enim is erit nostrae dēliciae!

nēmō mītiōrem
20   sē unquam praebuit
quam Marcus cum labōrem
ā nōbīs requīrit.
nec clāmitat nec castīgat,
nec probra cōnicit.
25   prōstrātus enim nōs ōrat
ut cōmitās adsit:
"subvenīte mihi, virī benevolī,
et omnibus erit, iūrō, plūs stīpendiī!"'

TITUS: verba rīdicula, sed quam grāta mihi sunt miserō!

sīc beātē vīvitur!

WORD LIST

*frīgidus, -a, -um, cold
flāre, to blow
nūbilus, -a, -um, cloudy
*genū, -ūs, *n.,* knee
*horrēre, to shudder
*dēsum, -esse, -fuī, be lacking
*voluptās, -ātis, *f.,* pleasure
*dēsīderium, -iī, *n.,* longing
*fatīgāre, to tire, weary
cantus, -ūs, *m.,* music, song
ūnicus, -a, -um, unique, without parallel
pūgiō, -ōnis, *m.,* dagger
īnfēnsus, -a, -um, hostile
remeāre, to return

*centuria, -ae, *f.,* century, company of soldiers
dēliciae, -ārum, *f.pl.,* darling, pet
requīrō, -ere, -quīsīvī, -quīsītum, ask for, demand
probrum, -ī, *n.,* insult, abuse
prōstrātus, -a, -um, prostrate, throwing oneself on the ground
cōmitās, -ātis, *f.,* friendliness, kindness, courtesy
*benevolus, -a, -um, kind, well-disposed
*iūrāre, to swear
stīpendium, -iī, *n.,* pay
*rīdiculus, -a, -um, amusing, funny, droll

NOTES

15 **in diēs,** *daily, day by day.* **cottīdiē,** *daily,* means that something is happening *on every day*; **in diēs,** with an adjective or adverb in the comparative degree, suggests that something is increasing (or decreasing) from day to day.
20 **sē praebuit mitiōrem,** has shown himself gentler.

Exercise 31b

[*Someone is heard approaching. It is* GĀIUS SAUFEIUS, *the Macedonian who shares with* TITUS *the sentry duty on this part of the wall.*]

GĀIUS: heus tū! quid agis?
TITUS: satis bene.
GĀIUS: nōnne tīrō es?
TITUS: ita vērō; Hispāniam relīquī abhinc quīndecim diēs.
5 GĀIUS: trīstis esse vidēris.
TITUS: nōn est cūr gaudeam.
GĀIUS: nōnne vīdistī ūllōs hostēs hodiē?
TITUS: nūllōs vīdī, sed paucōs Selgovārum per agrōs errantēs.
GĀIUS: ōlim vidēbis et laetior tū eris. quid es factūrus hāc nocte perāctīs
10 vigiliīs?
TITUS: nesciō.
GĀIUS: quīn mēcum venīs, prīmum ad balnea, deinde ad tabernam? omnēs ibi comitēs conveniēs.
TITUS: quid ibi faciēmus?
15 GĀIUS: vīnum bibēmus et multam ad noctem cantābimus, ego dē Macedoniā, tū dē Hispāniā, aliī dē Germāniā vel Āfricā. sīc beātē vīvētur ab omnibus. gaudē, mī amīce. vīta nostra brevis est.

WORD LIST
tīrō, -ōnis, *m.,* recruit
*beātē, happily

NOTES
6 **nōn est cūr** (with subjunctive), there is no reason why.
8 **Selgovārum;** the **Selgovae** were a tribe living in the area now covered by the Border counties of Scotland.
9 **perāctīs vigiliīs,** when sentry duty is over.

Exercise 31c

redde Latīnē :

After I left Spain, I travelled to Gaul.
As soon as I came here, I knew that the British weather was cold.
If I had stayed in Spain, I should now be happy.

When I saw you, I knew that you were a recruit.
If you come with me, you will meet many comrades.
When we meet our comrades, we shall sing far into the night.
Upon my word, if I were to sing, my comrades would not be happy!
When the soldiers sing, the centurion laughs.

Hadrian's Wall at Cuddy's Crag in Northumberland.

Lesson 32

THE ROMANS IN SCOTLAND

About A.D. 140, when Antoninus Pius was emperor and Lollius Urbicus governor of Britain, it was decided that the pressure on Hadrian's Wall had to be relieved and an advance made to the line between the Clyde and Forth which Agricola had occupied almost sixty years before. The intention was to contain the warlike tribes of the Caledonians and Maeatae as far as possible within their own territory and to prevent them from raiding the country to the south, as they had done to the great annoyance of the Romans.

Most of Agricola's forts were reoccupied, but on this occasion the defence system was strengthened by the construction of a turf wall. The Roman historians appear to have taken little notice of this campaign and only one brief reference to it is to be found in the works of a rather obscure historian:

'per lēgātōs suōs plūrima bella gerit; nam Britannōs per Lollium Urbicum vicit lēgātum aliō mūrū caespiticiō summōtīs barbarīs ductō.'

caespiticius, -a, -um, of turf
summoveō, -ēre, -mōvī, -mōtum,
   dislodge, move back

Archaeologists, however, have added to our knowledge of this period and several inscriptions unearthed by them bear the name of Lollius Urbicus; for example this one found at a Roman fort in Redesdale in the Cheviot Hills.

IMPeratori CAESari Tito AELIO HADriano ANTONINO
AUGusto PIO Patri Patriae SUB Quinto LOLlio
URBICO LEGato AUGusti PRO PRAEtore COHors
I (prima) LINGonum EQuitata Fecit

(Note that only the parts of words shown in capital letters are found in the original inscription.)

Three times during the next sixty years the wall of Antoninus Pius was overrun and in part, at least, destroyed. On the last occasion the northern tribes continued as far south as Eboracum (York), plundering and burning as they went.

It was to meet such a situation as this that the Emperor Septimius Severus came to Britain in 208. The preparations, however, that he made to invade Caledonia were so impressive that the tribesmen surrendered unconditionally.

The ditch of the Antonine Wall at Watling Lodge near Falkirk.

Even before he came to Britain Severus had been a sick man, but such was his determination to put the troublesome Caledonians in their place that he was carried in a litter 'to the extreme end of the Isle of Britain', as one Roman historian tells us. The expedition, however, proved too much for him and he died at York in 211.

Here are two references to his illness and death from the writings of the *Scriptores Historiae Augustae*.

Exercise 32a

(*a*) periit Eborācī in Britanniā, subāctīs gentibus quae Britanniae vidē-
bantur īnfestae, annō imperiī XVIII, morbō gravissimō exstīnctus iam
senex.

    corpus eius ā Britanniā Rōmam usque cum prōvinciālium reverentiā
susceptum est: nōnnūllī tamen urnam auream modo fuisse dīcunt Sevērī   5
reliquiās continentem, cum Septimius illīc, ubi vītā fūnctus est, esset
incēnsus.

(b) ultima verba eius dīcuntur haec fuisse: 'turbātam rem pūblicam ubīque
accēpī, pācātam etiam Britannīs relinquō, senex et pedibus aeger, firmum
10   imperium Antōnīnīs meīs relinquēns sī bonī erunt, imbēcillum, sī malī.'

WORD LIST

*subigō, -ere, -ēgī, -āctum, subdue,
conquer
prōvinciālis, -is, *m.*, provincial, inhabitant of a province
reverentia, -ae, *f.*, reverence, respect
*suscipere, to bear
urna, -ae, *f.*, urn (for ashes of dead)
*aureus, -a, -um, of gold

reliquiae, -ārum, *f.pl.*, remains, ashes of
dead
*ultimus, -a, -um, last
*turbātus, -a, -um, disturbed, troubled,
in disorder
pācātus, -a, -um, peaceful
*firmus, -a, -um, strong
imbēcillus, -a, -um, weak

NOTES

2   **exstinctus,** having died *or* succumbed. **exstinguī** the passive of **exstinguere,** *to put
out a light*, means literally to be snuffed out, i.e. to die.
6   **vitā fūnctus est,** he completed his life—still another way of saying 'he died'.
fungor, fungī, fūnctus sum (ablative) means to complete.
10   **Antōnīnīs meīs,** Severus's two sons. Severus had adopted them into the Antonine
family into which, in admiration of Marcus Aurelius (Antoninus), he had first had
himself adopted. The high hopes he had of his sons were sadly disappointed, for
within a year of his death the elder, who has gone down to history by his nickname
Caracalla, had murdered his brother Geta and thus secured for himself the imperial
power.

Exercise 32b

*The emperor Severus had presentiments of death some time before he visited
Britain, and constantly consulted the stars. An unusual incident in Britain
seemed to him to confirm his fear of approaching death.*

post mūrum apud Luguvallium vīsum in Britanniā ad proximam
mānsiōnem redībam, nōn sōlum victor sed etiam in aeternum pāce
fundātā. animō volvēbam quid ōminis mihi occurreret cum Aethiops
quīdam ē numerō mīlitum, cuius fāma inter scurrās erat clāra propter
5   iocōs, mihi occurrit cum corōnā ē cupressū factā. quem cum ego īrātus
removērī ab oculīs iussissem, et colōre eius et ōmine corōnae tāctus, ille
clāmāvit iocī causā, 'tōtum fuistī; tōtum vīcistī; iam deus estō victor!'

WORD LIST

*proximus, -a, -um, nearest
mānsiō, -ōnis, f., station, halting place
*sōlum, only
fundāre, to establish
animō volvere, to ponder, consider, lit.
  turn over in one's mind
ōmen, -inis, n., omen, sign
*occurrō, -ere, -currī, -cursum, run to
  meet, present itself

*fāma, -ae, f., reputation
scurra, -ae, m., buffoon, jester
*clārus, -a, -um, famous, notorious
iocus, -ī, m., joke, jest
*corōna, -ae, f., wreath, garland
cupressus, -ūs, f., cypress
*removēre, to remove
*color, -ōris, m., colour

NOTES

1 **post mūrum apud Luguvallium vīsum,** after visiting the wall at Carlisle.
2 **in aeternum,** for all time.
3 **quid ōminis,** what (of) omen, i.e. what sort of omen.
6 **tāctus,** affected, moved.
7 **tōtum fuistī,** you have been everything.
  estō, thou shalt be! This is an example of the future imperative of **esse.**

For the rest of the third century there was comparative peace in the north, though at no time did the tribesmen welcome the refinements of Roman life, as the Britons of the south had done, among whom the toga was commonplace, the Latin language widely spoken, and baths, amphitheatres and temples evidence of their eager acceptance of the **Pāx Rōmāna.**

Towards the end of the century danger came from another direction. Pictish and Saxon pirates began to raid the south-east shores of Britain. A fleet was assembled to guard the coast from the Wash to the Isle of Wight (which came to be known as the Saxon Shore) and forts built to house both sailors and soldiers whose responsibility it was to intercept raiders by land and sea. For a time these precautions were fairly successful, but in 367 a great combined attack by Saxons, Picts and Scots caused widespread distress throughout the coastal regions.

Exercise 32c

(duo agrestēs, Dinias et Alaun, dum fugiunt perterritī, omnibus rēbus āmissīs, in silvā conveniunt. quid faciant in hōc tantō discrīmine aliquamdiū dubitant. quō sē vertant? redeantne in agrōs suōs an salūtem petant alibī? barbarī enim omnēs in partēs errant neque quicquam relinquunt tūtum.)   5

DINIAS: quid faciēmus? quō tandem ībimus?
ALAUN: nesciō, sed fugiāmus statim. nōn interest quō eāmus, dummodo

illōs Saxŏnēs procul ā tergō relinquāmus.

DINIAS: nihil certē nōbīs iam superest. casa incēnsa est, uxor līberīque
10 aut occīsī aut abductī, bovēs exāctī.

ALAUN: et messis dīrepta. sī hīc manēbimus, ad ultimam inopiam
addūcēmur.

DINIAS: estne tibi quod edāmus? ēsuriō enim neque quicquam multīs
hōrīs comēdī.

15 ALAUN: nihil nisi pānis et cāseī paululum quod in prandium parāveram.
vix effūgī tribus barbarīs persequentibus. forte, dum currō, in
cavum incidī atque ibi latēbam fruticibus tēctus dum praeterīrent.
timēbam tamen domum redīre cibum comparātum nē caperer ā
barbarīs.

20 DINIAS: quid nōbīs fīet, sī Rōmānī nōn satis validī sunt ut illōs repellant?
audīvī enim Nectaridum, comitem ōrae maritimae, occīsum et
Fullofaudēn ducem circumventum īnsidiīs hostium esse.

ALAUN: ōlim maiōrēs nostrī Rōmānōs molestē ferēbant vī et armīs patriam
subigentēs.

25 DINIAS: nunc salūtem nostram in Rōmānīs pōnimus.

ALAUN: ēheu, nōs miserī quid exspectāre possumus sī Pictī ā septentriōnibus, Scottī ab occidente, Saxŏnēs ab oriente patriam invādent
et Rōmānōs superābunt? quō fugiāmus, sī vītam agere volumus
tranquillam.

30 DINIAS: ad merīdiem iter faciāmus. ibi fortasse tūtī ac serēnī vīvēmus.

ALAUN: iam advesperāscit. sī noctū contendēmus, hostēs fortasse fallēmus.
eāmus fortī animō. nihil est auxiliī nisi in nōbīs ipsīs.

WORD LIST

agrestis, -is, *m.,* rustic, countryman
discrīmen, -inis, *n.,* danger, crisis
*tūtus, -a, -um, safe
*dummodo (*with subjunctive*), provided
that
casa, -ae, *f.,* hut, cottage, cabin
exigō, -ere, -ēgī, -āctum, drive out *or*
away
messis, -is, *f.,* harvest, crops
*inopia, -ae, *f.,* need, poverty, scarcity
ēsurīre, to be hungry
comedō, -ere, -ēdī, -ēsum, eat up,
consume
cavum, -ī, *n.,* hole, hollow

*tēctus, -a, -um, covered, hidden
*validus, -a, -um, strong
*ōra, -ae, *f.,* shore, coast
*circumvenīre, to surround
*insidiae, -ārum, *f.pl.,* ambush,
treachery
*pōnō, -ere, posuī, positum, place,
stake
*tranquillus, -a, -um, quiet, peaceful,
calm
serēnus, -a, -um, serene, cheerful, glad
*advesperāscit, evening approaches
*fallō, -ere, fefellī, falsum, escape the
notice of

NOTES

3 **quō sē vertant? redeantne in agrōs suōs?** Where are they to turn? Are they to return to their own lands? The present subjunctive in a direct question indicates that the questioner is deliberating—'What am I to do?' The imperfect subjunctive—**quō sē verterent?** would mean 'Where were they to turn?'

7 **nōn interest,** it does not matter; it is not important.

13 **neque quicquam,** and nothing (*lit.* and not anything).

15 **paululum,** diminutive of **paulum; a** very little.
   in prandium, for lunch.

18 **cibum comparātum,** to get food: **comparātum** is the supine which is used after verbs of motion, e.g. **redīre,** to indicate *purpose.*

21 **Nectaridum comitem ōrae maritimae,** Nectaridus, Count of the Saxon Shore.

22 **Fullofaudēn ducem,** Duke Fullofaudes.

23 **molestē ferēbant,** *lit.* bore with difficulty, i.e. resented.

26 **ā septentriōnibus.** To indicate direction the Romans used the heavenly bodies; thus the **septentriōnēs,** the seven stars of the Great or Little Bear (the Plough) near the north pole stood for the north. The **occidēns (sōl),** the setting sun, and **oriēns (sōl),** the rising sun, became west and east respectively; **merīdiēs,** i.e. **medi-diēs,** noon (*or* the sun at noon), was used to indicate south.

Distance slab marking the eastern end of Antonine's Wall, found at Bridgeness on the Firth of Forth. 'For the Emperor Caesar Titus Aelius Hadrianus Antoninus Augustus Pius, Father of his country, the Legion Second Augusta built (this wall) for a distance of 4 miles, 652 paces.'

167

Lesson 33

THE ROMAN WITHDRAWAL FROM BRITAIN

When it became evident to the Emperor Valentinian that order could not be restored in Britain unless powerful reinforcements were sent at once, he entrusted to Count Theodosius, one of his moxt experienced generals, the task of clearing the country of the predatory barbarians.

This he did successfully and the wall and forts were rebuilt. Life, however, changed for the civil settlements that had grown up outside the forts. The settlements themselves, destroyed in the raids, were not restored; the women and children were accommodated in the reconstructed forts which came to resemble miniature fortified towns; and the garrisons, now granted the right to cultivate the surrounding land, combined the duties of soldiers and farmers.

These new developments could not be expected to improve, or even maintain the alertness and effectiveness of the garrisons, but, to compensate for this, a greater measure of independence was given to tribes such as the Dumnonii and Notadini who had been under Roman protection and given proof of their loyalty.

For a time the attacks of the Scots, Picts and Saxons slackened, but about 390, when some of the legions had been withdrawn to defend other parts of the Roman Empire, they were renewed. Italy itself was then under threat from hordes of barbarians who swept on relentlessly from the far east and in time overran Europe. By 410, when Rome was sacked by Alaric, the province of Britain must have come to realise that little further assistance could be expected from the Romans. This did not prevent the Britons, however, from sending piteous appeals for help to Rome as late even as 446, and on occasion with temporary success.

Exercise 33a

frācta est autem Rōma ā Gothīs annō mīllēsimō centēsimō sexāgēsimō quārtō suae conditiōnis, ex quō tempore Rōmānī dēstitērunt in Britanniā rēgnāre, post annōs fermē quadringentōs septuāgintā ex quō Gāius Iūlius Caesar eandem īnsulam adiit. habitābant autem intrā vallum quod
5 Sevērum trāns īnsulam fēcisse commemorāvimus, ad plagam merīdiānam, quod cīvitātēs, pontēs et strātae ibīdem factae usque hodiē testantur.

WORD LIST

*conditiō, -ōnis, *f.*, state, existence
*rēgnāre, to rule
*dēsistō, -ere, dēstitī, cease

*fermē, almost
*quadringentī, -ae, -a, four hundred
*intrā (*prep. with acc.*), within, inside

*vallum, -ī, *n.*, rampart, fortification, wall
*commemorāre, to relate, mention
plaga, -ae, *f.*, region, district
merīdiānus, -a, -um, southern

strāta (via), -ae, *f.*, paved street
ibidem, in the same place
*testārī, to bear witness to, give evidence of

NOTES

1 **annō millēsimō** . . . , calculate the year A.D. in which the Roman withdrawal took place.
2 **ex quō** . . . , from the time when . . . .

Exercise 33b

Response to an Appeal for Help and a Warning

vērum priōrēs hostēs, ubi Rōmānōs mīlitēs abiisse cōnspexērunt, mox advectī nāvibus inrumpunt terminōs caeduntque omnia, et quasi mātūram segetem obvia quaeque metunt, calcant, trānseunt: unde rūrsus mittuntur Rōmam lēgātī, flēbilī vōce auxilium implōrantēs nē penitus misera patria dēlērētur. rūrsus mittitur legiō quae inopīnāta tempore autumnī adveniēns 5
magnās hostium strāgēs dedit eōsque quī ēvādere poterant omnēs trāns maria fugāvit, quī prius anniversāriās praedās trāns maria nūllō obsistente cōgere solēbant.

tum Rōmānī dēnūntiāvērunt Brettōnibus nōn sē ultrā ob eōrum dēfēnsiōnem tam labōriōsīs expedītiōnibus posse fatīgārī. ipsōs potius 10
monent ut armīs captīs certārent cum hostibus quī nōn aliam ob causam quam quod ipsī inertiā solverentur, eīs possent esse fortiōrēs.

WORD LIST

*prior, prius, former
advehor, -ī, -vectus sum, sail in, *lit.* be carried towards
*terminus, -ī, *m.*, boundary
metō, -ere, mow down
calcāre, to tread, trample upon
flēbilis, -is, -e, tearful, piteous
*penitus, utterly
inopīnātus, -a, -um, unexpected
*autumnus, -ī, *m.*, autumn
*strāgēs, -is, *f.*, slaughter
*ēvādere, to escape

*fugāre, to put to flight, drive away
*prius (*adv.*), formerly, previously
anniversārius, -a, -um, yearly, annual
*cōgere, to bring together, collect
dēnūntiāre, to give notice
*ultrā, further, longer
dēfēnsiō, -ōnis, *f.*, defence
labōriōsus, -a, -um, difficult, trouble-some
expedītiō, -ōnis, *f.*, expedition, campaign
*potius, rather
*causa, -ae, *f.*, reason

NOTES

3 **obvia quaeque,** everything they met (*lit.* each thing in their path).
unde, in consequence of this.
7 **nūllō obsistente,** without resistance (no one resisting).
12 **quod solverentur,** because they were weakened, demoralised. **solvere,** originally means to loosen, then to relax *or* weaken.

Exercise 33c

(a) The Romans Leave

quia et hoc sociīs quōs dērelinquere cōgēbantur aliquid commodī
adlātūrum esse putābant, mūrum ā marī ad mare rēctō trāmite inter
urbēs quae ibi ob metum hostium factae fuerant, ubi et Sevērus quondam
vallum fēcerat, firmō dē lapide collocāvērunt.

5   et in lītore Ōceanī ad merīdiem quō nāvēs eōrum habēbantur, quia et
inde barbarōrum inruptiō timēbātur, turrēs per intervalla ad prōspectum
maris collocant et valēdīcunt sociīs tamquam ultrā nōn reversūrī.

Scottī Pictīque cognitā reditūs dēnegātiōne redeunt cōnfestim ipsī et
omnem aquilōnālem extrēmamque īnsulae partem prō indigenīs ad mūrum
10 usque capessunt.

(b) The Appeal that Failed (A.D. 446)

Aetiō ter cōnsulī gemitūs Britannōrum.

'nōs repellunt barbarī ad mare, repellit mare ad barbarōs: inter haec
oriuntur duo genera fūnerum; aut iugulāmur aut mergimur.' neque haec
tamen agentēs quicquam ab illō auxiliī impetrāre potuērunt, utpote quī
15 gravissimīs eō tempore bellīs cum Blaedlā et Attilā rēgibus Hunōrum esset
occupātus.

WORD LIST

dērelinquere, to abandon
*commodum, -ī, *n.*, benefit, advantage
trāmes, -itis, *m.*, path, line
*ob (+*acc.*), because of
*quondam, once, formerly
*collocāre, to erect
inruptiō, -ōnis, *f.*, invasion
*turris, -is, *f.*, tower
valēdīcō, -ere, -dīxī, -dictum (*dat.*),
  say farewell

*cōnfestim, immediately
aquilōnālis, -is, -e, northern
indigena, -ae, *m.*, native
capessō, -ere, -essīvī, -essītum, seize
repellō, -ere, reppulī, repulsum, drive
  back
*fūnus, -eris, *n.*, death
iugulāre, to cut the throat
mergō, -ere, mersī, mersum, drown

NOTES

4 **firmō dē lapide,** of solid stone.
6 **ad prōspectum maris,** to command a view of the sea.
7 **tamquam ultrā nōn reversūrī,** since they would return no more (*lit.* as being
  likely to return no more).
8 **cognitā reditūs dēnegātiōne,** learning of the intimation not to return.
9 **prō indigenīs,** in place of the natives.
13 **haec agentēs,** making these pleas—**agere** in the sense of 'to plead'.

Map of Roman Britain, showing the main towns and tribes and the principal roads.

171

Lesson 34

Exercise 34a

Britain's debt to Rome did not cease with the fall of the city and the withdrawal of the legions from Britain. In 597 Augustine came, bringing, as he said, 'the best news'. With this a new and peaceful invasion of Britain by Rome began.

itaque Augustīnus cum famulīs Christī quī erant cum eō, rediit in opus verbī pervēnitque Britanniam, ubi erat eō tempore rēx Aedilberct in Cantiā potentissimus.

est autem ad orientālem Cantiae plagam Tanatos īnsula. in hāc
5 adplicuit servus Dominī Augustīnus et sociī eius, virī, ut ferunt, fermē quadrāgintā. accēpērunt autem, praecipiente beātō papā Gregoriō, dē gente Francōrum interpretēs, et mittēns ad Aedilberctum mandāvit sē vēnisse dē Rōmā ac nūntium ferre optimum quī sibi obtemperantibus aeterna in caelīs gaudia et rēgnum sine fīne cum Deō vīvō et vērō futūrum
10 sine ūllā dubietāte prōmitteret. quī haec audiēns, manēre illōs in eā quam adierant īnsulā, et eīs necessāria ministrārī, dōnec vidēret quid eīs faceret, iussit. nam et anteā fāma ad eum Christiānae religiōnis pervēnerat, utpote quī et uxōrem habēret Christiānam dē gente Francōrum rēgiā, vocābulō Bercta.

WORD LIST

famulus, -ī, *m.*, servant	***obtemperāre,** to obey
*potēns, -entis, powerful	**dubietās, -ātis,** *f.*, doubt
orientālis, -is, -e, eastern	***necessāria, -ōrum,** *n.pl.*, necessities, requirements
adplicuit (adplicāre), landed	
*praecipiō, -ere, -cēpī, -ceptum, advise	***ministrāre,** to supply
interpres, -pretis, *m.*, interpreter	**vocābulum, -ī,** *n.*, name
mandāvit (mandāre), sent word	

NOTES

1 **in opus verbī,** to the task of the Word, i.e. the service of the Gospel.

3 **Cantia,** Kent.

4 **Tanatos,** Isle of Thanet.

7 **mittēns,** sending: in classical Latin one would have found **cum misisset,** but in later Latin the present participle is used much less strictly—very like its English equivalent.

mandāvit; the usual meaning is *to entrust*; from meaning 'to entrust a message to someone to deliver' it comes to mean, as it does here, 'to send word to'.

11 **dōnec vidēret quid eīs faceret,** until he should see what to do with them.

12 **utpote quī habēret** . . . , seeing that he had . . . .

Exercise 34b

post paucōs diēs vēnit ad īnsulam rēx et residēns sub dīvō iussit Augustīnum cum sociīs ad suum ibīdem advenīre colloquium. cumque ad iussiōnem rēgis residentēs, verbum eī vītae ūnā cum omnibus quī aderant eius comitibus praedicārent, respondit ille dīcēns: 'pulchra sunt quidem verba et prōmissa quae adfertis; sed quia nova sunt et incerta, nōn hīs 5 possum adsēnsum tribuere, relictīs eīs quae tantō tempore cum omnī Anglōrum gente servāvī. vērum quia dē longē hūc peregrīnī vēnistis et, ut ego mihi videor perspexisse, ea quae vōs vēra et optima crēdēbātis, nōbīs quoque commūnicāre dēsīderāstis, nōlumus molestī esse vōbīs: quīn potius benignō vōs hospitiō recipere et quae vīctuī sunt vestrō 10 necessāria, ministrāre cūrāmus: nec prohibēmus quīn omnēs quōs potestis fideī vestrae religiōnis praedicandō sociētis.'

WORD LIST

residō, -ere, -sēdī, sit
divum, -ī, *n.*, the open sky
*colloquium, -iī, *n.*, conference
iussiō, -ōnis, *f.*, order, bidding
prōmissa, -ōrum, *n.*, promises
adsēnsus, -ūs, *m.*, assent, agreement
*tribuō, -ere, -uī, -ūtum, grant, give
peregrīnus, -ī, *m.*, foreigner

*perspiciō, -ere, -spexī, -spectum, observe
commūnicāre, to share, communicate
*molestus, -a, -um, troublesome
*benignus, -a, -um, kindly
*hospitium, -iī, *n.*, hospitality
victus, -ūs, *m.*, support, sustenance
sociāre, to attach, associate

NOTES

2 **ad suum colloquium,** to conference with him.
3 **verbum vītae,** the Word of Life.
9 **dēsīderāstis** *for* **dēsīderāvistis,** you have desired.
10 **quīn potius,** on the contrary, rather.
11 **nec prohibēmus quīn . . . sociētis,** we do not prevent you from attaching . . . .
12 **praedicandō,** by preaching.

Revision Exercises

A Word Test
Give the Latin for:
(a) hand, foot, head, leg, nose, mouth, eye, finger.
(b) midday, summer, winter, sun, moon, wind, dawn, storm, evening.
(c) weapon, army, to retreat, warship, standard-bearer, sword, helmet, fort,
    legion, breastplate.
(d) garment, baker, innkeeper, butcher, smith, clothier, sausage, robe, woollen.

B Revise Conditional Sentences
1 In each sentence fill the blank, using the appropriate part of the verb which
  is printed in brackets.
2 *redde Anglicē:*

Example: sī amīcus noster ——, domum redībit.   (vīvere)
        sī amīcus noster **vīvit,** domum redībit.
        If our friend is alive, he will return home.

sī centuriō mīlitēs cantantēs ——, rīdēbit.	(audīre)
sī ab Hispāniā nōn discessissem, nōn iam miser ——.	(esse)
sī mihi licēret redīre, libenter ——.	(abīre)
sī centuriō 'abī' mihi ——, quam laetus discēdam.	(dīcere)
sī vesperī mēcum vēneris, ad multam noctem cum comitibus vīnum ——.	(bibere)
sī barbarī mīlitēs cantantēs ——, perterritī fugiant.	(audīre)
sī diū in hāc terrā ——, ipse barbarus erō.	(manēre)

C Revise the uses of **ut**
1 *redde Anglicē:*
fac ut tibi imperāvī.
currāmus ut ad balnea quam celerrimē perveniāmus.
tam celeriter currēbāmus ut prīmī ad balnea pervenīrēmus.
ut ad balnea pervēnimus, hominem ēgredientem vīdimus.
calor tantus erat ut multī in forō conciderint.

2 *redde Latīnē:*
The country-folk were so afraid of the Saxons that they fled to the woods.
They remained there until the enemy should go away.
Then they returned to inspect their homes.
When (*ut*) they saw their homes, they stood dumbfounded.
They had all been burned so that nothing remained.

V The Language of Europe

Perhaps the city or town in which you live, or the school which you attend, has an ancient charter dating from the Middle Ages. If so, you will probably find that it is written in Latin. If, some day, you become a serious student of history, you will find that, until about two hundred years ago, treaties between nations were written in Latin; so were English laws until the fifteenth century. Until the end of the seventeenth century scientific writings in all Western countries were in Latin. Until very recently Latin was the official language of the Roman Catholic Church throughout the world. To this day lawyers employ many Latin words and phrases.

There were two main reasons why Latin was so widely used in the Middle Ages and still survives today. In the first place, it expresses ideas clearly, accurately and in few words. For example, someone chosen for an important position may be appointed **ad vitam aut culpam;** find out what this means, and see how many words you would need to say the same thing in English. Secondly, Latin was understood by educated people in all the countries of Western Europe. Where the Romans came as conquerors they stayed as civilisers, and when some people in the conquered countries learned to read and write, it was in Latin they did so. In this way Latin became the language in which educated people wrote throughout the Roman Empire. And when the Romans themselves were compelled by the barbarian invasions to withdraw from the outposts of their empire, Latin remained as the language of education and culture. Scientists and scholars in our own age must often wish that there were a common language in which they could communicate with their fellow-researchers in other countries.

In the next few lessons you will learn something of the types of subject on which the medieval writers wrote, and read some extracts adapted from their works.

The language underwent many changes through the centuries—as any language does. New words were introduced, old words changed their meaning; spelling and pronunciation changed. Grammatical constructions were less strictly observed; often an old and a new method of expression are found side by side. Unfamiliar features of the language will be pointed out to you in the notes to each passage. From this point onwards long vowels are not marked in this book.

Lesson 35

Exercise 35

The King and the Bishop (St Aidan)

Oswinus, rex Northumbriae, olim equum optimum donaverat antistiti
Aidano in quo ille, quamvis ambulare solitus, vel amnes transire vel
viam peragere posset. cui cum paulo post pauper quidam occurreret
elimosynam petens, desiliens iussit equum pauperi dari; erat enim multum
5 misericors ac velut pater miserorum. hoc cum regi esset nuntiatum,
dicebat episcopo cum forte ingressuri essent ad prandium, 'cur, domine
antistes, equum regium, quem debebas proprium habere, pauperi dedisti?
nonne habuimus equos viliores plurimos qui ad pauperum dona suffi-
cerent?' cui statim episcopus, 'quid loqueris,' inquit, 'rex? num tibi carior
10 est ille filius equae quam ille filius Dei?' quibus dictis intrabant ad
prandium.

post prandium rex recordans verbum quod dixerat illi antistes,
festinans ad eum ante pedes episcopi conruit postulans ut sibi placatus
esset. 'numquam,' inquit, 'posthac aliquid loquar de hoc aut indicabo
15 quantum de pecunia nostra filiis Dei tribuas.' quod videns episcopus
multum perturbatus surgens levavit eum promittens se illi esse placatum.

tum episcopus tristis esse coepit ad lacrimarum effusionem. quem cum
presbyter suus lingua patria, quam rex et domestici eius non noverant,
quare lacrimaretur interrogasset, 'scio,' inquit, 'quia non multo tempore
20 victurus est rex; numquam enim ante haec vidi humilem regem; non digna
haec gens est talem habere rectorem.' nec multo post dira antistitis
praesagia tristi regis morte impleta sunt.

WORD LIST

dono, -are, -avi, -atum, make a gift of
antistes, -itis, *m.,* priest
quamvis, although
amnis, -is, *m.,* stream
peragere (viam), to travel by road
elimosyna, -ae, *f.,* alms
misericors, -cordis, tender-hearted
episcopus, -i, *m.,* bishop
proprius, -a, -um, one's own
vilis, -is, -e, cheap
donum, -i, *n.,* gift
sufficio, -ere, -feci, -fectum, be good
   enough

recordari, to recall
conruere, to fall down
indicare, to suggest
tribuo, -ere, -ui, -utum, allot
levare, to raise up
presbyter, -eri, an elder (of the church)
lingua, -ae, *f.,* language
patrius, -a, -um, native
domestici, -orum, *m.,* courtiers
rector, -oris, *m.,* ruler
dirus, -a, -um, dreadful
praesagium, -ii, *n.,* foreboding
impleo, -ere, -evi, -etum, fulfil

NOTES

1 **Oswinus:** Oswin was king of Deira, the southern half of Northumbria, from A.D. 641 to 651.

2 **Aidanus:** St Aidan, a monk of Iona, was sent to Northumbria to re-establish Christianity in that kingdom, which had lapsed into paganism. He established his headquarters at Lindisfarne on the island off the coast of Northumberland now known as Holy Isle.

3 **cui,** translate as though this were **ei.**

6 **episcopo . . . antistes;** the words **episcopus,** *bishop,* and **antistes,** *priest,* are used without distinction to refer to the same person.

7 **proprium habere,** to have as your own.

8 **ad pauperum dona,** for gifts to beggars.

13 **ut sibi placatus esset,** that he might be forgiven, reconciled.

17 **ad lacrimarum effusionem,** to the extent of shedding tears.

18 **lingua patria,** the Scots language, which Aidan, as a monk of Iona in Scotland, would regard as his native tongue.

19 **scio quia;** in Medieval Latin verbs meaning *to know, say, think,* etc. are often followed by a clause introduced by **quia** or **quod,** meaning *that*—just like English.

20 **victurus,** from **vivere** to live; not to be confused with **vĭcturus,** from **vincere,** to conquer.

Lesson 36

Exercise 36

The story which follows is one of the **exempla,** *illustrations, taken from the sermons of a French priest, Jacques de Vitry, born in the later part of the twelfth century, who became Bishop of Tusculum, an Italian city not far from Rome.*

A Priest outwitted by his worldly brother

audivi quod quidam prelatus in Francia optimum equum habuit; frater autem eius miles valde desiderabat eum ut uteretur eo in torneamentis et nullo modo potuit optinere. tandem cum multis precibus optinuit quod frater eius tribus diebus equum sibi commodaret. et accedens ad capel-
5 lanum prelati diligenter interrogabat cuiusmodi verba frater dum equitaret diceret saepius. at ille cogitabat et respondit: 'dominus meus equitando dicit horas suas nec ullum verbum saepius dicit quam illud quod dicit in principio cuiuslibet horae, id est: "Deus, in adiutorium meum intende".'

tunc miles cepit (=coepit) equum equitare et saepe dicens illa verba,
10 quociens (=quotiens) dicebat, fortiter cum calcaribus equum pungebat. ita in triduo equum instruxit ut quocienscumque dicebat, 'Deus, in adiutorium meum intende', equus timens calcaria magnos saltus dabat et vix poterat retineri.

postea cum prelatus ille equum equitaret, frater eius comitabatur eum
15 ut finem videret. cum autem prelatus diceret, 'Deus, in adiutorium meum intende,' equus magnos saltus dare cepit (=coepit) et eum fere deiecit. cum autem saepe hoc fecisset, dixit miles: 'Domine, iste equus non competit vobis; vos enim gravis persona estis et, si forte caderetis, multum laedi possetis.' tunc prelatus valde tristis dixit: 'equus iste valde suaviter
20 me ferre solebat; nunc autem—nescio quomodo istud accidit illi—doleo quod equum bonum amisi; sed cum ita sit, accipe illum; magis autem competit militibus, quam prelatis.' et ita miles equum optatum optinuit.

WORD LIST

prelatus, -i, *m.,* priest
valde, very much, very
torneamentum, -i, *n.,* tournament
capellanus, -i, *m.,* secretary
horae, -arum, *f.,* prayers
calcar, -aris, *n.,* spur
pungo, -ere, pupugi, punctum, prick
triduum, -i, *n.,* space of three days
instruo, -ere, -struxi, -structum, train

quocienscumque, as often as
saltus, -us, *m.,* leap
fere, almost
competit, is suitable
suaviter, gently
accidit, it has happened
optatus, -a, -um, coveted, desired
(**optare,** wish for)

NOTES

1 **audivi quod,** see Ex. 35, line 19.

3 **optinere—obtinere,** by the twelfth century when this story was written, this verb, which in classical Latin means *to hold*, had come to mean *to obtain*.

8 **horae,** from meaning the hours or set times at which the prayers were to be offered, **horae** came to mean the prayers themselves. **in principio cuiuslibet horae,** at the beginning of any and every prayer.

10 **fortiter,** violently.
 cum calcaribus, with the spurs. In classical Latin the ablative without **cum** would be used.

11 **Deus, in adiutorium meum intende,** Lord, direct thyself to my help. This was obviously a standard introduction to prayer.

18 **vobis,** the use of the plural to refer to single people is common in Medieval Latin. This survives in the French use of **vous.**
 persona, this interesting word originally meant a theatrical mask, then the character who wore the mask, and thus any individual—our English *person.*

Lesson 37

Exercise 37

A Story Teller's Trick

rex quidam habuit fabulatorem suum qui singulis noctibus quinque sibi
narrare fabulas consueverat. contigit tandem quod rex, curis quibusdam
sollicitus, dormire non posset, pluresque solito quaesivit audire fabulas.
ille autem tres enarravit sed parvas. quaesivit rex etiam plures. ille vero
5 noluit. dixerat enim, sicut rex iusserat, multas. ad haec rex: 'plurimas iam
narravisti sed brevissimas; vellem te aliquam rem narrare quae multis
producatur verbis et sic te dormire permittam.' concessit fabulator et sic
incepit.

'erat quidam rusticus qui mille solidos habuit. hic proficiscens bis mille
10 oves emit. accidit, eo redeunte, quod magna inundatio aquarum esset.
cum igitur neque per pontem neque per vadum transire posset, abiit
sollicitus quaerens quo cum ovibus suis transire posset. invenit tandem
exiguam naviculam et duas oves imponens aquam transiit.'

his dictis fabulator obdormivit. rex autem illum excitans fabulam
15 quam inceperat finire iussit. fabulator ad haec:

'fluctus ille magnus est, navicula autem parva, et grex ovium innumera-
bilis. permitte rusticum suas transferre oves; tum quam incepi fabulam
ad finem perducam.'

WORD LIST

fabulator, -oris, *m.,* story-teller	**vadum, -i,** *n.,* ford
contigit, it happened	**exiguus, -a, -um,** tiny
cura, -ae, *f.,* care, worry	**navicula, -ae,** *f.,* little boat
produco, -ere, -xi, -ctum, draw out	**obdormire,** to fall asleep
concedo, -ere, -cessi, -cessum, agree	**finire,** to finish
solidus, -i, *m.,* a gold coin; *tr.* 'pound'	**fluctus, -us,** *m.,* river
ovis, -is, *f.,* sheep	**grex, gregis,** *m.,* flock
accidit, it happened	**innumerabilis, -is, -e,** countless
inundatio, -onis, *f.,* flood	**finis, -is,** *m.,* end

NOTES

1 **singulis noctibus,** every night.

3 **plures solito,** more than usual.

7 **dormire permittam:** how would this have been expressed in Latin of the classical
period? See page 105.

12 **quaerens quo . . . transire posset,** lit. seeking a means by which he might cross,
i.e. a means of crossing.

13 **imponens,** putting on board.

Lesson 38

Exercise 38

Erasmus (Desiderius Erasmus Rotterodamus) was the most famous classical scholar of Western Europe in the fifteenth century. Born in Holland in 1466 he travelled all over Europe, living and writing at different periods in Germany, England, Switzerland and Italy. He wrote books on grammar, edited texts of Greek and Latin authors, produced the first edition of the Greek New Testament; but his best-known work is the 'Colloquia', Conversations, on one of which the following passage is based.

'It's nice to get up in the morning . . . .'

QUĪNTUS: hodie volebam te convenire, sed negabant famuli te domi esse.

GĀIUS: non mentiti sunt omnino. non eram quidem tibi domi, sed eram mihi maxime.

QUĪNTUS: quid aenigmatis est istud quod refers?

GĀIUS: nonne meministi illud vetus proverbium, 'non dormio 5 omnibus'? fugitne te iocus ille Nasicae? Nasica olim amicum Ennium invisere volens ad domum eius se contulit. cum autem ancilla iussu domini negavisset eum esse domi, Nasica sensit et discessit. sed cum Ennius vicissim ingressus domum Nasicae rogaret puerum num esset intus, Nasica ipse clamavit de 10 conclavi, 'non sum domi'. cumque Ennius, agnita voce, dixisset, 'impudens, nonne agnosco te loquentem?' 'immo,' inquit Nasica, 'tu impudentior qui non habes fidem mihi, cum ego crediderim tuae ancillae.'

QUĪNTUS: eras fortasse occupatior? 15

GĀIUS: immo suaviter otiosus.

QUĪNTUS: rursus me torques aenigmate.

GĀIUS: dicam igitur aperte. nec dicam ficum aliud quam ficum.

QUĪNTUS: dic.

GĀIUS: altum dormiebam. 20

QUĪNTUS: quid ais? atqui octava hora praeterierat iam, cum sol surgat hoc mense ante quartam.

GĀIUS: liberum est soli per me quidem surgere vel media nocte, modo liceat mihi dormire usque ad satietatem.

QUĪNTUS: qua hora soles relinquere lectum? 25

GĀIUS: inter quartam et nonam.

QUĪNTUS: spatium satis amplum! unde venisti in hanc consuetudinem?

GĀIUS: quod solemus producere convivia, lusus, iocos in multam noctem.

30 QUĪNTUS: vix umquam vidi hominem prodigiorem te.

GĀIUS: videtur mihi parsimonia magis quam prodigalitas. interim nec absumo candelas nec detero vestes.

QUĪNTUS: praepostera frugalitas est servare vitrum ut perdas gemmas. ille philosophus sapiit qui, rogatus quid esset pretiosissimum, respondit 'tempus'!

WORD LIST

mentior, -iri, -titus sum, tell lies
aenigma, -atis, *n.,* riddle
invisere, to call upon, visit
se contulit (conferre), made his way
vicissim, in turn
conclave, -is, *n.,* room
impudens, -entis, impudent, shameless
occupatus (*compar.* **-ior**), busy
suaviter, pleasantly
torqueo, -ere, torsi, tortum, tease, torture
aperte, openly
atqui, and yet
satietas, -atis, *f.,* satisfaction

spatium, -ii, *n.,* range, interval
consuetudo, -inis, *f.,* custom
convivium, -ii, *n.,* feast
lusus, -us, *m.,* sport
prodigus, -a, -um, extravagant
parsimonia, -ae, *f.,* economy
absumo, -ere, -sumpsi, -sumptum, waste
candela, -ae, *f.,* candle
detero, -ere, -trivi, -tritum, wear
praeposterus, -a, -um, absurd
sapio, -ere, -ii, be wise
pretiosus, -a, -um, precious

NOTES

2 **tibi,** to you; **mihi,** to myself.

4 **quid aenigmatis?** what sort of riddle?

6 **fugitne te: fugere** here means *to escape notice.*
Nasica, a famous member of the Scipio family.

7 **Ennius,** 'father of Roman poetry', lived 239–169 B.C.

8 **sensit,** understood.

11 **agnita voce,** recognising his voice. **agnita** is the perfect participle passive of **agnoscere.**

13 **cum ego crediderim,** although I believed . . . .

18 **nec dicam ficum aliud quam ficum.** What is the equivalent English proverb?

21 **atqui,** and yet: do not confuse with **atque.**

23 **liberum est soli** . . . , the sun is at liberty to . . . .
modo liceat mihi, provided that I am allowed.

24 **usque ad** . . . , 'right up to'—until I am completely satisfied.

27 **spatium amplum,** a wide range.

Summary of Grammar

I THE NOUN

FIRST DECLENSION
puella, puellae, *f.*, a girl

	Singular	*Plural*
Nom.	puell-a	puell-ae
Acc.	puell-am	puell-ās
Gen.	puell-ae	puell-ārum
Dat.	puell-ae	puell-īs
Abl.	puell-ā	puell-īs

Note
Nouns of the First Declension are feminine except names of males and nouns denoting male occupations, e.g. **Casca, agricola,** *farmer;* **nauta,** *sailor;* **poēta,** *poet.*

SECOND DECLENSION

	dominus-ī	**puer, puer-ī**	**magister-trī**	**bellum-ī**
	m., lord, master	*m.,* boy	*m.,* master, teacher	*n.,* war
		Singular		
Nom.	domin-us	puer	magister	bell-um
Acc.	domin-um	puer-um	magistr-um	bell-um
Gen.	domin-ī	puer-ī	magistr-ī	bell-ī
Dat.	domin-ō	puer-ō	magistr-ō	bell-ō
Abl.	domin-ō	puer-ō	magistr-ō	bell-ō
		Plural		
Nom.	domin-ī	puer-ī	magistr-ī	bell-a
Acc.	domin-ōs	puer-ōs	magistr-ōs	bell-a
Gen.	domin-ōrum	puer-ōrum	magistr-ōrum	bell-ōrum
Dat.	domin-īs	puer-īs	magistr-īs	bell-īs
Abl.	domin-īs	puer-īs	magistr-īs	bell-īs

Notes
1 Nouns of the Second Declension ending in **-us** and **-er** are mostly masculine; those ending in **-um** are all neuter.
2 Vocative case: nouns of the second declension ending in **-us** have a separate ending for the Vocative, e.g. **dominĕ, Marcĕ; fīlius** and proper names ending in **-ius** have vocative ending in **-ī,** e.g. **fīlī, Iūlī.** In all other Latin nouns the vocative has the same form as the nominative.

THIRD DECLENSION

(*a*) *Increasing nouns*

	dux, duc-is *m.*, leader	**arbor, arbor-is** *f.*, tree	**corpus, corpor-is** *n.*, body
		Singular	
Nom.	dux	arbor	corpus
Acc.	duc-em	arbor-em	corpus
Gen.	duc-is	arbor-is	corpor-is
Dat.	duc-ī	arbor-ī	corpor-ī
Abl.	duc-e	arbor-e	corpor-e
		Plural	
Nom.	duc-ēs	arbor-ēs	corpor-a
Acc.	duc-ēs	arbor-ēs	corpor-a
Gen.	duc-um	arbor-um	corpor-um
Dat.	duc-ibus	arbor-ibus	corpor-ibus
Abl.	duc-ibus	arbor-ibus	corpor-ibus

Note

pater, -tris, *m.*, father; **māter, -tris,** *f.*, mother; **frāter, -tris,** *m.*, brother; **senex, senis,** *m.*, old man; **iuvenis, -is,** *m.*, young man; **canis, -is,** *m.*, dog, are included in this group; i.e. they have the ending **-um** in the genitive plural.

(*b*) *Non-increasing nouns*

	cīvis, cīvis, *m.*, citizen		**nāvis, nāvis,** *f.*, ship	
	Singular	*Plural*	*Singular*	*Plural*
Nom.	cīvis	cīvēs	nāvis	nāvēs
Acc.	cīvem	cīvēs	nāvem	nāvēs
Gen.	cīvis	cīvium	nāvis	nāvium
Dat.	cīvī	cīvibus	nāvī	nāvibus
Abl.	cīve	cīvibus	nāve	nāvibus

Note that nouns of this group have **-ium** in the genitive plural.

(*c*) *Nouns of one syllable ending in two consonants*

	urbs, urb-is, *f.*, city	
	Singular	*Plural*
Nom.	urbs	urb-ēs
Acc.	urb-em	urb-ēs
Gen.	urb-is	urb-ium
Dat.	urb-ī	urb-ibus
Abl.	urb-e	urb-ibus

Note

nox, noctis, *f.*, night, is included in this group which has the ending **-ium** in the genitive plural.

FOURTH DECLENSION

manus, manūs, *f.*, hand

cornū, cornūs, *n.*, horn, wing (of an army)

	Singular	Plural	Singular	Plural
Nom.	man-us	man-ūs	corn-ū	corn-ua
Acc.	man-um	man-ūs	corn-ū	corn-ua
Gen.	man-ūs	man-uum	corn-ūs	corn-uum
Dat.	man-uī	man-ibus	corn-ū	corn-ibus
Abl.	man-ū	man-ibus	corn-ū	corn-ibus

Notes

1 **manus** is feminine, but most nouns of the fourth declension ending in **-us** are masculine.
2 Nouns of the fourth declension ending in **-u** are neuter.
3 **domus, -ūs,** *f.*, a house, has abl. sing. **domō,** acc. pl. **domūs** or **domōs,** gen. pl. **domuum** or **domōrum.** N.B. locative case **domī,** at home.

FIFTH DECLENSION

diēs, diēī, *m.*, day

rēs, reī, *f.*, thing

	Singular		Plural	
Nom.	di-ēs	di-ēs	rēs	rēs
Acc.	di-em	di-ēs	rem	rēs
Gen.	di-ēī	di-ērum	reī	rērum
Dat.	di-ēī	di-ēbus	reī	rēbus
Abl.	di-ē	di-ēbus	rē	rēbus

II THE ADJECTIVE

I ADJECTIVES OF THE FIRST AND SECOND DECLENSIONS

Examples: **parvus, parva, parvum,** small
pulcher, pulchra, pulchrum, beautiful
miser, misera, miserum, wretched
The case endings are the same as those of nouns of the First and Second Declensions.

Notes

(*a*) Forms of **alius, alia, aliud:**

Nom.	alius	alia	aliud
Acc.	alium	aliam	aliud
Gen.	alīus	alīus	alīus
Dat.	aliī	aliī	aliī
Abl.	aliō	aliā	aliō

The plural **aliī, aliae, alia** is quite regular.

(b) The adjectives **alter, -era, -erum**, one *or* the other of two; **ūnus, -a, -um**, one; **sōlus, -a, -um**, alone; **tōtus, -a, -um**, whole; **ūllus, -a, -um**, any; **nūllus, -a, -um**, no, none, also have **-ius** in genitive singular, **-ī** in dative singular.

2 ADJECTIVES OF THE THIRD DECLENSION

Examples: (1) **audāx, audācis,** bold
           ingēns, ingentis, huge
       (2) **fortis, fortis, forte,** brave
       (3) **ācer, ācris, ācre,** keen, fierce

Adjectives of the above types have the ending **-ī** in the ablative singular, **-ia** in the nominative and accusative plural neuter and **-ium** in the genitive plural.

Notes
(a) Forms of **pauper, pauperis,** poor—masculine and feminine only.

	Singular	*Plural*
Nom.	pauper	pauperēs
Acc.	pauperem	pauperēs
Gen.	pauperis	pauperum
Dat.	pauperī	pauperibus
Abl.	paupere	pauperibus

So with **dīves, dīvit-is,** rich.

(b) Forms of **vetus, veteris,** old, of long standing.

	M. and F.	*N.*	*M. and F.*	*N.*
Nom.	vetus	vetus	veterēs	vetera
Acc.	veterem	vetus	veterēs	vetera
Gen.	veteris	veteris	veterum	veterum
Dat.	veterī	veterī	veteribus	veteribus
Abl.	vetere	vetere	veteribus	veteribus

III COMPARISON OF ADJECTIVES

Type 1:	**longus,**	long	**longior**	**longissimus**
	fortis,	brave	**fortior**	**fortissimus**
Type 2:	**miser,**	wretched	**miserior**	**miserrimus**
	pulcher,	beautiful	**pulchrior**	**pulcherrimus**
Type 3:	**facilis,**	easy	**facilior**	**facillimus**

Only a few adjectives belong to type 3, the commonest being **facilis**, easy, **difficilis**, difficult, **similis**, like, **dissimilis**, unlike.

Irregular :	**magnus,**	great	**maior**	**maximus**
	parvus,	small	**minor**	**minimus**
	bonus,	good	**melior**	**optimus**
	malus,	bad	**peior**	**pessimus**
	multus,	much	**plūs**	**plūrimus**
	multī,	many	**plūrēs**	**plūrimī**

The case-forms of a comparative adjective are as follows:

	Singular		_Plural_	
	_M._ and _F._	_N._	_M._ and _F._	_N._
Nom.	fortior	fortius	fortiōrēs	fortiōra
Acc.	fortiōrem	fortius	fortiōrēs	fortiōra
Gen.	fortiōris	fortiōris	fortiōrum	fortiōrum
Dat.	fortiōrī	fortiōrī	fortiōribus	fortiōribus
Abl.	fortiōre	fortiōre	fortiōribus	fortiōribus

IV COMPARISON OF ADVERBS

longē,	far	**longius,**	farther	**longissimē,**	farthest
fortiter,	bravely	**fortius,**	more bravely	**fortissimē,**	most bravely
facile,	easily	**facilius,**	more easily	**facillimē**	most easily
bene,	well	**melius,**	better	**optimē**	best
male,	badly	**peius,**	worse	**pessimē,**	worst
magnopere,	greatly	**magis,**	more	**maximē,**	most

V THE PRONOUN

I PERSONAL PRONOUNS

	ego, I	**nōs,** we	**tū,** you (sing.)	**vōs,** you (pl.)
Nom.	ego	nōs	tū	vōs
Acc.	mē	nōs	tē	vōs
Gen.	meī	nostrī, nostrum	tuī	vestrī, vestrum
Dat.	mihi	nōbīs	tibi	vōbīs
Abl.	mē	nōbīs	tē	vōbīs

is, ea, id, he, she, it; they

	Singular			_Plural_		
	_M._	_F._	_N._	_M._	_F._	_N._
Nom.	is	ea	id	eī (iī)	eae	ea
Acc.	eum	eam	id	eōs	eās	ea
Gen.	eius	eius	eius	eōrum	eārum	eōrum
Dat.	eī	eī	eī	eīs (iīs)	eīs (iīs)	eīs (iīs)
Abl.	eō	eā	eō	eīs (iīs)	eīs (iīs)	eīs (iīs)

First and Second Persons: **mē, nōs; tē, vōs;** same as personal pronouns.
Third Person: *Singular and Plural,* **sē**

Acc.	sē
Gen.	suī
Dat.	sibi
Abl.	sē

3   EMPHASISI. 'G PRONOUNS

ipse, ipsa, ipsum, self

	Singular			*Plural*		
	M.	*F.*	*N.*	*M.*	*F.*	*N.*
Nom.	ipse	ipsa	ipsum	ipsī	ipsae	ipsa
Acc.	ipsum	ipsam	ipsum	ipsōs	ipsās	ipsa
Gen.	ipsīus	ipsīus	ipsīus	ipsōrum	ipsārum	ipsōrum
Dat.	ipsī	ipsī	ipsī	ipsīs	ipsīs	ipsīs
Abl.	ipsō	ipsā	ipsō	ipsīs	ipsīs	ipsīs

īdem, eadem, ĭdem, the same

	Singular			*Plural*		
Nom.	īdem	eadem	ĭdem	eīdem (iīdem)	eaedem	eadem
Acc.	eundem	eandem	idem	eōsdem	eāsdem	eadem
Gen.	eiusdem	eiusdem	eiusdem	eōrundem	eārundem	eōrundem
Dat.	eīdem	eīdem	eīdem	eīsdem (iīsdem)	eīsdem	eīsdem
Abl.	eōdem	eādem	eōdem	eīsdem	eīsdem	eīsdem

4   POSSESSIVE ADJECTIVES AND PRONOUNS

First Person: **meus, mea, meum,** my
                noster, nostra, nostrum, our
Second Person: **tuus, tua, tuum,** your (belonging to you singular)
                vester, vestra, vestrum, your (belonging to you plural)
Third Person: **eius** (*genitive sing.* of **is, ea, id**) his, her, its
                eōrum, eārum (*genitive pl.* of **is, ea, id**), their
                suus, sua, suum, his (own), her (own), their (own)
                (property of subject of nearest verb).

(a) **hic, haec, hoc,** this

	Singular			Plural		
	M.	F.	N.	M.	F.	N.
Nom.	hic	haec	hoc	hī	hae	haec
Acc.	hunc	hanc	hoc	hōs	hās	haec
Gen.	huius	huius	huius	hōrum	hārum	hōrum
Dat.	huic	huic	huic	hīs	hīs	hīs
Abl.	hōc	hāc	hōc	hīs	hīs	hīs

(b) **is, ea, id,** that

See personal pronouns; the personal pronoun of the third person is really a demonstrative pronoun meaning *that man, woman, thing.*

(c) **ille, illa, illud,** that (yonder)

	Singular			Plural		
	M.	F.	N.	M.	F.	N.
Nom.	ille	illa	illud	illī	illae	illa
Acc.	illum	illam	illud	illōs	illās	illa
Gen.	illīus	illīus	illīus	illōrum	illārum	illōrum
Dat.	illī	illī	illī	illīs	illīs	illīs
Abl.	illō	illā	illō	illīs	illīs	illīs

6 RELATIVE PRONOUNS

qui, quae, quod, who, which

	Singular			Plural		
	M.	F.	N.	M.	F.	N.
Nom.	quī	quae	quod	quī	quae	quae
Acc.	quem	quam	quod	quōs	quās	quae
Gen.	cuius	cuius	cuius	quōrum	quārum	quōrum
Dat.	cui	cui	cui	quibus	quibus	quibus
Abl.	quō	quā	quō	quibus	quibus	quibus

VI THE VERB

Regular Verbs

PRINCIPAL PARTS

1st Conjugation	**laud-ō, laudāre, laudāvī, laudātum,** praise
2nd Conjugation	**mone-ō, monēre, monuī, monitum,** warn
3rd Conjugation (a)	**dūc-ō, dūcere, dūxī, ductum,** lead
(b)	**capi-ō, capere, cēpī, captum,** take
4th Conjugation	**audi-ō, audīre, audīvī, audītum,** hear

INDICATIVE ACTIVE

Present :   laud-ō, laudā-s, lauda-t; laudā-mus, laudā-tis, lauda-nt
mone-ō, monē-s, mone-t; monē-mus, monē-tis, mone-nt
dūc-ō, dūc-is, dūc-it; dūc-imus, dūc-itis, dūc-unt
capi-ō, capi-s, capi-t; capi-mus, capi-tis, capi-unt
audi-ō, audī-s, audi-t; audī-mus, audī-tis, audi-unt

Future :   laudā-⎫
        monē-⎭ bō, -bis, -bit; -bimus, -bitis, -bunt

        dūc-⎫
        capi- ⎬ am, -ēs, -et; -ēmus, -ētis, -ent
        audi- ⎭

Imperfect :   laudā-⎫ bam, -bās, -bat; -bāmus, -bātis, -bant
            monē-⎭

            dūc-⎫
            capi- ⎬ ēbam, -ēbās, -ēbat; -ēbāmus, -ēbātis, -ēbant
            audi- ⎭

Perfect :   laudāv-⎫
        monu-⎪
        dūx- ⎬ ī, -istī, -it; -imus, -istis, -ērunt
        cēp- ⎪
        audīv-⎭

Fut. Perf. :   laudāv-⎫
            monu-⎪
            dūx- ⎬ erō, -eris, -erit; -erimus, -eritis, -erint
            cēp- ⎪
            audīv-⎭

Pluperfect :   laudāv-⎫
            monu-⎪
            dūx- ⎬ eram, -erās, -erat; -erāmus, -erātis, -erant
            cēp- ⎪
            audīv-⎭

INDICATIVE PASSIVE

Present :

laud-or	laudā-ris	laudā-tur	laudā-mur	laudā-minī	lauda-ntur
mone-or	monē-ris	monē-tur	monē-mur	monē-minī	mone-ntur
dūc-or	dūc-eris	dūc-itur	dūc-imur	dūc-iminī	dūc-untur
capi-or	cap-eris	cap-itur	cap-imur	cap-iminī	capi-untur
audi-or	audī-ris	audī-tur	audī-mur	audī-minī	audi-untur

Future :
lauda̅-
mone̅- } bor, -beris, -bitur; -bimur, -bimini̅, -buntur

du̅c-
capi- } ar, -e̅ris, -e̅tur; -e̅mur, -e̅mini̅, -entur
audi-

Imperfect :
lauda̅-
mone̅- } bar, -ba̅ris, -ba̅tur; -ba̅mur, -ba̅mini̅, -bantur

du̅c-
capi- } e̅bar, -e̅ba̅ris, -e̅ba̅tur; -e̅ba̅mur, -e̅ba̅mini̅, -e̅bantur
audi-

Perfect :

lauda̅tus(-a-um)			lauda̅ti̅(-ae-a)		
monitus			moniti̅		
ductus	}	sum, es, est	ducti̅	}	sumus, estis, sunt
captus			capti̅		
audi̅tus			audi̅ti̅		

Fut. Perf. :

lauda̅tus(-a-um)			lauda̅ti̅(-ae-a)		
monitus			moniti̅		
ductus	}	ero̅, eris, erit	ducti̅	}	erimus, eritis, erunt
captus			capti̅		
audi̅tus			audi̅ti̅		

Pluperfect :

lauda̅tus(-a-um)			lauda̅ti̅(-ae-a)		
monitus			moniti̅		
ductus	}	eram, era̅s, erat	ducti̅	}	era̅mus, era̅tis, erant
captus			capti̅		
audi̅tus			audi̅ti̅		

SUBJUNCTIVE ACTIVE

Present :
laud-em, -e̅s, -et; -e̅mus, -e̅tis, -ent

mone-
du̅c-
capi- } am, -a̅s, -at; -a̅mus, -a̅tis, -ant
audi-

Imperfect:

laudā-
monē-
dūce-
cape-
audī- } rem, -rēs, -ret; -rēmus, -rētis, -rent

Perfect:

laudāv-
monu-
dūx-
cēp-
audīv- } erim, -eris, -erit; -erimus, -eritis, -erint

Pluperfect:

laudāv-
monu-
dūx-
cēp-
audīv- } issem, -issēs, -isset; -issēmus, -issētis, -issent

SUBJUNCTIVE PASSIVE

Present:

laud-er, -ēris, -ētur; -ēmur, -ēminī, -entur

mone-
dūc-
capi-
audi- } ar, -āris, -ātur; -āmur, -āminī, -antur

Imperfect:

laudā-
monē-
dūce-
cape-
audī- } rer, -rēris, -rētur; -rēmur, -rēminī, -rentur

Perfect:

laudātus(-a-um)
monitus
ductus } sim, sīs, sit
captus
audītus

laudātī(-ae-a)
monitī
ductī } sīmus, sītis, sint
captī
audītī

192

Pluperfect :

laudātus(-a-um)			laudātī(-ae-a)	
monitus			monitī	
ductus	essem, essēs, esset		ductī	essēmus, essētis, essent
captus			captī	
audītus			audītī	

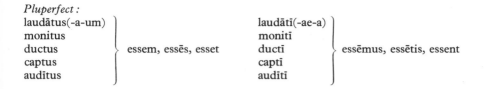

IMPERATIVE

Active		*Passive*	
laudā	laudāte	laudāre	laudāminī
monē	monēte	monēre	monēminī
dūc	dūcite	dūcere	dūciminī
cape	capite	capere	capiminī
audī	audīte	audīre	audīminī

Note

dūcere, dīcere and **facere** have a short form of the imperative singular—**dūc, dic, fac.** All other verbs of the third conjugation have imperative singular ending in **-e,** e.g. **lege, cinge.**

INFINITIVE

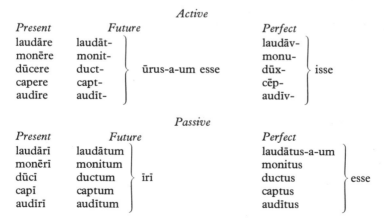

Active

Present	*Future*		*Perfect*	
laudāre	laudāt-		laudāv-	
monēre	monit-		monu-	
dūcere	duct-	ūrus-a-um esse	dūx-	isse
capere	capt-		cēp-	
audīre	audīt-		audīv-	

Passive

Present	*Future*		*Perfect*	
laudārī	laudātum		laudātus-a-um	
monērī	monitum		monitus	
dūcī	ductum	īrī	ductus	esse
capī	captum		captus	
audīrī	audītum		audītus	

PARTICIPLES

	Active	
Present	*Future*	*Perfect*
laudāns-antis	laudātūrus-a-um	—
monēns-entis	monitūrus-a-um	—
dūcēns-entis	ductūrus-a-um	—
capiēns-entis	captūrus-a-um	—
audiēns-entis	audītūrus-a-um	—

	Passive	
—	—	laudātus-a-um
—	—	monitus-a-um
—	—	ductus-a-um
—	—	captus-a-um
—	—	audītus-a-um

Irregular Verbs

I   *(a)* **sum, esse, fui,** to be

INDICATIVE

Present :   sum, es, est; sumus, estis, sunt
Future :   erō, eris, erit; erimus, eritis, erunt
Imperfect :   eram, erās, erat; erāmus, erātis, erant
Perfect :   fu-ī, fu-istī, fu-it; fu-imus, fu-istis, fu-ērunt
Fut. Perf. :   fu-erō, fu-eris, fu-erit; fu-erimus, fu-eritis, fu-erint
Pluperf. :   fu-eram, fu-erās, fu-erat; fu-erāmus, fu-erātis, fu-erant

SUBJUNCTIVE

Present :   sim, sīs, sit; sīmus, sītis, sint
Imperfect :   essem, essēs, esset; essēmus, essētis, essent
Perfect :   fu-erim, fu-eris, fu-erit; fu-erimus, fu-eritis, fu-erint
Pluperf. :   fu-issem, fu-issēs, fu-isset; fu-issēmus, fu-issētis, fu-issent

IMPERATIVE   *Sing.* es   *Plur.* este

INFINITIVE

Present :   esse
Perfect :   fu-isse
Future :   futūrus -a -um esse *or* fore

PARTICIPLE

Future :   futūrus -a -um

(b) **possum, posse, potui,** to be able

INDICATIVE

Present :   possum, potes, potest; possumus, potestis, possunt
Future :   pot-erō, pot-eris, etc.
Imperfect :   pot-eram, pot-erās, etc.
Perfect :   potu-ī, potu-istī, etc.
Fut. Perf. :   potu-erō, potu-eris, etc.
Pluperf. :   potu-eram, potu-erās, etc.

SUBJUNCTIVE

Present :   possim, possīs, etc.
Imperfect :   possem, possēs, etc.
Perfect :   potu-erim, potu-eris, etc.
Pluperf. :   potu-issem, potu-issēs, etc.

INFINITIVE

Present :   posse
Perfect :   potuisse

PARTICIPLE

The present participle **potēns -entis** is an adjective meaning *powerful*. There are no other participles.

2   ferō, ferre, tulī, lātum, bear

INDICATIVE

	Active		*Passive*	
Present :	ferō	ferimus	feror	ferimur
	fers	fertis	ferris	feriminī
	fert	ferunt	fertur	feruntur
Future :	feram, ferēs, etc.		ferar, ferēris, etc.	
Imperfect :	ferēbam, -bās, etc.		ferēbar, -bāris, etc.	
Perfect :	tulī, -istī, etc.		lātus sum, es, etc.	
Fut. Perf. :	tulerō, -eris, etc.		lātus erō, eris, etc.	
Pluperfect :	tuleram, -erās, etc.		lātus essem, essēs, etc.	

SUBJUNCTIVE

Present :	feram, ferās, etc.	ferar, ferāris, etc.
Imperfect :	ferrem, ferrēs, etc.	ferrer, ferrēris, etc.
Perfect :	tulerim, tuleris, etc.	lātus sim, sīs, etc.
Pluperfect :	tulissem, tulissēs, etc.	lātus essem, essēs, etc.

IMPERATIVE	fer	ferre
	ferte	feriminī

INFINITIVE

Present:	ferre	ferrī
Future:	lātūrus-a-um esse	lātum īrī
Perfect:	tulisse	lātus-a-um esse

PARTICIPLES

Present Active: ferēns, -entis
Future Active: lātūrus, -a, -um
Perfect Passive: lātus, -a, -um

3 (a) **volō, velle, voluī,** wish, be willing
   (b) **nōlō, nōlle, nōluī,** refuse, be unwilling
   (c) **mālō, mālle, māluī,** prefer
   (d) **eō, īre, īvī, itum,** go
   (e) **fīō, fierī, factus sum,** be made, become

INDICATIVE

		Present		
volō	nōlō	mālō	eō	fīō
vīs	nōnvīs	māvīs	īs	fīs
vult	nōnvult	māvult	it	fit
volumus	nōlumus	mālumus	īmus	—
vultis	nōnvultis	māvultis	ītis	—
volunt	nōlunt	mālunt	eunt	fīunt

		Future		
volam	nōlam	mālam	ībō	fīam
volēs	nōlēs	mālēs	ībis	fīēs
etc.	etc.	etc.	etc.	etc.

		Imperfect		
volēbam	nōlēbam	mālēbam	ībam	fīēbam

		Perfect		
voluī	nōluī	māluī	īvī(iī)	factus sum

		Fut. Perf.		
voluerō	nōluerō	māluerō	īverō	factus erō

		Pluperfect		
volueram	nōlueram	mālueram	īveram	factus eram

SUBJUNCTIVE

Present

velim	nōlim	mālim	eam	fīam
velīs	nōlīs	mālīs	eās	fīās
velit	nōlit	mālit	eat	fīat
velīmus	nōlīmus	mālīmus	eāmus	fīāmus
velītis	nōlītis	mālītis	eātis	fīātis
velint	nōlint	mālint	eant	fīant

Imperfect

vellem	nōllem	māllem	īrem	fierem

Perfect

voluerim	nōluerim	māluerim	īverim	factus sim

Pluperfect

voluissem	nōluissem	māluissem	īvissem	factus essem

IMPERATIVE

—	nōlī	—	ī	—
—	nōlīte	—	īte	—

INFINITIVE

Present :	velle	nōlle	mālle	īre	fierī
Future :	—	—	—	itūrus esse	factum īrī
Perfect :	voluisse	nōluisse	māluisse	īvisse	factus-a-um esse

PARTICIPLES

Présent :	volēns-entis	nōlēns-entis	—	iēns, euntis	—
Future :	—	—	—	itūrus-a-um	—
Perfect :	—	—	—	—	factus-a-um

VII NUMERALS

	Cardinal			Ordinal	
I	ūnus, -a, -um	1	prīmus, -a, -um	1st
II	duo, duae, duo	2	secundus	2nd
III	trēs, trēs, tria	3	tertius	3rd
IV	quattuor	4	quārtus	4th
V	quīnque	5	quīntus	5th
VI	sex	6	sextus	6th
VII	septem	7	septimus	7th
VIII	octō	8	octāvus	8th
IX	novem	9	nōnus	9th
X	decem	10	decimus	10th
XI	ūndecim	11	ūndecimus	11th
XII	duodecim	12	duodecimus	12th
XIII	tredecim	13	tertius decimus	13th
XIV	quattuordecim	14	quārtus decimus	14th
XV	quīndecim	15	quīntus decimus	15th
XVI	sēdecim	16	sextus decimus	16th
XVII	septendecim	17	septimus decimus	17th
XVIII	duodēvīgintī	18	duodēvīcēsimus	18th
XIX	ūndēvīgintī	19	ūndēvīcēsimus	19th
XX	vīgintī	20	vīcēsimus	20th
XXI	vīgintī ūnus	21	vīcēsimus prīmus	21st
XXX	trīgintā	30	trīcēsimus	30th
XL	quadrāgintā	40	quadrāgēsimus	40th
L	quīnquāgintā	50	quīnquāgēsimus	50th
LX	sexāgintā	60	sexāgēsimus	60th
LXX	septuāgintā	70	septuāgēsimus	70th
LXXX	octōgintā	80	octōgēsimus	80th
XC	nōnāgintā	90	nōnāgēsimus	90th
C	centum	100	centēsimus	100th
CV	centum quīnque	105	centēsimus quīntus	105th
CC	ducentī, -ae, -a	200	ducentēsimus	200th
D	quīngentī, -ae, -a	500	quīngentēsimus	500th
M	mīlle	1,000	mīllēsimus	1,000th
MM	duo mīlia, -ium	2,000	bis mīllēsimus	2,000th

Declension of **ūnus, duo, trēs:**

(1) For the declension of **ūnus** see page 186.

(2) Declension of **duo** and **trēs**.

	M.	F.	N.	M.	F.	N.
Nom.	duo	duae	duo	trēs	trēs	tria
Acc.	duōs	duās	duo	trēs	trēs	tria
Gen.	duōrum	duārum	duōrum	trium	trium	trium
Dat.	duōbus	duābus	duōbus	tribus	tribus	tribus
Abl.	duōbus	duābus	duōbus	tribus	tribus	tribus

Notes

1 Cardinal numbers from **quattuor** to **centum** are indeclinable.

2 The hundreds from **ducenti** to **nōngenti** are declined like **bonus, -a, -um** except that the genitive plural ends in **-um**, e.g. **ducentum,** of two hundred.

3 **mille** is an indeclinable adjective; **mille milités** is 1000 soldiers; **mille militum,** of 1000 soldiers.

   milia is a neuter plural noun of the third declension.
   So, **duo milia militum,** 2 000 soldiers,
      lit. two thousands of soldiers.
      duōrum milium militum, of 2 000 soldiers
      cum duōbus milibus militum, with 2 000 soldiers.

4 The ordinal numbers are declined like **bonus, -a, -um.**

Summary of Syntax

I THE CASES

1 **The Accusative:**
   (a) Case of the Object:
   urbem amō. *I love the city.*
   (b) After certain prepositions, e.g. **ad,** *to, towards;* **in,** *into;* **per,** *through;* **post,** *after;* etc.
   (c) Extent of time or space:
   trēs hōrās ambulāvī. *I walked for three hours.*
   tria mīlia passuum ambulāvī. *I walked for three miles.*

2 **The Genitive:**
   (a) Possessive case:
   domus Vesōniī, *the house of Vesonius* (or *Vesonius's house*).
   (b) Genitive of value:
   hic liber trium dēnāriōrum est, *this book is worth three denarii.*
   (c) Partitive genitive (indicates a part or share):
   multī cīvium periērunt, *many of the citizens perished.*
   multum pecūniae, *much (of) money.*
   (d) Description:
   vir summae audāciae, *a man of very great daring.*
   puer decem annōrum, *a boy of ten years.*

3 **The Dative:**
   (a) Case of the Indirect Object:
   dā mihi librum. *Give me the book.*
   (b) Possession:
   sunt Vesōniō multī et bonī servī. *Vesonius has many good slaves.*
   (c) After certain verbs, e.g.
   imperāre, *to command;* **persuādēre,** *to persuade;* **parcere,** *to spare;* **crēdere,** *to believe.*
   (d) Predicative Dative:
   hoc tibi exemplō sit. *Let this be (for an) example to you.*

4 **The Ablative:**
   (a) With certain prepositions, e.g. **ā, ab,** *by, from;* **cum,** *with;* **dē,** *concerning;* **ē, ex,** *out of;* **prō,** *on behalf of;* etc.
   (b) Manner:
   puerī summā celeritāte currēbant. *The boys ran at top speed.*
   (c) Time:
   (i) **septimā hōrā profectī sumus.** *We set out at the seventh hour.*
   (ii) **duābus hōrīs rediimus.** *We returned in two hours.*
   (d) Place:
   domō (Nōlā) profectī sumus. *We set out from home (Nola).*

(*e*) Ablative Absolute:

nōbīs dormientibus, latrō domum intrāvit. *While we were sleeping, a robber entered the house.*

(*f*) Price:

librum tribus dēnāriīs ēmī. *I bought the book for three denarii.*

(*g*) Description:

nubēs magnitūdine inūsitātā. *A cloud of unusual size.*

II INDIRECT STATEMENT

Latin —Accusative and Infinitive construction.

English—normally noun clause introduced by *that* (which may be omitted) dependent on verb indicating speech, thought, senses, e.g. **tē vēra dīcere crēdō.** *I believe that you are telling the truth.* (*I believe you to be telling the truth.*)

Notes

1 Tense of infinitive indicates tense of direct speech:

tē vēra **dīcere** crēdō (crēdēbam, crēdam)—vēra **dīcis.**
tē vēra **dīxisse** crēdō (crēdēbam, crēdam)—vēra **dīxistī.**
tē vēra **dictūrum esse** crēdō (crēdēbam, crēdam)—vēra **dīcēs.**

2 Reflexive pronouns:

mē ventūrum esse prōmittō. *I promise that I will come.*
sē ventūrum esse prōmittit. *He promises that he will come.*
so with **nōs, tē, vōs.**

3 **negat** puer sē hodiē lūdere.
The boy *says* that he is *not* playing today.

negāre, *to deny,* is usually to be translated *to say that . . . not.*

N.B. **negō . . . umquam.** *I say that . . . never.*
negō . . . quemquam. *I say that . . . no one.*
negō . . . quicquam. *I say that . . . nothing.*
negō . . . ūllum, -am, -um. *I say that . . . no.*

III PARTICIPLES

1 Normal Verbs

Active	*Passive*
Present : **laudāns, -antis, monēns,** etc.	
Future : **laudātūrus, -a, -um, monitūrus,** etc.	
Perfect :	**laudātus-a-um, monitus,** etc.

2 Deponent Verbs (active meaning)

Present : **hortāns, -antis, loquēns,** etc.
Future : **hortātūrus, -a, -um, locūtūrus,** etc.
Perfect : **hortātus-a-um, locūtus,** etc.

Notes

1 **Present Participle:**
   ad rētia **sedēns** librum legēbam.
   While sitting at the nets, I was reading a book.
   (not used loosely as it often is in English, e.g. *Hearing the news, I hurried home,* which
   really means *having heard* or *after having heard.*)

2 **Perfect Participle Passive:**
   librum **lēctum** dēposuī. When I had read the book, I put it down *or* Having read
   the book I put it down (the literal translation 'I put down the read book' is not natural
   English).

IV ABLATIVE ABSOLUTE

1 *Absolute,* i.e. *detached* phrases in Ablative Case (no participle):
   Caesare duce. *With Caesar as leader; under the leadership of Caesar.*
   Rūfō vīvō. *With Rufus alive; so long as Rufus is alive.*

2 **With Present Participle:**
   fēle dormiente, mūrēs lūdēbant. *While the cat was asleep, the mice played.*

3 **With Perfect Participle Passive:**
   librō lēctō, cubitum abiī. *When I had read the book, I went off to bed.*

Note
The Latin Ablative Absolute should normally be translated into English by a clause
introduced by *since* (because) *when, while, if, although* etc.

V THE SUBJUNCTIVE

Independent Subjunctive, i.e. subjunctive in a principal verb.

1 The subjunctive makes a cautious statement:
   dīcat aliquis . . . . *Someone may say . . . .*
   dīcerēs tōtam urbem ardēre. *You (i.e. one) would have said that the whole city was on
   fire.*

2 (a) The present subjunctive expresses a wish:
   fēlīcēs **sīmus.** *May we be fortunate.*
   fēlix **sīs.** *May you be fortunate.*
   vīvat rēgīna. *Long live the queen.*
   Negative **nē: nē** dēcipiāmur. *May we not be deceived.*

   (b) The present subjunctive in the 1st and 3rd persons gives a command.
   1st person: (exhortation) **festīnēmus.** *Let us hurry.*
   3rd person: captīvus hūc **dūcātur.** *Let the prisoner be brought here.*
   Negative **nē: nē festīnēmus.** *Let us not hurry.*

Summary of Command

Person	Positive	Negative
1st (Exhortation)	**festinēmus.** *Let us hurry.*	**nē festinēmus.** *Let us not hurry.*
2nd	**festina!** *Hurry!* (sing.) **festināte!** *Hurry!* (pl.)	**nōli festināre.** *Don't hurry.* (sing.) **nōlite festināre.** *Don't hurry.* (pl.)
3rd	captīvus hūc **dūcātur.** *Let the prisoner be brought here.*	**nē** captīvus hūc **dūcātur.** *Let not the prisoner be brought here.*

cum with Subjunctive

cum meaning *since* is found with all tenses of the subjunctive; with imperfect and pluperfect tenses it can also mean *when*. *These subjunctives are translated by the corresponding tense of the indicative in English.*
cum dēfessus sim, dormiam paulīsper. *Since I am tired, I shall sleep for a short time.*
cum ōrātōrem **audīvissem,** domum rediī. *When I had heard the orator, I returned home.*

VI PURPOSE

Final (i.e. Purpose) Clauses

Examples:
1 ad tabernam eāmus **ut pānem emāmus.**
   Let us go to the shop *to buy bread.*
2 fūgimus **nē** ab hostibus **caperēmur.**
   We fled *so that we might not be captured* by the enemy.

Summary of Construction

Introducing Word	Sequence of Tenses	
	Principal Verb	Subordinate Verb
UT, in order that **NĒ,** lest, in order that—not **nē quis,** in order that no one **nē quid,** in order that nothing **nē ūllus,** in order that no **nē umquam,** in order that never **nē usquam,** in order that nowhere	Present Future Perfect (true Perfect) Fut. Perfect Imperfect Perfect (Past Definite) Pluperfect	Present Subjunctive Imperfect Subjunctive

Notes

1 A final (purpose) clause may often be translated into English by the present infinitive (see Example 1 above) but in classical Latin the present infinitive is not used to express purpose.

2 The relative pronoun with the present or imperfect subjunctive may express purpose, e.g.

> servum mīsī **quī** pānem **emeret.**
>
> *I sent a slave to buy bread.*

(What would be the meaning of **servum mīsī quī pānem emēbat**?)

3 When the final clause contains an adjective or adverb in the comparative degree **quō** takes the place of **ut**, e.g.

> festīnēmus **quō celerius domum perveniāmus.**
>
> *Let us hurry to reach home more quickly.*

4 After a verb implying motion the supine expresses purpose:

> **cubitum abiī.** *I went off to bed.*
>
> (lit. *to lie down.* **cubitum** is the supine of **cubāre,** *to lie down.*)

VII   INDIRECT COMMAND

Examples: 1 **dominus coquō imperāvit ut cibum parāret.**
   The master ordered the cook to prepare food.
   Direct: **cibum parā.** *Prepare food.*

   2 **amīcus mē rogāvit nē discēderem.**
   My friend asked me not to go away.
   Direct: **nōlī discēdere.** *Don't go away.*

Summary of Indirect Command

Verb	*Person Commanded— Case*	*Construction*
monēre, to advise **rogāre,** to ask **ōrāre,** to beg **hortārī,** to urge	Accusative Accusative Accusative Accusative	**ut** or **nē** with present or imperfect subjunctive as in FINAL (PURPOSE) CLAUSES
imperāre, to command **persuādēre,** to persuade	Dative Dative	as for FINAL CLAUSES
petere, to seek **postulāre,** to demand	**ā, ab** with ablative	as for FINAL CLAUSES
iubēre, to order **vetāre,** to forbid, to order . . . not	Accusative	Present Infinitive

VIII RESULT—CONSECUTIVE CLAUSES

Example: aqua **tam** frīgida est **ut** natāre nōn possīmus.
The water is *so* cold *that* we cannot swim.

Construction

Principal Clause; 'so', etc.	Subordinate Clause	
	Introduced by	*Verb*
tam, so (usually with adjective or adverb) **adeō,** so, to such an extent (usually with verb) **ita,** so, in such a way (usually with verb) **tantus-a-um,** so great **tālis, -is, -e,** such, of such a kind **tot,** so many **totiēns,** so often	**ut,** that **ut . . . nōn,** that not **ut . . . numquam,** that . . . never **ut . . . nēmō,** that . . . no one **ut . . . nihil,** that . . . nothing **ut . . . nūllus,** that . . . no	subjunctive present imperfect perfect as the sense requires

IX SUMMARY OF USES OF *UT*

1 With indicative:
   (*a*) **parātus sum, ut vidēs,** I am ready, as you see.
       ut, meaning *as*, is found with any tense of indicative.
   (*b*) **ut domum vēnī, iānuam claudī iussī.**
       When I got home, I ordered the door to be closed.
       ut, meaning *when*, is found usually with perfect indicative.

2 With subjunctive:
   (*a*) Purpose: **ad pistrīnam eō ut pānem emam.**
                 I am going to the baker's *to buy* bread.
                 —negative **nē.**
   (*b*) Indirect command or request:
       Vesōnius omnibus imperāvit (omnēs ōrāvit) ut festīnārent.
                 Vesonius told (begged) everyone to hurry.
                 —negative **nē.**
   (*c*) Result: **strepitus tantus est ut dormīre nōn possim.**
                 The noise is *so* great *that* I cannot sleep.

X DIRECT QUESTIONS

Type 1
Asked by means of interrogative words, e.g.
> **quis** portam pulsat? *Who is knocking at the door?*
> **ubi** studētis? *Where do you study (go to school)?*

The commonest interrogative words are:

quis?	who?	**cūr?**	why?
quid?	what?	**quōmodo?**	how? in what way?
ubi?	where?	**quālis?**	of what kind?
quō?	where to?	**quantus?**	how big?
unde?	where from?	**quot?**	how many?
quandō?	when?	**quotiēs?**	how often?

Type 2

Statement	*Question*
studētis domī.	**studētisne domī?**
You study (go to school) in your home town.	*Do you study in your home town?*
	nōnne studētis domī?
	Don't you study in your home town?
	Surely you study . . . ?
	num studētis domī?
	Do you really study . . . ?
	Surely you don't study . . . ?

Note
> **utrum** domī **an** Mediōlānī studētis?
> *Whether do you study in your home town or in Milan?*
> **utrum** domī studētis **annōn?**
> *(Whether) do you study in your home town or not?*

XI INDIRECT QUESTIONS
Structure

Main Clause	*Interrogative word*	*Subordinate noun clause*
nesciō, *I do not know* Main verbs: ask, e.g. **rogāre** tell, e.g. **dīcere** know, e.g. **scīre** senses, e.g. **audīre,** to hear	**quis,** *who* Introducing words: **quis, quae, quid; cūr;** **ubi, quō, unde;** **quandō; quantus;** **quālis; quot.** N.B. **num, -nĕ,** whether **utrum . . . an,** whether . . . or **utrum . . . necne,** whether . . . or not	**sīs,** *you are* Verb in subjunctive (see below)

Tense of Subjunctive:

General rule—translate into English by corresponding tense of indicative.

nesciō quis
I do not know who
$\left\{\begin{array}{l}\end{array}\right.$
superāverit, *has won, won, was winning.*
(quis superāvit? or **superābat?)**
superet, *is winning.* **(quis superat?)**
superātūrus sit, *will win.* **(quis superābit?)**

nesciēbam quis
I did not know who
$\left\{\begin{array}{l}\end{array}\right.$
superāvisset, *had won.* **(quis superāvit?)**
superāret, *was winning.* **(quis superat?)**
superātūrus esset, *would win.* **(quis superābit?** or **quis superātūrus est?)**

XII TIME, PLACE, SPACE

1 TIME

(a) **tertiā hōrā,** at the third hour; **quintō diē,** on the fifth day; **decimō annō,** in the tenth year.
The ablative case indicates the time at which something happens.

(b) **tribus hōrīs,** in three hours; **quinque diēbus,** in five days; **decem annīs,** in ten years.
The ablative case also indicates the time within which something happens.

(c) **trēs hōrās,** for three hours; **quinque diēs,** for five days; **decem annōs,** for ten years.
The accusative case indicates the time throughout which something goes on.

2 PLACE

Prepositions indicate place *in* or *at*, *to*, *from*, e.g. **in urbe,** *in the city;* **ad iānuam,** *at the door;* **ad** or **in urbem,** *to (into) the city;* **ā** or **ē forō,** *from (out of) the forum;* **ab** or **ex urbe,** *from (out of) the city.*

Names of towns and small islands, also **domus,** *home,* **rūs,** *the country,* are not accompanied by a preposition, e.g. **Rōmae,** *at Rome;* **domī,** *at home;* **rūrī,** *in the country;* also **humī,** *on the ground*—locative case (see note overleaf).

Rōmam, *to Rome;* **domum (eō),** *(I go) home;* **rūs,** *to the country*—accusative case.
Rōmā, *from Rome;* **domō,** *from home;* **rūre,** *from the country*—ablative case.

How to recognise the Locative case:

Name	*Locative case*
1 Place names of first and second declensions singular	same form as genitive, e.g. **Rōmae, Corinthī**
2 Place names of any declension plural	same form as ablative, e.g. **Athēnis, Gādibus**
3 All other place names (towns and small islands), also **domus, rūs, humus**	ending **-ī**, e.g. **Carthāginī, domī, rūrī, humī**

3 SPACE

tria mīlia passuum ambulāvimus.
We walked for three miles.
domus vīgintī pedēs alta est.
The house is twenty feet high.

Accusative indicates extent of space.

Note
haec domus **decem pedibus** altior est quam illa.
This house is ten feet higher than that one (i.e. *higher* by *ten feet*).

XIII PRICE AND VALUE

The **ablative** indicates *price*.
Iūlia pallam **sexāgintā dēnāriīs** ēmit.
Julia bought the robe for sixty denarii.

The **genitive** indicates value.
palla **sexāgintā dēnāriōrum** erat.
The robe was worth sixty denarii.

Note
tantī, quantī, plūris, minōris, are used to indicate both price and value.

XIV ROMAN MONEY

The **as,** the original unit of money, was obsolete by the time of Augustus.

$2\frac{1}{2}$ **assēs**   — 1 **sēstertius**
  4 **sēstertii** — 1 **dēnārius**
 25 **dēnāriī** — 1 **aureus**
1 000 **sēstertii** — 1 **sēstertium**

XV CONDITIONAL SENTENCES

Three Types

A. Open: If *a* is, was, will be true, *b* is, was, will be true.

      sī mē **amās,** mē **adiuvābis.** *If you love me, you will help me.*

      —INDICATIVE in both clauses.

B. Unfulfilled:

(1) If *a* were true (but it is not), *b* would be true (but it is not).

      sī mē **amārēs,** mē **adiuvārēs.**

      If you loved me (but you do not), you would be helping me (but you are not).

      —IMPERFECT SUBJUNCTIVE in both clauses.

(2) If *a* had been true (but it was not), *b* would have been true (but it was not).

      sī mē **amāvissēs,** mē **adiūvissēs.**

      If you had loved me (but you did not), you would have helped me (but you did not).

      —PLUPERFECT SUBJUNCTIVE in both clauses.

(3) If *a* had been true (but it was not), *b* would now be true (but it is not).

      sī mē **adiūvissēs,** iam tūtus **essem.**

      If you had helped me (but you did not), I should now be safe (but I am not).

      —PLUPERFECT SUBJUNCTIVE—IMPERFECT SUBJUNCTIVE.

C. Improbable:

If *a* were to be true, *b* would be true.

sī mē **rogēs,** tē **adiuvem.**

If you were to ask me, I should help you.

—PRESENT SUBJUNCTIVE in both clauses.

Negative: **nisi** *or* **sī nōn.**

XVI EXPRESSIONS OF TIME

(Temporal Clauses)

1 **cum,** meaning *when* is found with present, future, future perfect indicative and with imperfect and pluperfect subjunctive.

    Examples: **cum** otiōsus **sum,** trīstis sum.

               When I am idle, I am unhappy.

               Caesar, **cum** ad Graeciam **nāvigāret,** ā praedōnibus captus est.

               When Caesar was sailing to Greece, he was captured by pirates.

    N.B. **cum** meaning *since* or *although* is found with all tenses of the subjunctive.

2 **ubi,** *when, as soon as*
  simul ac, *as soon as*   are found with the indicative, usually the perfect tense
  ut, *when, as*   (past definite).
  postquam, *after*

3 **dum,** *while,* is found with present, future, imperfect indicative.

    N.B. (1) **dum redeō,** multī mihi obviam vēnērunt.

               While I *was* returning, many people came to meet me (i.e. they came at some point during my journey).

         (2) **dum redībam,** dē rē pūblicā cōgitābam.

               While I was returning, I was thinking about the state (i.e. all the time that I was returning, I was thinking).

General Word List

ā, ab (+*abl.*), from, by

abdūcō, -ere, -dūxī, -ductum, lead away, carry off

abeō, -īre, -iī, -itum, go away

abhinc, from this time, ago

abiciō, -ere, -iēcī, -iectum, throw away

absum, -esse, āfuī, be away, be absent

ac (atque), and

accēdō, -ere, -cessī, -cessum, go or come to, approach

accendō, -ere, -cendī, -cēnsum, set on fire

accidō, -ere, -cidī, happen

accipiō, -ere, -cēpī, -ceptum, receive, welcome

acclāmāre, to acclaim

accurrō, -ere, -currī, -cursum, run up to

accūsāre, to accuse

aciēs, -ēī, *f.*, line of battle, battle-array, battlefield

ad (+*acc.*), to, towards, at

addō, -ere, -didī, -ditum, add

addūcō, -ere, -dūxī, -ductum, bring to, induce, prevail upon

adductus, -a, -um, influenced, persuaded

adeō, so much, to such a degree

adeō, -īre, -iī, -itum, go or come to, approach

adhūc, hitherto, till now, still

adiciō, -ere, -iēcī, -iectum, add

adiuvō, -āre, -iūvī, -iūtum, help, assist

admiror, -ārī, -ātus sum, admire, wonder at

admittō, -ere, -mīsī, -missum, commit

admonēre, to warn, advise

admoveō, -ēre, -mōvī, -mōtum, move to or near, apply

adoptāre, to adopt (children)

adstō, -āre, -stitī, stand by or near

adsum, -esse, -fuī, be present, at hand

adulēscentia, -ae, *f.*, youth

advehor, -vehī, -vectus sum, be conveyed towards, sail to

adveniō, -īre, -vēnī, -ventum, arrive at

adventāre, to approach, draw near

adversus, -a, -um, hostile, unfavourable; **rēs adversae,** failure, disaster

advesperāscit, evening approaches

advocāre, to summon

aedificium, -iī, *n.*, building

aeger, -gra, -grum, sick, ill

aegrē, with difficulty, scarcely

aegrotāre, to be ill

āēr, āeris, *m.*, air (*acc. sing.* **āera**)

aestās, -ātis, *f.*, summer

aestimāre, to reckon, put a value upon

aestus, -ūs, *m.*, tide

aetās, -ātis, *f.*, age

aeternus, -a, -um, everlasting, eternal; **in aeternum,** for all time

affābilis, -is, -e, approachable

afferō, -ferre, attulī, allātum, bring to or upon

affirmāre, to declare, assure

afflictāre, to batter, damage

ager, -grī, *m.*, field, open country

agitāre, to shake, stir, trouble

agitātiō, -ōnis, *f.*, movement, exercise

agitātor, -ōris, *m.*, driver

agmen, -inis, *n.*, army on the march, column

agnōscō, -ere, agnōvī, agnitum, recognise

agō, -ere, ēgī, āctum, pass, spend (time), act, plead; **quid agis?** how are you? **āctum est dē mē,** it is all up with me, I am done for; **fēriās agere,** to be on holiday; **grātiās agere,** to thank; **partēs agere,** to act a part (in a play); **agere dē,** to discuss; **age, agite,** come!

agrestis, -is, *m.*, countryman, peasant

āla, -ae, *f.*, wing

alibī, elsewhere

aliquamdiū, for some (considerable) time

aliquī, -a, -od, some, any

aliquis, -a, -id, someone, anyone, something, anything; **aliquid novī,** something (of) new alius, -a, -ud, another, other; alii . . . alii, some . . . others

alō, -ere, aluī, altum *or* alitum, support, feed, rear

alter, -era, -erum, one of two, the one, the other

alternus, -a, -um, one after the other, alternate

altitūdō, -inis, *f.*, height, depth

altus, -a, -um, high, deep

amāre, to love

ambiguus, -a, -um, uncertain, obscure

ambō, -ae, -ō, both

ambulāre, to walk

amictus, -a, -um (amicīre), clothed

amīcus, -a, -um, friendly

amīcus, -ī, *m.*, friend

amita, -ae, *f.*, aunt

amittō, -ere, -mīsī, -missum, lose

amoenus, -a, -um, pleasant, lovely, charming

amphitheātrum, -ī, *n.*, amphitheatre

amplius, more, further

ancilla, -ae, *f.*, maidservant

ancora, -ae, *f.*, anchor

angustus, -a, -um, narrow, difficult; in rēbus angustis, in time of difficulty

anhēlāre, to pant, gasp

anima, -ae, *f.*, breath

animadvertō, -ere, -vertī, -versum, notice, observe

animal, -ālis, *n.*, creature, beast

animus, -ī, *m.*, mind; bonō animō esse, to be of good cheer

anniversārius, -a, -um, yearly

annus, -ī, *m.*, year

ante (+*acc.*), before

ante (*adv.*), before, previously

anteā, formerly, previously

aper, -prī, *m.*, wild boar

aperiō, -īre, -ruī, -rtum, open, reveal

apis, -is, *f.*, bee

apodytērium, -ii, *n.*, undressing room in a public bath

appāreō, -ēre, -uī, appear, become visible

appellāre, to call, name, appeal to

appetō, -ere, -īvī, -ītum, desire, have an appetite for

applicō, -āre, -cuī, -citum, land

appōnō, -ere, -posuī, -positum, serve (a meal)

appropinquāre (+*dat.*, *or* ad+*acc.*), to approach

aptus, -a, -um, fit, suitable

apud (+*acc.*), among, in the presence of, at the house of

aqua, -ae, *f.*, water

aquila, -ae, *f.*, eagle, standard of Roman legion

aquilōnālis, -is, -e, northerly, northern

arbor, -oris, *f.*, tree

architectūra, -ae, *f.*, architecture, art of building

ārdeō, -ēre, ārsī, ārsum, burn, be on fire

ārea, -ae, *f.*, courtyard

argentum, -ī, *n.*, silver

āridum, -ī, *n.*, dry land

āridus, -a, -um, dry

arma, -ōrum, *n.pl.*, weapons, arms

armāmenta, -ōrum, *n.pl.*, ship's tackle

armātus, -a, -um, armed, equipped

ars, artis, *f.*, art, skill

artus, -ūs, *m.*, limb

as, assis, *m.*, as, a copper coin

ascendō, -ere, -ndī, -ēnsum, climb

āscrībō, -ere, -scrīpsī, -scrīptum, enrol, enlist

asinus, -ī, *m.*, ass

aspectus, -ūs, *m.*, sight, appearance

aspergō, -ere, -rsī, -rsum, sprinkle, scatter

aspis, -idis, *f.*, viper, adder

assēnsus, -ūs, *m.*, assent, agreement

assentior, -īrī, -sēnsus sum, agree

assiduus, -a, -um, incessant, continuous; assiduē, continuously

assuēfacere, to accustom (someone) to

assultāre, to leap at, attack

astrologus, -ī, *m.*, astrologer

āter, ātra, ātrum, black

ātrium, -ii, *n.*, hall

atrōx, -ōcis, terrible, savage, violent

attentē, attentively

attonitus, -a, -um, astonished, thunderstruck

auctor, -ōris, *m.,* originator, beginner; **libellus sine auctōre,** an anonymous pamphlet

audācia, -ae, *f.,* boldness, daring

audāx, -ācis, bold, daring; **audācter,** boldly

audeō, -ēre, ausus sum, dare

audiō, -ire, -ivi, -itum, hear

auferō, -ferre, abstuli, ablātum, take away, carry off, steal

aufugiō, -ere, -fūgi, -fugitum, flee away

augeō, -ēre, -xi, -ctum, increase

aureus, -a, -um, golden

aurum, -i, *n.,* gold

aut . . . aut, either . . . or

autem (*second word in sentence*), but, moreover, however, now

autumnus, -i, *m.,* autumn

auxilium, -ii, *n.,* help, assistance

avis, -is, *f.,* bird

avunculus, -i, *m.,* uncle

avus, -i, *m.,* grandfather

axis, -is, *m.,* axle

balnea, -ōrum, *n.pl.,* public baths

barbarus, -i, *m.,* barbarian, foreigner

bāsium, -ii, *n.,* kiss

beātus, -a, -um, happy, blessed; **beātē,** happily

bellum, -i, *n.,* war; **bellum indicere** (+*dat.*), to declare war upon

bene, well; **bene habet,** all right, agreed

beneficium, -ii, *n.,* act of kindness, service

benevolus, -a, -um, kind, benevolent

benignitās, -ātis, *f.,* kindness

benignus, -a, -um, kind, generous

bēstia, -ae, *f.,* wild beast

bēstiārius, -ii, *m.,* beast-fighter

bibō, -ere, bibi, drink

bigae, -ārum, *f.pl.,* two-horsed chariot

bis, twice

blandiri (+*dat.*), to coax, flatter

blandus, -a, -um, wheedling, flattering

bombus, -i, *m.,* a buzzing

bonus, -a, -um, good

bona, -ōrum, *n.pl.,* goods, property

bōs, bovis, *m. or f.,* ox, bull, cow

brevis, -is, -e, short; **brevi (tempore),** in a short time, soon

brūtus, -a, -um, stupid

bubulcus, -i, *m.,* ox-driver, one who ploughs with oxen

cachinnus, -i, *m.,* loud laugh, guffaw

cadō, -ere, cecidi, cāsum, fall

caedō, -ere, cecidi, caesum, cut, beat, kill

caelum, -i, *n.,* sky, heaven, weather

caeruleus, -a, -um, dark-blue

caespiticius, -a, -um, made of turf

calcāre, to tread down, trample upon

calceus, -ei, *m.,* shoe

calēre, to be warm or hot

cal(i)dārium, -ii, *n.,* room for taking warm baths

calidus, -a, -um, warm, hot

cāligō, -inis, *f.,* fog, gloom

callidus, -a, -um, cunning, clever

calor, -ōris, *m.,* warmth, heat

candidus, -a, -um, shining white, bright

canis, -is, *m. or f.,* dog

cantāre, to sing, croak

cantus, -ūs, *m.,* song, music

capessō, -ere, -sivi, -situm, seize (eagerly), take in hand

capilli, -ōrum, *m.pl.,* hair

capiō, -ere, cēpi, captum, take, seize; **arma capere,** to take up arms; **cōnsilium capere,** to form a plan

captivus, -i, *m.,* prisoner

caput, -itis, *n.,* head

carmen, -inis, *n.,* song

casa, -ae, *f.,* hut, cottage

cāseus, -ei, *m.,* cheese

castellum, -i, *n.,* fort

castigāre, to scold, chide

castra, -ōrum, *n.pl.,* camp

casus, -ūs, *m.,* event, contingency, misfortune, adventure

catēna, -ae, *f.,* chain, fetter

cathedra, -ae, *f.,* armchair

caupō, -ōnis, *m.,* innkeeper

caupōna, -ae, *f.,* inn, tavern

causa, -ae, *f.,* reason, excuse, case

causidicus, -i, *m.,* lawyer, advocate

cavea, -ae, *f.,* spectators' seats

caveō, -ēre, cāvī, cautum, take care; **cavē canem,** beware of the dog
caverna, -ae, *f.,* cave, cavern
cavum, -ī, *n.,* hollow, hole
cēlāre, to conceal, hide
celebrāre, to celebrate, honour
celeritās, -ātis, *f.,* speed, quickness
celer, -eris, -ere, swift, quick
celeriter, quickly, speedily; **quam celerrimē,** as quickly as possible
cēna, -ae, *f.,* dinner
cēnāre, to dine
centēsimus, -a, -um, hundredth
centuria, -ae, *f.,* company of soldiers, century
centuriō, -ōnis, *m.,* centurion
cēra, -ae, *f.,* wax
cērae, -ārum, *f.pl.,* writing tablet
certāre, to fight, contend
certē, certainly, at least
certō, with certainty, really
cessāre, to loiter, be idle, stop
cēterī, -ae, -a, the rest
cibus, -ī, *m.,* food
cingō, ere, cinxī, cinctum, surround, enclose
cinis, -eris, *m.,* ashes
circā (*adv.*), round about, all around; *prep.+acc.*), round, about
circum = circā
circumdō, -dăre, -dedī, -datum, surround
circumeō, -īre, -iī, -itum, go round, inspect
circumspectāre, to look round or about
circumstāre, to stand around, surround
circumvenīre, to surround, encircle
circus, -ī, *m.,* circus, race-course
cisium, -iī, *n.,* light two-wheeled carriage
cista, -ae, *f.,* chest, box
cithara, -ae, *f.,* lyre
cīvis, -is, *m. or f.,* citizen
cīvitās, -ātis, *f.,* state, city
clādēs, -is, *f.,* disaster, defeat, slaughter
clāmāre, to shout, cry aloud
clāmitāre, to cry aloud, shout repeatedly
clāmor, -ōris, *m.,* loud shout, cry
clārus, -a, -um, clear, loud, famous
claudō, -ere, -sī, -sum, shut, close

clēmēns, -tis, gentle, kind, merciful
clēmentia, -ae, *f.,* kindness, moderation
coccum, -ī, *n.,* scarlet dye
coepī, -isse, have begun, began
coercēre, to restrain, check
cōgitāre, to think, reflect upon
cōgitātiō, -ōnis, *f.,* thought
cognōmen, -inis, *n.,* surname, nickname
cognōscō, -ere, -gnōvī, -gnitum, learn, ascertain
cōgō, -ere, coēgī, coāctum, compel, gather; **agmen cōgere,** to bring up the rear
cohibēre, to restrain, hold back
cohortor, -ārī, -ātus sum, encourage, incite
collēgium, -iī, *n.,* guild, company
collīdō, -ere, -sī, -sum, knock or dash together
colligō, -ere, -lēgī, -lēctum, gather, collect; **sē colligere,** to recover one's senses or courage
collis, -is, *m.,* hill
collocāre, to place, station, erect
colloquium, -iī, *n.,* talk, conference
colloquor, -ī, -locūtus sum, converse, confer, negotiate with
collum, -ī, *n.,* neck
colōnia, -ae, *f.,* colony, settlement
color, -ōris, *m.,* colour, complexion
columna, -ae, *f.,* column, pillar
comedō, -ere, -ēdī, -ēsum, eat, consume
comes, -itis, *m. or f.,* companion, comrade; count
cōmitās, -ātis, *f.,* friendliness, kindness, courtesy
comitor, -ārī, comitātus sum, accompany, attend
commemorāre, to relate, mention
commercium, -iī, *n.,* trade; **iūs commercii,** right to trade
commerēre, to be guilty of
committere, to be guilty of, commit; **proelium committere,** to join battle
commodāre, to lend
commodum, -ī, *n.,* benefit, advantage
commoveō, -ēre, -mōvī, -mōtum, disturb, agitate
commūnicāre, to share, communicate

comparāre, to procure, obtain, prepare

compēs, -edis, *f.,* fetter or shackle

compleō, -ēre, -ēvī, -ētum, fill

complūrēs, -a, several

compluvium, -ii, *n.,* open space in roof of a Roman house

compōnō, -ere, -posuī, -positum, compose, arrange, settle

comportāre, to carry or bring together

comprehendō, -ere, -ndī, -ēnsum, seize, arrest

comprobāre, to prove, confirm

concēdō, -ere, -cessī, -cessum, grant, yield

concidō, -ere, -cidī, fall down, sink down

concipiō, -ere, -cēpī, -ceptum (animō), imagine, conceive

concitāre, to stir up

conclāmāre, to shout together or loudly

concurrō, -ere, -currī, -cursum, run together, rush in a body

conditiō, -ōnis, *f.,* state, existence

condō, -ere, -didī, -ditum, found, establish; **condere mānēs,** to lay a ghost

condūcere, to rent, hire

cōnferō, -ferre, -tulī, collātum, bring together; bestow, confer, contribute; **sē cōnferre,** to go off, betake oneself to

cōnfestim, immediately

cōnficiō, -ere, -fēcī, -fectum, finish, exhaust; **cōnfectus, -a, -um,** exhausted

cōnfīdō, -ere, -fīsus sum (+*dat.*), trust

cōnfirmāre, to corroborate, strengthen, cheer

congregāre, to gather together

congressus, -ūs, *m.,* meeting, encounter

cōniciō, -ere, -iēcī, -iectum, throw, hurl

coniūnx, -iugis, *f.,* wife; *m.,* husband

coniūrāre, to conspire

coniūrātiō, -ōnis, *f.,* conspiracy

cōnor, -ārī, cōnātus sum, try, attempt

cōnscendō, -ere, -dī, -sum (nāvem), embark

cōnsector, -ārī, cōnsectātus sum, hunt down

cōnsequor, -ī, -secūtus sum, overtake

cōnsīdō, -ere, -sēdī, -sessum, sit down

cōnsilium, -ii, *n.,* plan, advice; **cōnsilium capere (inīre),** to adopt a plan

cōnsobrīnus, -ī, *m.,* cousin

cōnspectus, -ūs, *m.,* sight, view; **in cōnspectum venīre,** to come into view

cōnspiciō, -ere, -spexī, -spectum, behold, observe

cōnstāns, -antis, steady, faithful, steadfast

cōnstat inter omnēs, everybody knows

cōnsternātiō, -ōnis, *f.,* dismay, alarm

cōnstituō, -ere, -uī, -ūtum, decide, resolve

cōnstruō, -ere, -uxī, -uctum, build, erect

cōnsuēscō, -ere, -ēvī, -ētum, become accustomed; *perfect tense,* be accustomed

cōnsul, -ulis, *m.,* consul

cōnsulō, -ere, -luī, -ltum, consult, ask the advice of

cōnsultum, -ī, *n.,* decree; **senātūs cōnsultum,** a decree of the senate

contemnō, -ere, -psī, -ptum, despise

contendō, -ere, -tendī, -tentum, hasten, march, contend, fight

contentus, -a, -um, content, satisfied

contestor, -ārī, -testātus sum, call to witness

continēns, -entis, *f.,* continent, mainland

contineō, -ēre, -tinuī, -tentum, contain, keep

contrā (*adv.*), in return, on the other hand; (*prep.*+*acc.*), against

contrahō, -ere, -traxī, -tractum, collect, assemble; **frontem contrahere,** to frown

contubernālis, -is, *m.,* mate, husband

contumēlia, -ae, *f.,* insult

contundō, -ere, -tudī, -tū(n)sum, bruise

conveniō, -īre, -vēnī, -ventum, meet, assemble

coquō, -ere, -xī, -ctum, cook

coquus, -ī, *m.,* cook

corōna, -ae, *f.,* wreath, garland

corpulentus, -a, -um, stout

corpus, -oris, *n.,* body; **corpus cūrāre,** to refresh oneself

coruscus, -a, -um, flashing, glittering

corvus, -ī, *m.*, raven
cottīdiē, daily
covinnus, -ī, *m.*, chariot
crās, tomorrow
creāre, to elect, choose
crēber, -bra, -brum, frequent
crēbrēscō, -ere, -bruī, become frequent, increase
crēdō, -ere, -didī, -ditum (+*dat.*), believe
crēta, -ae, *f.*, chalk
crimen, -inis, *n.*, accusation, charge, offence
cristātus, -a, -um, crested
cruciāre, to torture
crūdēlitās, -ātis, *f.*, cruelty
crūs, -ūris, *n.*, leg
crux, crucis, *f.*, cross
cubiculum, -ī, *n.*, bedroom
cubō, -āre, -buī, -bitum, lie down; cubitum īre, to go to bed
cucumis, -is, *m.*, cucumber
culcita, -ae, *f.*, mattress
culīna, -ae, *f.*, kitchen
culpāre, to blame
cum (*conj.*), when, whenever, since; (*prep.*+*abl.*), with
cumulus, -ī, *m.*, heap
cūnctārī, to delay, hesitate
cūnctātiō, -ōnis, *f.*, delay, hesitation
cupidus, -a, -um (+*gen.*), fond of, eager for
cupiō, -ere, -īvī, -ītum, desire
cupressus, -ī, *f.*, cypress
cūr, why?
cūrāre, to care for, attend to
cūria, -ae, *f.*, senate-house
currō, -ere, cucurrī, cursum, run
currus, -ūs, *m.*, chariot
cursus, -ūs, *m.*, running, speed of foot, course
custōdīre, to guard

damma, -ae, *f.*, deer
damnāre, to condemn
dē (+*abl.*), about, concerning, from
dēbēre, to owe, be under an obligation; īre dēbuī, I ought to have gone

dēcēdō, -ere, -cessī, -cessum, depart, retire; ē (dē) vītā dēcēdere, to die
decem, ten
decimus, -a, -um, tenth
dēdecus, -oris, *n.*, disgrace, dishonourable act
dēditiō, -ōnis, *f.*, surrender; in dēditiōnem accipere, to receive in surrender
dēditus, -a, -um, devoted to
dēfēnsiō, -ōnis, *f.*, defence
dēferō, -ferre, -tulī, -lātum, report
dēfessus, -a, -um, tired, weary
dēficiō, -ere, -fēcī, -fectum, be eclipsed
dēfīgō, -ere, -fīxī, -fīxum, fix, turn intently upon
dēflectō, -ere, -flexī, -flexum, turn aside
dehinc, from this time forth, in future
dēiciō, -ere, -iēcī, -iectum, throw down
deinde, then, next
dēlectāre, to delight
dēleō, -ēre, -ēvī, -ētum, destroy
dēlīberāre, to discuss, consider
dēliciae, -ārum, *f.pl.*, pet, darling
dēligāre, to tie, moor
dēmittō, -ere, -mīsī, -missum, let drop, lower
dēmōnstrāre, to show
dēmum, at last, at length
dēnārius, -iī, *m.*, Roman silver coin worth ten asses
dēnegātiō, -ōnis, *f.*, denial, refusal
dēnsus, -a, -um, thick
dēnūntiāre, to announce, proclaim, give notice of
dēpōnō, -ere, -posuī, -positum, put or lay down
dērelinquō, -ere, -līquī, -lictum, abandon
dērīdeō, -ēre, -rīsī, -rīsum, laugh at, mock
dēscendō, -ere, -ndī, -nsum, climb down
dēscrībō, -ere, -psī, -ptum, allot, tax
dēserō, -ere, -seruī, -sertum, abandon
dēsīderāre, to desire
dēsīderium, -iī, *n.*, longing, yearning
dēsiliō, -īre, -uī, -sultum, jump down
dēsistō, -ere, -stitī, cease

dēspērāre, to despair

dēstināre, to doom

dēsum, -esse, -fui, be lacking

dētineō, -ēre, -tinui, -tentum, detain, hold back

deus, -i, *m.,* god

dēvertō, -ere, -rti, -rsum, lodge, put up at

dēvolāre, to fly down

dexter, -dext(e)ra, -dext(e)rum, right, right-hand; **ā dextrā,** on the right

dicō, -ere, dixi, dictum, say, tell; **dictum factum,** no sooner said than done

diēs, -ēi, *m.,* day; **in diēs,** daily, day by day (with words indicating increase or decrease)

differō, -ferre, distuli, dilātum, differ

difficilis, -is, -e, difficult

diffugiō, -ere, -fūgi, -fugitum, flee in different directions, disperse

digitus, -i, *m.,* finger

dignus, -a, -um (+*abl.*), worthy, deserving

diligenter, diligently, hard

dimittō, -ere, -misi, -missum, send away

dinōscō, -ere, distinguish, discern

diplōma, -ātis, *n.,* letter of recommendation, passport

diripiō, -ere, -ripui, -reptum, plunder

dirus, -a, -um, dreadful

discēdō, -ere, -cessi, -cessum, go away, depart

discipulus, -i, *m.,* pupil

discō, -ere, didici, learn

discrimen, -inis, *n.,* distinction, difference, danger, crisis

dispēnsātor, -ōris, *m.,* steward

dispergō, -ere, -si, -sum, scatter, spread

dispōnō, -ere, -posui, -positum, place in different places

dissimulāre, to conceal, hide

distinguō, -ere, -inxi, -inctum, adorn

distribuō, -ere, -ui, -ūtum, distribute

diū, for a long time; **diūtius,** for a longer time

diversus, -a, -um, different

dives, -itis, rich

dividō, -ere, -visi, -visum, divide

divinus, -a, -um, divine, god-like

divitiae, -ārum, wealth, riches

divum, -i, *n.,* sky, open air

dō, dăre, dedi, dătum, give; **praecipitem dăre,** to send headlong

doceō, -ēre, -ui, doctum, teach

doctus, -a, -um, learned

documentum, -i, *n.,* proof

dolēre, to ache, grieve

dolor, -ōris, *m.,* grief, pain

domesticus, -a, -um, domestic, relating to house or family

domesticus, -i, *m.,* member of a household

domina, -ae, *f.,* mistress

dominus, -i, *m.,* master, owner; **domine,** sir, sire!

domus, -ūs, *f.,* house, home; **domi,** at home; **domō,** from home; **domum,** homewards, home

dōnāre, to give as a present, present with

dōnec, until

dōnum, -i, *n.,* present, gift

dormiō, -ire, -ivi, -itum, sleep

dōs, dōtis, *f.,* dowry

dubietās, -ātis, *f.,* doubt

dubitāre, to doubt, hesitate

dubius, -a, -um, doubtful, uncertain

dūcō, -ere, dūxi, ductum, lead, guide, take; build (a wall)

dulcis, -is, -e, sweet, pleasant; fresh (of water)

dum, while

dummodo (*with subj.*), provided that

duo, -ae, -o, two

duodecim, twelve

duodecimus, -a, -um, twelfth

duodēviginti, eighteen

duovir, -i, *m.,* magistrate (in provincial town)

dūrus, -a, -um, hard, harsh

dux, ducis, *m.,* leader

ē, ex (+*abl.*), out of, from

ecce, lo! behold!

edepol, indeed, truly

ēdictum, -i, *n.,* proclamation, decree

ĕdō, -ere, ēdi, ēsum, eat

ēdō, -ere, -didī, -ditum, give forth, utter

ēdŭcāre, to educate, bring up

effascināre, to bewitch

efferō, -ferre, extulī, ēlātum, carry out for burial

efficiō, -ere, -fēcī, -fectum, perform, cause, produce

effigiēs, -ēī, *f.,* ghost

effodiō, -ere, -fōdī, -fossum, dig out or up

effugiō, -ere, -fūgī, -fugitum, escape, flee away

effundor, -ī, -fūsus sum, rush out

ego, I

ēgredior, -ī, -gressus sum, go out, come out, leave

ēgregius, -a, -um, excellent, admirable

ēgressus, -ūs, *m.,* departure

ēheu, alas!

ei, ah! woe!

ēlātus, -a, -um, carried away, transported

elephantus, -ī, *m.,* elephant

ēmittō, -ere, -mīsī, -missum, send out, let loose

emō, -ere, ēmī, ēmptum, buy

enim, for *(second word in sentence)*

eō, thither, to that place

eō, īre, īvī, itum, go

epistula, -ae, *f.,* letter

epulae, -ārum, *f.pl.,* banquet, feast

equitātus, -ūs, *m.,* cavalry

equus, -ī, *m.,* horse

errāre, to wander, be mistaken; **dē viā errāre,** to lose one's way

error, -ōris, *m.,* mistake, fault

ēruō, -ere, -ruī, -rutum, dig out, search out

ēruptiō, -ōnis, *f.,* sortie

ēsurīre, to be hungry

etiam, even, also, yes

euge, well done! bravo!

ēvādō, -ere, -vāsī, -vāsum, escape

ēveniō, -īre, -vēnī, -ventum, happen, turn out

ēvolāre, to fly out

exanimāre, to alarm, drive out of one's senses (with fear)

exanimis, -is, -e, lifeless

excēdō, -ere, -cessī, -cessum, depart, withdraw; **ē vītā excēdere,** to die

excipiō, -ere, -cēpī, -ceptum, take up, receive

excitāre, to rouse, awaken

exclāmāre, to call out

excōgitāre, to think out, devise

excutiō, -ere, -cussī, -cussum, examine, shake off

exemplum, -ī, *n.,* example, sample, specimen

exeō, -īre, -iī, -itum, go out

exercēre, to train, exercise

exercitus, -ūs, *m.,* army

exigō, -ere, -ēgī, -āctum, drive out or away

exitium, -iī, *n.,* end, destruction

exonerāre, to unload, relieve of one's burden

expedītiō, -ōnis, *f.,* expedition, military operation

expellō, -ere, -pulī, -pulsum, drive out, banish

expendō, -ere, -ndī, -ēnsum, spend

expergīscor, -ī, -perrēctus sum, wake up

experior, -īrī, -pertus sum, test

expōnō, -ere, -posuī, -positum, explain

exprobrāre, to reproach with, blame for

expugnāre, to take by storm

exsiliō, -īre, -luī, leap out

exspectāre, to wait for, await

exstinguō, -ere, -īnxī, -īnctum, put out (a fire)

exstinguī *(passive),* to die, perish

exstruō, -ere, -ūxī, -uctum, erect

extendō, -ere, -tendī, -tentum (tēnsum), stretch or spread out

extrā ($+acc.$), outside

extrahō, -ere, -traxī, -tractum, take or draw out

extrēmus, -a, -um, last, furthest

exuō, -ere, -uī, -ūtum, take off, strip, shake off

exūrō, -ere, -ussī, -ustum, burn out or up

faber, -brī, *m.,* fireman, workman, craftsman

fabricāre, to forge, fashion
fābula, -ae, *f.,* story, play
facilis, -is, -e, easy, good-natured; **facile,** easily
faciō, -ere, fēcī, factum, do, make
factiō, -ōnis, *f.,* party, team
faenum, -ī, *n.,* hay
falcātus, -a, -um, equipped with scythes
fallō, -ere, fefellī, falsum, deceive, escape the notice of; **fidem fallere,** to break one's word
falsus, -a, -um, false, untrue
fāma, -ae, *f.,* rumour, report, reputation
famēs, -is, *f.,* hunger
familia, -ae, *f.,* household
famulus, -ī, *m.,* servant
farina, -ae, *f.,* flour; **farīnam subigere,** to knead the dough
fascis, -is, *m.,* bundle
fatigāre, to tire, weary
faucēs, -ium, *f.pl.,* throat
faveō, -ēre, fāvī, fautum, favour, support (a team)
favor, -ōris, *m.,* favour, applause
febris, -is, *f.,* fever
fēcundus, -a, -um, fertile
fēlēs, -is, *f.,* cat
fēlicitās, -ātis, *f.,* good fortune, success
fēlix, -icis, fortunate, happy; **fēliciter,** fortunately, successfully, Good Luck!
fēmina, -ae, *f.,* woman
fĕmur, -inis, *n.,* thigh
fēriae, -ārum, *f.pl.,* holiday; **fēriās agere,** to keep holiday
fermē, almost
ferō, ferre, tulī, lātum, bear, carry, bring; **ferunt,** they say; **molestē ferre,** to be angry or annoyed at
ferōx, -ōcis, fierce, spirited
ferrum, -ī, *n.,* iron, chains
fervens, -entis, burning, hot
festināre, to hasten, hurry
fēstus, -a, -um, festive, festal
fīcus, -ī, *f.,* fig
fidēlis, -is, -e, faithful, loyal
fidēs, -ēī, *f.,* faithfulness, loyalty, faith; **fidem fallō, -ere, fefellī, falsum,** break one's word
fīlia, -ae, *f.,* daughter

fīlius, -ii, *m.,* son
fingō, -ere, finxī, fictum, invent, devise
fīnis, -is, *m.,* end; **fīnēs, -ium,** *m.pl.,* land, territory
fiō, fierī, factus sum, become, happen
firmus, -a, -um, strong
flamma, -ae, *f.,* flame
flāre, to blow
flēbilis, -is, -e, tearful, doleful
flōs, flōris, *m.,* flower
flūmen, -inis, *n.,* river
fluō, -ere, -uxī, -uxum, flow
fōcilāre, to restore to life
folium, -ii, *n.,* leaf
fōns, -tis, *m.,* fountain
forās, outwards, out of doors (motion); **foris,** out of doors (rest)
fōrma, -ae, *f.,* shape, appearance
fōrmāre, to mould, fashion
fortasse, perhaps
forte, by chance
fortis, -is, -e, brave; **fortiter,** bravely
fortūna, -ae, *f.,* good or bad fortune, successful outcome
forum, -ī, *n.,* market place; the Roman Forum
fragor, -ōris, *m.,* crash
frangō, -ere, frēgī, frāctum, break, tear to pieces, shatter, crush
frāter, -tris, *m.,* brother
fraus, -dis, *f.,* trick, stratagem
frequentāre, to visit often or in crowds; to fill with a crowd, people
fricō, -āre, -cuī, -c(ā)tum, rub
frictus, -a, -um, roasted
frigidus, -a, -um, cold
frigus, -oris, *n.,* cold
frōns, -tis, *f.,* forehead, brow; **frontem contrahere,** to frown
frūctus, -ūs, *m.,* fruit
frūmentum, -ī, *n.,* corn
frūstrā, in vain
frutex, -icis, *m.,* shrub, bush
fuga, -ae, *f.,* flight; **in fugam dare,** to put to flight
fugāre, to rout, put to flight
fugiō, -ere, fūgī, fugitum, flee, run away
fulgeō, -ēre, -lsī, shine, gleam

fullō, -ōnis, *m.,* fuller
fullōnica, -ae, *f.,* a fuller's shop; a fuller's trade
fulmen, -inis, *n.,* flash of lightning, thunderbolt
fūmus, -i, *m.,* smoke
fūnambulus, -i, *m.,* rope-walker
fundāre, to establish, secure
fundus, -ī, *m.,* farm
fungor, -ī, fūnctus sum, perform, complete; **vitā fungī,** to complete one's life, to die
fūnis, -is, *m.,* rope
fūnus, -eris, *n.,* funeral, death
fur, fūris, *m.,* thief
furnus, -i, *m.* (baker's) oven
fūror, -ārī, -ātus sum, steal
fūrtivus, -a, -um, stealthy, secret
fūrtum, -ī, *n.,* theft
fuscus, -a, -um, dark, swarthy
fūstis, -is, *m.,* cudgel, club
futūra, -ōrum, *n.pl.,* the future; **in futūrum,** for the future, for all time to come

galea, -ae, *f.,* helmet
gallicē, in the fashion of the Gauls, in the Gallic manner
gallicinium, -ii, *n.,* cock-crow, break of day
gallus, -ī, *m.,* cock
gaudeō, -ēre, gāvīsus sum, rejoice, be glad
gaudium, -ii, *n.,* joy, gladness
gelidus, -a, -um, cold, freezing
gemitus, -ūs, *m.,* groan
gemma, -ae, *f.,* jewel, precious stone
generāre, to produce
gēns, gentis, *f.,* race, family
genū, -ūs, *n.,* knee
genus, -eris, *n.,* kind, birth, family
gerō, -ere, gessī, gestum, wear, conduct; **bellum gerere,** to wage war; **rem bene gerere,** to be successful; **rem male gerere,** to be unsuccessful; **rēs gestae,** exploits, career, achievements
gestus, -ūs, *m.,* bearing
gladiātor, -ōris, *m.,* gladiator

gladiātōrius, -a, -um, of gladiators, gladiatorial
gladius, -ii, *m.,* sword
glōria, -ae, *f.,* fame, renown
glōrior, -ārī, -ātus sum, boast
glōriōsus, -a, -um, boastful
gradus, -ūs, *m.,* step
grammaticus, -ī, *m.,* teacher (of literature), secondary school teacher
grātia, -ae, *f.,* favour; **grātiās agere,** to give thanks; **dīs grātiās,** thanks (be) to the gods
grātus, -a, -um, pleasing
gravis, -is, -e, heavy, serious, important; **graviter,** seriously
gravitās, -ātis, *f.,* seriousness
gustāre, to taste

habeō, -ēre, -ui, -itum, have, consider, regard; **bene habet,** all right, agreed!; **prō certō habēre,** to be sure
habitātiō, -ōnis, *f.,* lodging, house-rent
habitāre, to live, dwell
haereō, -ēre, haesī, haesum, stick, remain in one place
hama, -ae, *f.,* water-bucket
(h)arēna, -ae, *f.,* sand, arena in an amphitheatre
haud, not; **haud procul,** not far
hērēs, -ēdis, *m. or f.,* heir, heiress
hesternus, -a, -um, of yesterday; **hesternā nocte,** last night
hetaeria, -ae, *f.,* club, fraternity
heus, hullo there! listen!
hīc, here
hic, haec, hoc, this; he, she, it
hiemāre, to winter
hiems, -emis, *f.,* winter
hilaris, -is, -e, cheerful; **hilariter,** gaily, cheerfully
hinc, hence, from here
hodiē, today
holus, -eris, *n.,* vegetables
homō, -inis, *m.,* man, person
honestus, -a, -um, honourable; **honestē,** honourably, worthily
honor, -ōris, *m.,* honour, distinction
honōrāre, to honour
hōra, -ae, *f.,* hour

horrēre, to bristle, shudder
hortor, -ārī, -ātus sum, urge, encourage
hortus, -ī, *m.,* garden
hospes, -itis, *m.,* host, guest
hospitium, -iī, *n.,* hospitality, lodging
hostis, -is, *m.,* enemy
hūc, hither, to this place; **hūc illūc,** hither and thither
humāre, to bury
humus, -ī, *f.,* ground, earth; **humī,** on the ground

iaceō, -ēre, iacuī, lie, lie down
iactāre, to throw
iam, already, now
iānitor, -ōris, *m.,* doorkeeper
iānua, -ae, *f.,* door
ibi, there
ibidem, in the same place
idem, eadem, ĭdem, same
identidem, again and again, repeatedly
ientāculum, -ī, *n.,* breakfast
igitur (*second word in sentence*), therefore
ignārus, -a, -um, ignorant, unaware
ignis, -is, *m.,* fire
ignōrantia, -ae, *f.,* ignorance, lack of knowledge
ignōscō, -ere, -gnōvī, -gnōtum (+*dat.*), pardon, forgive
ignōtus, -a, -um, unknown
ille, illa, illud, that (yonder); he, she, it
illic, yonder, there
illūc, to that place
illūcēscit, it grows light, day breaks
imāgō, -inis, *f.,* statue, portrait
imbēcillus, -a, -um, weak, feeble
imber, -bris, *m.,* shower of rain
imitor, -ārī, -ātus sum, imitate, copy
immemor, -oris (+*gen.*), forgetful, unmindful
imminēre, to threaten, be imminent
immittō, -ere, -mīsī, -missum, send in, let in
immō, rather, on the contrary
immōbilis, -is, -e, motionless
immōtus, -a, -um, motionless
impediō, -īre, -īvī, -ītum, hinder
impendō, -ere, -ndī, -ēnsum, spend
imperāre (+*dat.*), to command

imperātor, -ōris, *m.,* general, emperor
imperium, -iī, *n.,* power, command, empire
impetrāre, to gain a request
impetus, -ūs, *m.,* attack
implōrāre, to beseech, entreat
impluvium, -iī, *n.,* basin sunk in the floor of the atrium; it received the rain water let in by the **compluvium**
impōnō, -ere, -posuī, -positum, place upon, superimpose, give as a title, impose
importāre, to import, bring in
imprōvīsō, unexpectedly
imprūdēns, -entis, thoughtless, rash, careless
imus, -a, -um, lowest; **ad imum collem,** at or near the foot of the hill
in (+*abl.*), in, on, in the case of
in (+*acc.*), into, upon, for (the purpose of)
inaequālitās, -ātis, *f.,* inequality
inānis, -is, -e, vain, groundless, empty
incautus, -a, -um, unawares, off guard
incendium, -iī, *n.,* fire, conflagration
incendō, -ere, -cendī, -cēnsum, burn, set fire to
incertus, -a, -um, uncertain
incidō, -ere, -cidī, -cāsum, fall into or upon
incipiō, -ere, -cēpī, -ceptum, begin
incitāmentum, -ī, *n.,* inducement, incentive
incitāre, to rouse, induce
inclūdō, -ere, -clūsī, -clūsum, shut in, enclose
incognitus, -a, -um, unknown
incolumis, -is, -e, safe and sound, unharmed
incultus, -a, -um, uncivilised
incumbō, -ere, -cubuī, -cubitum (*dat.,* or **in**+*acc.*), devote oneself to
incūs, -ūdis, *f.,* anvil
inde, thence, from there, after that
index, -icis, *m.,* informer
indicāre, to point out, show
indicium, -iī, *n.,* sign
indigena, -ae, *m.* or *f.,* native
indomitus, -a, -um, untamed, unconquered

indūcō, -ere, -dūxī, -ductum, lead in, bring in

indulgeō, -ēre, -dulsī (+ *dat.*), indulge, gratify

inertia, -ae, *f.,* laziness, inactivity

inexpiābilis, -is, -e, unforgivable

infāmis, -is, -e, disreputable, having a bad reputation

infāns, -antis, *m. or f.,* child, infant

infantia, -ae, *f.,* infancy

infector, -ōris, *m.,* dyer

infectus, -a, -um, stained

infēnsus, -a, -um, hostile

infestus, -a, -um, dangerous, hostile

inficiō, -ere, -fēcī, -fectum, dye, stain

infirmus, -a, -um, weak

infundō, -ere, -fūdī, -fūsum, pour on

ingēns, -tis, huge, enormous

ingredior, -ī, -gressus sum, enter

iniciō, -ere, -iēcī, -iectum, throw in, on or over

initium, -iī, *n.,* beginning

iniūria, -ae, *f.,* wrong, injustice

innuō, -ere, -uī, nod to or at

inopia, -ae, *f.,* scarcity, lack

inopīnātus, -a, -um, unexpected

inquam (inquit, inquiunt), I (he, they) say(s)

inquiētus, -a, -um, restless

īnscrībō, -ere, -scrīpsī, -scrīptum, inscribe, engrave

īnsidiae, -ārum, *f.pl.,* ambush, trap, treachery

īnsignis, -is, -e, remarkable, distinguished

īnsiliō, -īre, -luī, leap into

īnsistō, -ere, -stitī, set foot upon

īnsolitus, -a, -um, unusual

īnsonō, -āre, -uī, make a noise

īnspiciō, -ere, -spexī, -spectum, look at, view

īnstituō, -ere, -uī, -ūtum, establish, found

īnstrūmentum, -ī, *n.,* apparatus

īnstruō, -ere, -xī, -ctum, marshal, draw up; **īnstructus, -a, -um,** furnished

īnsula, -ae, *f.,* island

integer, -gra, -grum, whole, untouched, fresh

intellegō, -ere, -ēxī, -ēctum, understand, perceive

intempestus, -a, -um, timeless; **intempestā nocte,** at dead of night

intendō, -ere, -ndī, -ntum, direct, concentrate

intentus, -a, -um, intent (upon); **intentē,** anxiously, intently

inter (+ *acc.*), between, among, during

interclūdō, -ere, -clūsī, -clūsum, cut off

interdiū, by day

intereā, meanwhile

interest, it concerns, is of importance

interficiō, -ere, -fēcī, -fectum, kill

interim, meanwhile

interpres, -etis, *m. or f.,* interpreter

interrogāre, to question, ask

intervallum, -ī, *n.,* interval, distance

intonō, -āre, -uī, thunder

intrā (+ *acc.*), within

intrāre, to enter

intus, within, inside

inultus, -a, -um, unavenged

inūrō, -ere, -ussī, -ustum, burn in, brand

inūsitātus, -a, -um, unusual

inūtilis, -is, -e, useless

invādō, ere, -vāsī, -vāsum, attack, fall upon

inveniō, -īre, -vēnī, -ventum, find

invideō, -ēre, -vīdī, -vīsum (+ *dat.*), envy

invidia, -ae, *f.,* ill-will, envy, jealousy

invidus, -a, -um, envious, jealous

invīsus, -a, -um, hated, hateful; unseen

invītāre, to invite

iocōsē, jestingly

iocus, -ī, *m.,* jest, joke

ipse, -a, -um, self

īra, -ae, *f.,* anger

īrātus, -a, -um, angry

irrītāre, to annoy

irrumpō, -ere, -rūpī, -ruptum, break in, invade

irruptiō, -ōnis, *f.,* invasion

is, ea, id, that; he, she, it

iste, -a, -ud, that (of yours)

ita, thus, so; **ita vērō,** yes indeed

itaque, and so, therefore
item, likewise
iter, itineris, *n.*, journey; **iter facere,** to travel, make a journey
iterum, again, a second time
iubeō, -ēre, iussī, iussum, order, command
iūcundus, -a, -um, pleasant
iudicāre, to judge, decide
iugulāre, to cut the throat
iugulum, -ī, *n.*, throat
iugum, -ī, *n.*, yoke of slavery
iūrāre, to swear
iūs iūrandum, iūris iūrandī, *n.*, oath
iussiō, -ōnis, *f.*, order, command
iussū, by order
iūstus, -a, -um, just, fair, upright; **iūstē,** justly, fairly
iuvenis, -is, *m.*, young man

labor, -ōris, *m.*, labour, toil, exertion
labōrāre, to work
labōriōsus, -a, -um, wearisome, difficult, troublesome
lābrum, -ī, *n.*, tub
lacrima, -ae, *f.*, tear
laedō, -ere, laesī, laesum, hurt, injure
laetus, -a, -um, glad, happy
lāna, -ae, *f.*, wool
lancea, -ae, *f.*, lance, spear
lāneus, -a, -um, woollen
laniēna, -ae, *f.*, a butcher's stall
lanius, -iī, *m.*, butcher
lapideus, -a, -um, of stone
lapis, -idis, *m.*, stone, milestone
lassitūdō, -inis, *f.*, weariness
lātē, far and wide
latebrae, -ārum, *f.pl.*, hiding-place
latēre, to lie hid
latitāre, to be hidden, concealed
lātrāre, to bark
lātrātus, -ūs, *m.*, barking
laudāre, to praise
lautus, -a, -um, elegant
lavō, -āre, lāvī, lavātum, wash
lectīca, -ae, *f.*, litter
lectīcārius, -iī, *m.*, litter-bearer
lectulus, -ī, *m.*, *diminutive of* **lectus,** bed, couch

lectus, -ī, *m.*, bed, bier
lēgātus, -ī, *m.*, envoy, deputy, lieutenant
legiō, -ōnis, *f.*, legion
legō, -ere, lēgī, lēctum, read
lentus, -a, -um, slow; **lentē,** slowly
leō, -ōnis, *m.*, lion
lepus, -oris, *m.*, hare
levāre, to relieve, lessen, raise
levis, -is, -e, light
lēx, lēgis, *f.*, law
libellus, -ī, *m.*, pamphlet, letter
libenter, gladly, willingly
liber, -brī, *m.*, book
liberāre, to set free
liberī, -ōrum, *m.pl.*, children
lībertās, -ātis, *f.*, freedom
lībertus, -ī, *m.*, freedman
licet, it is permitted; **tibi licet,** you may
ligneus, -a, -um, wooden
līmen, -inis, *n.*, threshold
lingua, -ae, *f.*, tongue, language
littera, -ae, *f.*, letter of the alphabet
litterae, -ārum, *f.pl.*, letter, epistle
litus, -oris, *n.*, shore
locus, -ī, *m.*, place, category; **loca, -ōrum,** *n.pl.*, district
longus, -a, -um, long; **nāvis longa,** warship; **longē,** far; **longius,** further
loquor, -ī, -cūtus sum, speak
lōrīca, -ae, *f.*, breastplate
lūceō, -ēre, -xī, shine, be bright
lucrum, -ī, *n.*, gain, profit
lūdō, -ere, lūsī, lūsum, play
lūdus, -ī, *m.*, school, game
lūmen, -inis, *n.*, light
lūna, -ae, *f.*, moon
lupus, -ī, *m.*, wolf
lūridus, -a, -um, pale, sickly yellow
lūsus, -ūs, *m.*, game; **per lūsum latitāre,** to play hide and seek
lutum, -ī, *n.*, mud
lūx, lūcis, *f.*, light, daylight; **prīmā lūce,** at dawn
luxuria, -ae, *f.*, extravagance

macellum, -ī, *n.*, food market
magicus, -a, -um, magic
magis, more; **eō magis,** the more

magister, -trī, *m.*, master (of pupils), captain (of ship)

magistrātus, -ūs, *m.*, magistrate

magnitūdō, -inis, *f.*, size

magnopere, greatly

magnus, -a, -um, large, big, great; **maior, maius,** greater; **maximus, -a, -um,** greatest

magus, -ī, *m.*, magician

maiōrēs, -um, *m.pl.*, ancestors

maledīcō, -ere, -dīxī, -dictum (+*dat.*), curse, revile

mālō, mālle, māluī, prefer

malus, -a, -um, bad; **male,** badly; **malum, -ī,** *n.*, evil, misfortune, calamity

manceps, -cipis, *m.*, stall-holder

mandāre, to entrust

mandāta, -ōrum, *n.pl.*, instructions

māne, early in the morning; **prīmō māne,** very early in the morning

maneō, -ēre, mānsī, mānsum, remain

mānēs, -ium, *m.pl.*, ghosts or shades of the departed

mannus, -ī, *m.*, small Gallic horse

mānsiō, -ōnis, *f.*, station, stopping- or halting-place

manus, -ūs, *f.*, hand

mare, maris, *n.*, sea (*abl.* **marī**)

margarīta, -ae, *f.*, pearl

maritimus, -a, -um, relating to the sea; **ōra maritima,** sea-coast

marmor, -oris, *n.*, marble

marmoreus, -a, -um, made of marble

māter, -tris, *f.*, mother

mātūrēscō, -ere, -ruī, become ripe, ripen

mātūrus, -a, -um, ripe

mātūtīnus, -a, -um, of the morning; **in mātūtīnum,** until morning

maximus, -a, -um, very great; **maximē,** very much, very greatly

medicus, -ī, *m.*, doctor

medius, -a, -um, middle; **in mediō,** in the middle

mehercule, upon my word!

melior, -ius, better (*adj.*); **melius,** better (*adv.*)

meminī, -isse, remember; **mementō, -tōte,** remember!

memoria, -ae, *f.*, memory

mēns, mentis, *f.*, mind

mēnsa, -ae, *f.*, table

mēnsis, -is, *m.*, month

mercātor, -ōris, *m.*, merchant

mercēs, -ēdis, *f.*, reward, fee, salary

mergō, -ere, -rsī, -rsum, drown

merīdiānus, -a, -um, southern

merīdiēs, -ēī, *m.*, midday, south; **merīdiē,** at midday

messis, -is, *f.*, harvest, crops

metō, -ere, messem fēcī, reap, mow

metus, -ūs, *m.*, fear

meus, -a, -um, my; *voc. masc.*, **mī**

mīles, -itis, *m.*, soldier

mīliārium, -iī, *n.*, milestone

mille, thousand; **mīlia,** thousands; **mille passūs,** one mile; **duo mīlia passuum,** two miles

mīllēsimus, -a, -um, thousandth

minimus, -a, -um, smallest, very little; **minimē,** least of all, by no means; **minimē vērō,** no indeed

ministra, -ae, *f.*, deaconess

ministrāre, to supply

minor, minus, smaller, less; **minōris,** at a smaller price, of less value

mīrābilis, -is, -e, wonderful

mīrāculum, -ī, *n.*, wonder, marvel

mīror, -ārī, -ātus sum, wonder at, admire

mīrus, -a, -um, wonderful; **nec mīrum,** and no wonder; **mīra,** wonderful things; **mīrē,** wonderfully, marvellously, strangely

misceō, -ēre, miscuī, mixtum, mix, mingle

miser, -a, -um, wretched; **ō mē miserum,** woe is me! bother!

misereor, -ērī, -ritus sum (+*gen.*), pity; **mē miseret** (+*gen.*), I pity (*lit.* it pities me of)

misericordia, -ae, *f.*, pity

mītis, -is, -e, mild, gentle

mittō, -ere, mīsī, missum, send

modicus, -a, -um, modest, sparse

modius, -iī, *m.*, corn measure, peck

modo, only; **modo . . . . modo,** now . . . . now, sometimes . . . . sometimes; **nōn**

modo . . . . sed etiam, not only . . . . but also

modus, -ī, *m.,* way, manner; **nūllō modō,** by no means

mola, -ae, *f.,* millstone, grindstone

molestus, -a, -um, troublesome, irksome, annoying; **molestē ferre,** to be angry or annoyed at

mollis, -is, -e, soft, spineless, effeminate

moneō, -ēre, -uī, -itum, advise, warn

mōns, montis, *m.,* mountain

mōnstrum, -ī, *n.,* monster, supernatural being

monumentum, -ī, *n.,* memorial, tomb

mora, -ae, *f.,* delay

morbus, -ī, *m.,* illness, disease

morior, morī, mortuus sum, die; **moritūrus, -a, -um,** about to die; **mortuus, -a, -um,** dead, having died

moror, -ārī, -ātus sum, delay, linger

mors, -tis, *f.,* death; **mortem obīre,** to die

mōs, mōris, *m.,* custom; **mōrēs,** character

mōtus, -ūs, *m.,* movement, tide, uprising, rebellion; **mōtus terrae,** earthquake

moveō, -ēre, mōvī, mōtum, move, set in motion, begin

mox, soon

mulceō, -ēre, -sī, -sum, stroke, charm, caress

multitūdō, -inis, *f.,* crowd, large number

multus, -a, -um, much; **multī,** many men, many people; **multa,** many things

mūlus, -ī, *m.,* mule

mūniō, -īre, -īvī, -ītum, fortify

mūrus, -ī, *m.,* wall

mūs, mūris, *m. or f.,* mouse

nam, for

nancīscor, -ī, nactus *or* **nanctus sum,** obtain (by chance)

nārrāre, to tell, relate

nāscor, -ī, nātus sum, be born; **nātus, -a, -um,** aged, old, e.g. **septem annōs nātus,** seven years old

nāsus, -ī, *m.,* nose

nātālis, -is, -e, relating to birth; **diēs nātālis,** birthday

natāre, to swim

nātūra, -ae, *f.,* nature

naufragium, -iī, *n.,* shipwreck

nauta, -ae, *m.,* sailor

nāvigāre, to sail

nāvigātiō, -ōnis, *f.,* voyage, sailing

nāvis, -is, *f.,* ship; **nāvis longa,** warship; **nāvis onerāria,** merchant ship

nē, lest, in case; **nē . . . . quidem,** not even

-ně, interrogative particle, e.g. **audīsně?** do you hear?

nebula, -ae, *f.,* mist, cloud

necāre, to kill (e.g. by poison)

necessārius, -a, -um, necessary; **necessāria,** *n.pl.,* necessities, requirements

necně, or not (*in indirect question*)

negāre, to say no, deny, refuse

neglegō, -ere, -lēxī, -lēctum, neglect, disregard

negōtium, -iī, *n.,* business

nēmō, no one

nemus, -oris, *n.,* wood, forest

nēnia, -ae, *f.,* ditty, popular or folk-song

neque (nec), nor, and not; **neque . . . . neque,** neither . . . . nor; **neque quisquam,** and no one; **neque umquam,** and never; **neque usquam,** and nowhere

nesciō, -īre, -īvī, not to know

nescioquis, someone or other

neuter, -tra, -trum, neither of two

nihil, nothing

nimis, too much

nimium, too, too much

nisi, unless

nitrum, -ī, *n.,* washing soda

nix, nivis, *f.,* snow

nōlō, nōlle, nōluī, be unwilling

nōmen, -inis, *n.,* name

nōmināre, to name

nōminātim, by name

nōndum, not yet

nōnne? not? surely

nōnnūllī, -ae, -a, some

nōnnumquam, sometimes

nōnus, -a, -um, ninth

nōs, we; **nōbiscum,** with us

nōscō, -ere, nōvī, nōtum, get to know, become acquainted; perfect tense **nōvī,** I know (*a person*)

noster, -tra, -trum, our; **nostrī, -ōrum,** *m.pl.,* our men

nota, -ae, *f.,* mark, brand

nōtus, -a, -um, well-known

novus, -a, -um, new; **aliquid novī,** something new; **nihil novī,** nothing new

nox, noctis, *f.,* night; **nocte (noctū),** by night; **ad multam noctem,** till late at night

nūbēs, -is, *f.,* cloud

nūbilus, -a, -um, cloudy, overcast

nūbō, -ere, nūpsī, nuptum (+*dat.*), marry (of a bride)

nūdāre, to strip, plunder

nūllus, -a, -um, no, none

num, surely . . . . not? (direct question); whether (indirect question)

numerus, -ī, *m.,* number

nummus, -ī, *m.,* coin, sesterce, penny

numquam (nunquam), never

nunc, now, at present; **nunc . . . . nunc,** at one time . . . . at another time

nūntiāre, to report

nūntius, -iī, *m.,* message, messenger

nūper, recently, lately

nusquam, nowhere

ob (+*acc.*), on account of

obeō, -īre, -iī, -itum, meet; **mortem obīre,** to die; **suprēmum diem obīre,** to die

ōbiciō, -ere, -iēcī, -iectum, offer, present

oblīvīscor, -ī, oblītus sum (+*gen.*), forget

obscūrāre, to darken, conceal

obscūrus, -a, -um, dark, dim

obsecrāre, to entreat earnestly, implore

obsistō, -ere, -stitī (+*dat.*), withstand, resist

obstinātiō, -ōnis, *f.,* stubbornness, persistence

obstruō, -ere, -struxī, -structum, block up; **obstructus, -a, -um,** blocked

obtemperāre, (*dat.*), to obey

obterō, -ere, -trīvī, -trītum, crush

obveniō, -īre, -vēnī, -ventum, fall to one's lot

obviam, in the way, meeting; **obviam venīre** (+*dat.*), to come to meet

obvius, -a, -um, in the way; **obvia quaeque,** everything they met

occāsiō, -ōnis, *f.,* chance, opportunity

occĭdō, -ere, -cĭdī, -cāsum, set (of the sun)

occidēns (sōl), setting sun, west

occīdō, -ere, -cīdī, -cīsum, kill

occlūdō, -ere, -sī, -sum, close, shut up

occulcāre, to trample down

occupātus, -a, -um, busy, engaged

occurrō, -ere, -currī, -cursum (+*dat.*), run to meet, present itself

occursāre (+*dat.*), to meet

Ōceanus, -ī, *m.,* Atlantic Ocean

ocrea, -ae, *f.,* metal greave

octāvus, -a, -um, eighth

octō, eight

oculus, -ī, *m.,* eye

odōror, -ārī, -ātus sum, smell out, scent

offendō, -ere, -endī, -ēnsum, knock into, meet with, displease

offēnsus, -a, -um, displeased

officīna, -ae, *f.,* workshop

officium, -iī, *n.,* duty

offirmāre, to make firm or resolute

olfaciō, -ere, -fēcī, -factum, smell

ōlim, once, once upon a time, some day

ōmen, -inis, *n.,* omen, sign

omittō, -ere, -mīsī, -missum, give up, leave out, disregard

omnis, -is, -e, all, every; **omnēs,** everyone; **omnia,** everything

onerāre, to load, burden

onerārius, -a, -um, of burden; **nāvis onerāria,** merchant vessel, transport

onus, -eris, *n.,* load, burden

opera, -ae, *f.,* pains, effort, service; **operam dare,** to attend to, study

operiō, -īre, -eruī, -ertum, cover, close; **opertus, -a, -um,** covered

operor, -ārī, -ātus sum, work

opēs, -um, *f.pl.,* wealth, resources

opinor, -ārī, -ātus sum, think, suppose

oportet, it is necessary, proper, it behoves

oppidāni, -ōrum, *m.pl.,* townspeople

oppidum, -ī, *n.,* town

opportūnē, at the right time, conveniently

opprimō, -ere, -pressī, -pressum, overwhelm, crush

oppugnāre, to attack

optimus, -a, -um, best, very good, excellent

opulentus, -a, -um, wealthy

opus, -eris, *n.,* work, task, building; **opus tessellātum,** mosaic

ōra, -ae, *f.,* shore; **ōra maritima,** sea-coast

ōrāre, to beseech, pray

ōrātiō, -ōnis, *f.,* speech; **ōrātiōnem habēre,** to deliver a speech

orbis (terrārum), orbis, *m.,* the earth

orbita, -ae, *f.,* (wheel-)rut, track

oriēns, -tis, *m.,* the rising sun, the east

orientālis, -is, -e, eastern

orior, -īrī, ortus sum, arise

ōrnāre, to decorate

ōs, ōris, *n.,* mouth, face

os, ossis, *n.,* bone

ostendō, -ere, -ndī, -ntum (-nsum), show

ostentāre, to show, make known

ōtiōsus, -a, -um, at leisure, idle

ovis, -is, *f.,* sheep

ōvum, -ī, *n.,* egg

pācātus, -a, -um, pacified, peaceful

paedagōgus, -ī, *m.,* guardian, tutor

paene, almost, nearly

paenitet, it repents; **mē paenitet stultitiae,** it repents me of my foolishness, i.e. I regret, am sorry for, my foolishness

palaestra, -ae, *f.,* wrestling-place, gymnasium

palla, -ae, *f.,* robe, mantle

pallidus, -a, -um, pale

pānis, -is, *m.,* bread, loaf

pannus, -ī, *m.,* garment, piece of cloth, patch

pār, paris, equal, like

parāre, to prepare; **parātus, -a, -um,** ready, prepared

parcō, -ere, pepercī (+*dat.*), spare

parēns, -entis, *m. or f.,* parent

parēre (+*dat.*), to obey

pars, partis, *f.,* part; **partēs agere,** to act a part in a play

parvulus, -a, -um, very little or small

parvus, -a, -um, small; **parvī facere,** to consider of little importance, make light of

passus, -ūs, *m.,* step, pace

patefaciō, -ere, -fēcī, -factum, open, reveal, disclose

pater, -tris, *m.,* father

patientia, -ae, *f.,* submission

patior, patī, passus sum, suffer, endure, allow

patria, -ae, *f.,* native land

patrimōnium, -iī, *n.,* inheritance

paucī, -ae, -a, few

paulātim, gradually, little by little

paulisper, for a short time

paululum, -ī, *n.,* a very little, trifle

paulum, a little; **paulō post,** a little later

pauper, -eris, poor

pavīmentum, -ī, *n.,* pavement

pavor, -ōris, *m.,* terror, dread

pāx, pācis, *f.,* peace; **tuā pāce,** by your leave; **pācem compōnere,** to make peace

pectus, -oris, *n.,* breast

pecūnia, -ae, *f.,* money

pecus, -oris, *n.,* cattle, herd, flock

pelagus, -ī, *n.,* open sea, ocean

pellō, -ere, pepulī, pulsum, drive, push

penitus, utterly, completely

per (+*acc.*), through, throughout

peragō, -ere, -ēgī, -āctum, complete, finish

percontor, -ārī, -ātus sum, ask, inquire

percurrō, -ere, -currī, -cursum, hurry through, skim over

percutiō, -ere, -cussī, -cussum, strike

perdō, -ere, -didī, -ditum, waste, lose

peregrīnus, -ī, *m.,* foreigner

pereō, -īre, -iī, -itum, perish

perficiō, -ere, -fēcī, -fectum, complete, accomplish, finish

perīculōsus, -a, -um, dangerous

perīculum, -ī, *n.,* danger

peristylium, -ii, *n.,* peristyle (pillared courtyard of wealthy Roman's house)

permittō, -ere, -mīsī, -missum (+*dat.*), allow

persequor, -ī, -secūtus sum, pursue

persevērāre, to persist, remain steadfast

perspiciō, -ere, -spexī, -spectum, observe, perceive

persuādeō, -ēre, -suāsī, -suāsum (+*dat.*), persuade, prevail upon

perterreō, -ēre, -uī, -itum, terrify; **perterritus, -a, -um,** terrified

perturbātiō, -ōnis, *f.,* confusion

perturbātus, -a, -um, disturbed

pervādō, -ere, -vāsī, -vāsum, pass through, spread through

perveniō, -īre, -vēnī, -ventum, reach, arrive at

pēs, pedis, *m.,* foot

petasus, -ī, *m.,* hat

petō, -ere, -īvī, -ītum, seek, make for, attack

philosophus, -ī, *m.,* philosopher

pila, -ae, *f.,* ball

piscis, -is, *m.,* fish

pistor, -ōris, *m.,* baker

pistrīna, -ae, *f.,* bakery

pius, -a, -um, dutiful

placentārius, -ii, *m.,* pastrycook

placēre (+*dat.*), to please

plaga, -ae, *f.,* region, district

plānitiēs, -ēi, *f.,* level ground, plain

plānus, -a, -um, level

plaudō, -ere, -sī, -sum, clap the hands, applaud

plaustrum, -ī, *n.,* cart

plausus, -ūs, *m.,* applause

plēbs, -is, *f.,* common people

plēnus, -a, -um (*gen. or abl.*), full, filled

plērīque, very many, the majority

plōrāre, to wail, lament

plōrātus, -ūs, *m.,* lamentation, wailing

pluit, it is raining

plūrimus, -a, -um, very much; **plūrimī, -ae, -a,** very many

plūs, plūris, more; **plūrēs,** more people; **plūra,** more things; **plūris,** of greater value

poena, -ae, *f.,* punishment, penalty; **poenās dare,** to pay the penalty

poliō, -īre, -īvī, -ītum, polish, smooth

pollex, -icis, *m.,* thumb; **pollice versō,** with thumb extended

pondus, -eris, *n.,* mass, weight

pōnō, -ere, posuī, positum, place, stake

pōns, pontis, *m.,* bridge

pontifex, -icis, *m.,* high priest

poples, -itis, *m.,* knee, hollow of the knee, ham

populus, -ī, *m.,* people

porcus, -ī, *m.,* pig

porta, -ae, *f.,* gate, doorway

portāre, to carry

porticus, -ūs, *f.,* portico, arcade, colonnade

portus, -ūs, *m.,* harbour

possum, posse, potuī, be able

post (+*acc.*), after; **post** (*adv.*), afterwards; **post merīdiem,** after midday, in the afternoon

posteā, afterwards

posterus, -a, -um, following, next; **posterī, -ōrum,** *m.pl.,* descendants, posterity

posthāc, after this, in future

postīcum, -ī, *n.,* back-door

postquam, after

postrēmō, lastly, finally

postrīdiē, on the following day

postulāre, to demand, request

potēns, -entis, powerful

potius, rather; **quīn potius,** on the contrary, rather

potissimum, before everything else, especially

prae (+*abl.*), for, because of (*with negatives*), e.g. **prae lacrimis loquī nōn poterat,** she was not able to speak for tears

praebeō, -ēre, -uī, -itum, show, present

praecēdō, -ere, -cessī, -cessum, go in front

praeceps, -cipitis, headlong; **praecipitem dare,** to send flying headlong

praecipiō, -ere, -cēpī, -ceptum, advise, instruct

praecipuē, especially

praeclārus, -a, -um, famous

praeda, -ae, *f.*, booty, plunder

praedĭcāre, to preach

praedīcō, -ere, -dīxī, -dictum, foretell, prophesy

praedium, -iī, *n.*, estate, farm

praedīvīnāre, to forecast

praefectus, -ī, *m.*, commander, prefect; **praefectus portūs,** harbour-master

praegrandis, -is, -e, very large, very big

praemittō, -ere, -mīsī, -missum, send in advance

praemium, -iī, *n.*, reward

praesēns, -entis, present, in person; **mē praesente,** in my presence

praesertim, especially

praesidium, -iī, *n.*, garrison, post

praestō, -āre, -stitī, perform, give, show

praesum, -esse, -fuī (+*dat.*), command, be set over

praeter (+*acc.*), except, besides

praetereā, besides

praetereō, -īre, -iī, -itum, pass by

praetextātus, wearing a **toga praetexta,** young

prandium, -iī, *n.*, lunch

prasina (factiō), the green (party, team)

prātum, -ī, *n.*, lawn, meadow

prāvus, -a, -um, perverse, wicked, vicious

precēs, -um, *f.pl.*, prayer, entreaty

pretiōsus, -a, -um, valuable, precious, costly

pretium, -iī, *n.*, price

prīdiē, on the day before

prīmus, -a, -um, first; **prīmō,** at first; **prīmum,** firstly; **prīmā lūce,** at dawn; **prīmō māne,** early in the morning

princeps, -ipis, *m.*, chief, leading citizen, emperor

prior, prius, first (of two), former; **prius** (*adv.*), formerly, previously

priusquam (*conj.*), before

prīvāre (+*abl.*), to deprive of

prīvātus, -ī, *m.*, private individual

prō (+*abl.*), for, on behalf of, in return for; **prō certō habēre,** to be sure

probāre, to approve of

probrum, -ī, *n.*, insult, reproach

probus, -a, -um, upright, honourable

prōcēdō, -ere, -cessī, -cessum, advance; **prōcēdēns, -tis,** advancing

prōcrāstināre, to put off (till tomorrow)

procul, far away, at a distance

prōdō, -ere, -didī, -ditum, betray

prōdūcō, -ere, -xī, -ctum, prolong

proelium, -iī, *n.*, battle

profectō, indeed, assuredly

proficīscor, -ī, -fectus sum, set out

prōgredior, -ī, -gressus sum, advance

prohibeō, -ēre, -uī, -itum, prevent, cut off

prōiciō, -ere, -iēcī, -iectum, throw out, abandon

prōiectus, -a, -um, thrown out, abandoned

prōmittō, -ere, -mīsī, -missum, promise; **prōmissa, -ōrum,** *n.pl.*, promises

prope (+*acc.*), near; **prope** (*adv.*), near, nearly

properē, quickly, hastily

prōpōnō, -ere, -posuī, -positum, place before

propter (+*acc.*), on account of, because of

prōscrībō, -ere, -scrīpsī, -scrīptum, proscribe, outlaw

prōspectus, -ūs, *m.*, view

prōspiciō, -ere, -spexī, -spectum, look out, take care

prōstrātus, -a, -um, prostrate, throwing oneself to the ground

prōtinus, immediately, at once

prōvideō, -ēre, -vīdī, -vīsum, provide, foresee

prōvincia, -ae, *f.*, province

prōvinciālis, -is, *m.*, provincial, inhabitant of a province

prōvocāre, to challenge

prōvolāre, to fly forth

proximus, -a, -um, next, nearest

prūdēns, -entis, wise, prudent; **prūdenter,** wisely

pūblicus, -a, -um, belonging to the state; **pūblicē,** at the state's expense; **rēs pūblica, reī pūblicae,** *f.*, state; **rēs pūblicae,** affairs of state

pudet, it shames; **mē pudet,** it shames me (of), i.e. I am ashamed of
pudīcus, -a, -um, virtuous
pudor, -ōris, *m.,* sense of shame
puer, -ī, *m.,* boy
pueritia, -ae, *f.,* boyhood, childhood
pūgiō, -ōnis, *m.,* dagger
pugna, -ae, *f.,* fight, combat
pugnāre, to fight, contend
pugnus, -ī, *m.,* fist
pulcher, -chra, -chrum, beautiful
pullus, -ī, *m.,* chicken
pulsāre, to knock at
pulvis, -eris, *m.,* dust
pūmex, -icis, *m.,* pumice-stone
pūniō, -īre, -īvī, -ītum, punish
putāre, to think

quadrāgintā, forty
quadringentī, -ae, -a, four hundred
quaerō, -ere, quaesīvī, quaesītum, seek, search for
quaesō, please, I beg you
quaestiō, -ōnis, *f.,* examination, investigation with torture
quālis, -is, -e, of what kind?
quam (*exclamatory*), how!
quam, than
quamquam, although
quamvīs, although
quandō, when?; **sī quandō,** if ever, whenever
quantulus, -a, -um, how little, how small?; **quantulum,** how small an amount or sum?
quantus, -a, -um, how big?
quārē, wherefore, why?
quārtus, -a, -um, fourth
quasi, as if
quassāre, to shake, wreck, shatter
quaternī, -ae, -a, four each
quatiō, -ere, quassī, quassum, shake
quattuor, four
quattuordecim, fourteen
-que, and
quemadmodum, how
quī, quae, quod, who, which
quia, because

quicumque, quaecumque, quodcumque, whoever, whatever
quīdam, quaedam, quoddam, a certain
quidem, indeed; **nē . . . quidem,** not even
quiēs, -ētis, *f.,* rest, peace
quiēscō, -ere, -ēvī, -ētum, rest, sleep
quīn, why not?; but that, from (with verbs of hindering, when negative)
quīndecim, fifteen
quīnquāgintā, fifty
quīnque, five
quīntus, -a, -um, fifth
quirītātus, -ūs, *m.,* shriek
quis, who?; **quid,** what?; **nē quis,** in case anyone; **sī quis,** if anyone
quisquam, quidquam (*or* **quicquam**), anyone, anything (in negative sentences)
quisque, quaeque, quidque (quodque), each
quisquis, quidquid (*or* **quicquid**), whoever, whatever
quō, where . . . to? whither?
quod, because
quōmodo, how?
quondam, once, formerly, at some future time
quoniam, since
quoque, also
quot, how many?
quotus, -a, -um, which? (in a series) e.g. **quota hōra est?** What hour is it? What time is it?

raeda, -ae, *f.,* carriage
raedārius, -iī, *m.,* coachman
rāmōsus, -a, -um, spreading, branching
rapīna, -ae, *f.,* booty, plunder
rapiō, -ere, -puī, -ptum, seize, snatch
ratiō, -ōnis, *f.,* account, reckoning; **ratiōnem subdūcere,** to balance an account
raucus, -a, -um, hoarse
rebelliō, -ōnis, *f.,* rebellion, revolt
recēdō, -ere, -cessī, -cessum, retire, withdraw
recipiō, -ere, -cēpī, -ceptum, receive back, recover; **sē recipere,** to retreat
recreāre, to revive, restore

rēctor, -ōris, *m.,* mahout, driver

rēctus, -a, -um, straight; **rēctā (viā),** straight, right on

recumbō, -ere, -cubui, lie down

recūsāre, to refuse

reddō, -ere, -didi, -ditum, give back, return, render

redeō, -īre, -ii, -itum, return, go back

reditus, -ūs, *m.,* return

referō, -ferre, rettuli, relātum, report, refer to

reficiō, -ere, -fēci, -fectum, repair, restore

rēgia, -ae, *f.,* palace

regiō, -ōnis, *f.,* district, quarter of a city

rēgius, -a, -um, royal

rēgnāre, to rule

rēgnum, -i, *n.,* kingdom

regō, -ere, rēxi, rēctum, rule, control

regredior, -i, -gressus sum, go back, return, retreat

religiō, -ōnis, *f.,* religion, cult

relinquō, -ere, -liqui, -lictum, leave (behind), bequeath, abandon

reliquiae, -ārum, *f.pl.,* remains

reliquus, -a, -um, remaining, other, rest

relūcēscit (relūxit), it grows (grew) lighter

remeāre, to return

remedium, -ii, *n.,* cure

remittō, -ere, -misi, -missum, send back, relax grip on, let go

removeō, -ēre, -mōvi, -mōtum, remove

repellō, -ere, reppuli, repulsum, drive back

repente, suddenly

reportāre, to bring back, take back

reputāre, to consider, think over

requirō, -ere, -quisivi, -quisitum, ask for, desire

rēs, rei, *f.,* thing, matter, circumstance; **rēs pūblica, rei pūblicae,** *f.,* state; **rēs pūblicae,** affairs of state; **rēs angustae,** straits, time of trouble; **rēs secundae,** good fortune, success, prosperity; **rem bene gerere,** to be successful; **rē vērā,** indeed, in truth

residō, -ere, -sēdi, -sessum, sit down

respiciō, -ere, -spexi, -spectum, look back

respondeō, -ēre, -spondi, -spōnsum, reply, answer

respōnsum, -i, *n.,* reply

restāre, to remain, be left

restituō, -ere, -ui, -ūtum, restore

rēte, -is, *n.,* net

rētiārius, -ii, *m.,* gladiator who fought with a net, 'catcher'

retineō, -ēre, -ui, -tentum, retain, keep

retrō, backwards

reverentia, -ae, *f.,* reverence, respect

revertor, -i, -versus sum, return

revocāre, to recall

rēx, rēgis, *m.,* king

rideō, -ēre, risi, risum, laugh, laugh at

ridiculus, -a, -um, laughable, amusing

risus, -ūs, *m.,* smile, laugh

ritĕ, duly, properly

rōbustus, -a, -um, strong, vigorous

rogāre, to ask

rogus, -i, *m.,* funeral pile, pyre

rota, -ae, *f.,* wheel

rotāre, to turn, whirl round

ruber, -bra, -brum, red

rudō, -ere, -ivi, -itum, bray

ruina, -ae, *f.,* collapse

rumpō, -ere, rūpi, ruptum, break

ruō, -ere, rui, rutum, rush

rūrsus, again

rūs, rūris, *n.,* the country; **rūs,** to the country; **rūri,** in the country; **rūre,** from the country

russāta (factiō), the red (party, team)

saccus, -i, *m.,* bag

saepe, often; **saepius,** again and again

saevitia, -ae, *f.,* cruelty, severity

saevus, -a, -um, cruel

sagāx, -ācis, clever

sagitta, -ae, *f.,* arrow

saltem, at least

saltus, -ūs, *m.,* mountain pasture

salūs, -ūtis, *f.,* safety

salūtāre, to greet

salvē (*pl.* **salvēte),** good morning! good day!

salvus, -a, -um, safe, unhurt

sānē, surely, truly, indeed

sanguis, -inis, *m.,* blood, bloodshed

sānus, -a, -um, healthy, sound

sapiō, -ere, -iī, be wise

sarciō, -īre, -rsī, -rtum, mend, repair

satis, enough, quite

scaena, -ae, *f.,* stage

scālae, -ārum, *f.pl.,* flight of steps

scelestus, -a, -um, wicked

sciō, scīre, scīvī, scītum, know

scrībō, -ere, scrīpsī, scrīptum, write

scrīptor, -ōris, *m.,* writer; **rērum scrīptor,** historian

scurra, -ae, *m.,* buffoon, jester

scūtum, -ī, *n.,* shield

sē, himself, herself, themselves; **sēcum,** with himself, herself, themselves; **inter sē,** among themselves

sēcrētus, -a, -um, separated, lonely, hidden; **in sēcrētum venīre,** to come aside, apart

secundum (+*acc.*), along, beside

secundus, -a, -um, second, favourable; **rēs secundae,** good fortune, success, prosperity

sed, but

sēdecim, sixteen

sedeō, -ēre, sēdī, sessum, sit

sēdēs, -is, *f.,* seat, home

sēditiō, -ōnis, *f.,* strife, quarrel

seges, -etis, *f.,* crop, standing corn

sēgnitia, -ae, *f.,* inactivity

sella, -ae, *f.,* seat, chair

semel, once, a single time

sēmis, -issis, *m.,* half an **as**

semper, always

senātus, -ūs, *m.,* the senate; **senātūs consultum,** a decree of the senate

senex, senis, *m.,* old man; **senior,** older, elderly

sententia, -ae, *f.,* opinion

sentiō, -īre, sēnsī, sēnsum, feel, realise, perceive, be conscious

sēparātim, separately

sepeliō, -īre, -īvī, sepultum, bury

sēpōnō, -ere, -posuī, -positum, set aside or apart

September, -bris, -bre, belonging to September; **mēnsis September,** the month of September

septentriōnēs, -um, *m.pl.,* the seven stars of the Great or Little Bear; the north

septuāgintā, seventy

sequor, -ī, -cūtus sum, follow

serēnus, -a, -um, serene, cheerful, glad

sermō, -ōnis, *m.,* conversation, talk

sērō, late, too late

servāre, to keep, save

servitūs, -ūtis, *f.,* slavery

servus, -ī, *m.,* slave; **servus ā manū,** secretary

sēstertius, -iī, *m.,* sesterce (a small silver coin, originally worth two and a half **assēs**)

sevēritās, -ātis, *f.,* strictness, severity

sevērus, -a, -um, serious

sexāgēsimus, -a, -um, sixtieth

sexāgintā, sixty

sextus, -a, -um, sixth

sī, if; **sī minus,** if not; **sī quandō,** if ever

sīc, thus, in this manner

sīcut, just as

signātus, -a, -um, sealed

significāre, to indicate, make known

signum, -ī, *n.,* signal, sign, figure, design

silentium, -iī, *n.,* silence, stillness

silva, -ae, *f.,* wood

silvester, -tris, -tre, wooded

similis, -is, -e, like

simplex, -icis, simple

simplicitās, -ātis, *f.,* simplicity

simul, at the same time; **simul ac (atque),** as soon as

simulāre, to pretend

sin, but if

sine (+*abl.*), without; **sine dubiō,** without doubt

sinister, -tra, -trum, left, left-handed; **ā sinistrā,** on the left

sinō, -ere, sīvī, situm, allow, permit

siphō, -ōnis, *m.,* fire-engine

sitis, -is, *f.,* thirst

situs, -a, -um, situated

sīve . . . sīve (seu . . . seu), whether . . . or

sociāre, to attach, associate

socius, -iī, *m.,* companion, ally

socordia, -ae, *f.*, indolence, stupidity
sōl, sōlis, *m.*, sun
sōlācium, -ii, *n.*, comfort, relief
sōlārium, -ii, *n.*, sunny spot, terrace, balcony
soleō, -ēre, solitus sum, be accustomed
sōlitūdō, -inis, *f.*, loneliness, solitude
sollicitus, -a, -um, troubled, anxious
solum, -ī, *n.*, soil, land
sōlus, -a, -um, alone; sōlum, only
solvō, -ere, solvī, solūtum, loosen, release, break up, weaken
somnium, -ii, *n.*, dream
somnus, -ī, *m.*, sleep
sordidātus, -a, -um, dirtied
sordidus, -a, -um, dirty
soror, -ōris, *f.*, sister
sors, sortis, *f.*, lot, chance
spargō, -ere, -rsī, -rsum, scatter, spread
speciēs, -ēī, *f.*, appearance
spectāculum, -ī, *n.*, sight, show
spectātor, -ōris, *m.*, spectator
spectāre, to look at
spērāre, to hope
spēs, -ēī, *f.*, hope
splendidus, -a, -um, magnificent
spoliāre, to rob
squālēre, to be dirty
statim, immediately
statiō, -ōnis, *f.*, picket, guard
statua, -ae, *f.*, statue
stilus, -ī, *m.*, pen
stīpendium, -ii, *n.*, pay
stō, stāre, stetī, stātum, stand
strāgēs, -is, *f.*, slaughter, massacre
strāta via, paved street
strepitus, -ūs, *m.*, din, noise
stridor, -ōris, *m.*, squeal, grunt
stringō, -ere, strīnxī, strictum, draw, unsheath
struō, -ere, -uxī, -uctum, build
studeō, -ēre, -uī (+*dat.*), study, attend school
studiōsus, -a, -um (+*gen.*), devoted to, fond of
studium, -ii, *n.*, study, desire, passion
stultus, -a, -um, foolish; stultē, foolishly
suāvis, -is, -e, sweet, agreeable, pleasant
sub (+*abl.*), under

subdūcō, -ere, -dūxī, -ductum, draw up, beach (ships); ratiōnēs subdūcere, to balance accounts; sē subdūcere, to withdraw
subiciō, -ere, -iēcī, -iectum, put under
subigō, -ere, -ēgī, -āctum, subdue, conquer; farīnam subigere, to knead dough
subitō, suddenly
subsequor, -ī, -secūtus sum, follow up
subveniō, -īre, -vēnī, -ventum (+*dat.*), come to the help of, assist
succidō, -ere, -cīdī, -cīsum, cut down or through
sūdor, -ōris, *m.*, sweat, exertion
suggerō, -ere, -gessī, -gestum, heap up
summoveō, -ēre, -mōvī, -mōtum, dislodge, move back
summus, -a, -um, highest, greatest, top of; summā celeritāte, with the utmost speed; ā summō monte, from the top of the mountain
sūmō, -ere, sūmpsī, sūmptum, take up or in hand, assume
sūmptus, -ūs, *m.*, expense
super (+*acc.*), above, over
superbus, -a, -um, proud, arrogant
superiaciō, -ere, -iēcī, -iectum (-iactum), throw upon
superior, -ius, superior
superāre, to overcome, conquer, surpass; superātus, -a, -um, overcome
superstitiō, -ōnis, *f.*, superstition
superstitiōsus, -a, -um, superstitious
supersum, -esse, -fuī, be left over, survive
supplicāre (+*dat.*), to worship
supplicium, -ii, *n.*, punishment, execution
suprā (+*acc.*), above
suprēmus, -a, -um, last; suprēmus diēs, day of death
surdus, -a, -um, deaf
surgō, -ere, surrēxī, surrēctum, rise, get up
suscipiō, -ere, -cēpī, -ceptum, undertake, take, bear
sustineō, -ēre, -uī, -tentum, withstand, support, endure

sūtor, -ōris, *m.*, shoemaker
sūtrīna, -ae, *f.*, shoemaker's stall
suus, -a, -um, his, her, its, their own;
  suī, his own people

taberna, -ae, *f.*, shop
tabernārius, -iī, *m.*, shopkeeper
tablīnum, -ī, *n.*, study, living-room
tabula, -ae, *f.*, list, account-book
taceō, -ēre, -uī, -itum, be silent
taedet, it wearies; mē taedet, it wearies
  me (of), i.e. I am wearied, tired (of)
taeter, -tra, -trum, foul, shocking
tālis, -is, -e, such
tam, so (*with adjectives and adverbs*)
tamen, however, nevertheless
tamquam, as if, on the ground that
tandem, at length, at last
tangō, -ere, tetigī, tāctum, touch,
  affect, move; tāctus, -a, -um, affected,
  moved
tantus, -a, -um, so great; tantī, worth
  so much; tantum, only
tēctum, -ī, *n.*, roof, house
tegō, -ere, tēxī, tēctum, cover; tēctus,
  -a, -um, covered, hidden
tēlum, -ī, *n.*, javelin, missile
tempestās, -ātis, *f.*, weather, storm
templum, -ī, *n.*, temple
tempus, -oris, *n.*, time
tenāx, -ācis, retentive
tenebrae, -ārum, *f.pl.*, darkness
teneō, -ēre, -uī, tentum, hold, keep
tenuātus, -a, -um, thinned out
ter, thrice, three times
tergum, -ī, *n.*, back; ā tergō, in the rear
terminus, -ī, *m.*, boundary
ternī, -ae, -a, three each
terra, -ae, *f.*, earth; terrā marīque, by
  land and sea
terreō, -ēre, -uī, -itum, frighten;
  territus, -a, -um, frightened
terribilis, -is, -e, terrible, terrifying
terror, -ōris, *m.*, terror, alarm
tertiānus, -a, -um, recurring every third
  day
tertius, -a, -um, third
tessellātus, -a, -um, set with small
  square stones, mosaic

testor, -ārī, -ātus sum, to bear witness
  to, give evidence of
testula, -ae, *f.*, fragment of tile
texō, -ere, -xuī, -xtum, weave
textor, -ōris, *m.*, weaver
theātrum, -ī, *n.*, theatre
thermae, -ārum, *f.pl.*, warm baths
tībīcen, -inis, *m.*, flute-play
timeō, -ēre, -uī, fear, be afraid
timidus, -a, -um, timid, faint-hearted
timor, -ōris, *m.*, fear
tingō, -ere, tīnxī, tīnctum, dye; tīnctus,
  -a, -um, dyed
tīrō, -ōnis, *m.*, recruit
titulus, -ī, *m.*, label, placard
toga, -ae, *f.*, toga, robe
tollō, -ere, sustulī, sublātum, raise,
  remove, take away
tomāculum, -ī, *n.*, sausage
tonat, it thunders
tonitruum, -ī, *n.*, thunder
tormentum, -ī, *n.*, torture; per tormenta quaerere dē, to examine under
  torture
torqueō, -ēre, torsī, tortum, torture,
  twist
tot, so many
tōtus, -a, -um, whole
tractāre, to treat
trādō, -ere, -didī, -ditum, hand over,
  relate, record
trāiciō, -ere, -iēcī, -iectum, pierce
trāmes, -itis, *m.*, path, line
tranquillus, -a, -um, quiet, peaceful,
  calm
trāns (+*acc.*), across
trānseō, -īre, -iī, -itum, cross
trānsferō, -ferre, -tulī, -lātum, change
  over
trānsfuga, -ae, *m.*, deserter
trānsportāre, to transport, bring over
trānsvehor, -ī, -vectus sum, sail over
  or across
tremor, -ōris (terrae), *m.*, earth tremor,
  earthquake
trepidāre, to be agitated, excited
trepidātiō, -ōnis, *f.*, alarm
trepidus, -a, -um, alarmed, anxious
trēs, trēs, tria, three

tribūnal, -ālis, *n.*, raised platform
tribūnus, -ī, *m.*, tribune
tribuō, -ere, -uī, -ūtum, grant, give
triclīnium, -iī, *n.*, dining-room
trigintā, thirty
triquetrus, -a, -um, triangular
tristis, -is, -e, sad
triumphāre, to celebrate a triumph
triumvir, -ī, *m.*, triumvir, one of three associates
trucīdāre, to slaughter, assassinate
trūdō, -ere, -sī, -sum, push, thrust
tū, you (*singular*)
tuba, -ae, *f.*, trumpet
tum, then
tumultus, -ūs, *m.*, confusion, disturbance, rebellion
tunc, then, at that time
tundō, -ere, tutudī, tū(n)sum, beat, hammer
tunica, -ae, *f.*, tunic, undergarment
turba, -ae, *f.*, crowd, confusion
turbātus, -a, -um, disturbed, troubled, in disorder
turbulentus, -a, -um, stormy, troublesome
turris, -is, *f.*, tower
tūtus, -a, -um, safe
tuus, -a, -um, your

ubi, where, where?
ubi, when, as soon as
ubīque, everywhere
ūllus, -a, -um, any
ultimus, -a, -um, last, extreme
ultiō, -ōnis, *f.*, revenge
ultrā (+*acc.*), beyond, longer; **ulterius,** further, longer
ululāre, to howl
ululātus, -ūs, *m.*, shrieking, wailing
umbra, -ae, *f.*, shade
umerus, -ī, *m.*, shoulder
umquam (unquam), ever
ūnā, together, at the same time
unde, where from?
ūndēvīgintī, nineteen
undique, from, *or* on, all sides
unguentum, -ī, *n.*, ointment, perfume

ūnicus, -a, -um, unique, alone in its kind
ūniversus, -a, -um, all together
ūnus, -a, -um, one; **omnēs ad ūnum,** all to a man
urbs, urbis, *f.*, city
urna, -ae, *f.*, urn (for ashes of dead)
ūrō, -ere, ussī, ustum, burn
ursus, -ī, *m.*, bear
usquam, anywhere
usque ad, until, right up to
ūsus, -ūs, *m.*, use, profit, experience; **ūsuī esse,** to be of use, useful
ut, as, when
ut (*with subj.*), in order that, so that, how
uter, utra, utrum, which of two
uterque, utraque, utrumque, each of two
ūtilis, -is, -e, useful, profitable
ūtor, -ī, ūsus sum (+*abl.*), use, practise, enjoy
utpote quī (*with subj.*), seeing that, inasmuch as
utrum . . . an, whether . . . or; **utrum . . . annōn,** whether . . . or not (*direct questions*); **utrum . . . necne,** whether . . . or not (*indirect questions*)
uxor, -ōris, *f.*, wife

vacuus, -a, -um, empty, vacant
valē (*pl.* **valēte**), goodbye, farewell
valedīcō, -ere, -dīxī, -dictum (+*dat.*), bid farewell
valēre iubeō, -ēre, iussī, iussum, bid farewell
validus, -a, -um, strong
vallum, -ī, *n.*, rampart, fortification, wall
vāstāre, to devastate, lay waste; **vāstātus, -a, -um,** devastated, laid waste
vāstus, -a, -um, huge, enormous
-vě, or
vectīgal, -ālis, *n.*, tax
vehō, -ere, vēxī, vectum, carry, convey
vel, or; **vel . . . vel,** either . . . or
vēlōcitās, -ātis, *f.*, swiftness, rapidity
velut, just as, like
vēnābulum, -ī, *n.*, hunting-spear
vēnālis, -is, -e, for sale

vēnātiō, -ōnis, *f.,* fight of wild beasts, hunting

vendō, -ere, vendidī, venditum, sell

venēnum, -ī, *n.,* poison

vēneō, -īre, -iī, be sold

veneta (factiō), the blue (party, team)

venia, -ae, *f.,* pardon

veniō, -īre, vēnī, ventum, come

vēnor, -ārī, -ātus sum, hunt

venter, -tris, *m.,* belly, stomach

ventus, -ī, *m.,* wind

verberāre, to beat

verbum, -ī, *n.,* word

verēcundia, -ae, *f.,* modesty

vereor, -ērī, veritus sum, fear

vernus, -a, -um, relating to spring

vērō, indeed

versāre, to turn about often

versipellis, -is, *m.,* werewolf, one who can change himself into a wolf

vertō, -ere, -tī, -sum, turn

vērum, but

vērus, -a, -um, true, real; **vēra dīcere,** to speak the truth

vescor, -ī (+*abl.*), feed on, eat

vesper, -erī (*or* **-eris**), *m.,* evening; **vesperī,** in the evening

vester, -tra, -trum, your

vestiārius, -ii, *m.,* clothier

vestibulum, -ī, *n.,* vestibule, entrance

vestīgium, -ii, *n.,* track, footprint

vestīmentum, -ī, *n.,* garment, article of clothing

vestis, -is, *f.,* garment

vetus, -eris, old, former

vexāre, to annoy, harass

via, -ae, *f.,* road, street, way

viāticum, -ī, *n.,* travelling expenses

vīcīnus, -ī, *m.,* neighbour

victor, -ōris, *m.,* conqueror; victorious

victōria, -ae, *f.,* victory

victus, -ūs, *m.,* nourishment, sustenance

vīcus, -ī, *m.,* village, street, district of a town

videō, -ēre, -vīdī, vīsum, see; **videor, -ērī, vīsus sum,** seem

vigil, -is, *m.,* watchman, policeman, fireman

vigilāre, to be awake, spend sleepless nights

vigilia, -ae, *f.,* sleeplessness, sentry duty

vīgintī, twenty

vīlitās, -ātis, *f.,* cheapness

vīlla, -ae, *f.,* country house

villus, -ī, *m.,* hair (shaggy)

vincō, -ere, vīcī, victum, conquer

vinculum, -ī, *n.,* fetter, chain; **in vincula cōnicere,** throw into prison

vīnum, -ī, *n.,* wine

violentia, -ae, *f.,* violence, fury

vir, virī, *m.,* man, husband

virīlis, -is, -e, of a man, manly; **toga virīlis,** the all-white toga of manhood assumed by Roman youths in their sixteenth year

virtūs, -ūtis, *f.,* courage, virtue

vīs, vim, vī, *f.,* power, force; **vī et armis,** by force of arms

vīsō, -ere, -sī, go to see, visit

vīta, -ae, *f.,* life; **ē vītā excēdere (dēcēdere),** to depart from life, die

vītāre, to avoid

vitrum, -ī, *n.,* glass, woad (a vegetable dye)

vīvō, -ere, vīxī, victum, live

vīvus, -a, -um, alive

vix, scarcely, with difficulty

vocābulum, -ī, *n.,* name

vocāre, to call, invite

volāre, to fly

volō, velle, voluī, wish, be willing

volūmen, -inis, *n.,* roll, book

voluntārius, -a, -um, willing, voluntary

voluptās, -ātis, *f.,* pleasure

volvō, -ere, -lvī, -lūtum, roll, turn around; **animō volvere,** to revolve in one's mind, consider

vōs, you (*pl.*); **vōbīscum,** with you

vōx, vōcis, *f.,* voice

vulnerāre, to wound

vulpēs, -is, *f.,* fox

vultus, -ūs, *m.,* face, countenance, expression

Names

Actium, -iī, *n.,* Actium, a promontory on the N.W. coast of Greece, off which Antony was defeated by Octavian in 31 B.C.

Aegyptus, -ī, *f.,* Egypt

Aethiops, -opis, *m.,* Ethiopian; negro

Aetius, -iī, *m.,* Aetius; called 'the last of the Romans'; rallied the forces of Gaul against Attila and his Huns whom he defeated in A.D. 451

Agrippīna, -ae, *f.,* Agrippina, mother of Nero

Alexander (Magnus), Alexandrī, *m.,* Alexander the Great, whose conquests extended as far as India

Amphitheātrum, -ī, *n.,* amphitheatre; generally the Flavian Amphitheatre (Colosseum) which was begun by the Emperor Vespasian

Antōninus (Marcus Aurēlius), Antōninī, *m.,* Marcus Aurelius Antoninus, Roman emperor A.D. 161–180

Antōnius (Marcus), Antōnii, *m.,* Mark Antony; renowned for his oratory; member of Second Triumvirate; committed suicide after the battle of Actium

Athēnae, -ārum, *f.pl.,* Athens

Atia, -ae, *f.,* Atia, mother of Augustus

Attila, -ae, *m.,* Attila, leader of the Huns, a wild people from Central Asia, who invaded Italy in A.D. 452

Augustus, -ī, *m.,* Augustus, first Roman emperor (31B.C.–A.D. 14)

Boudicca, -ae, *f.,* Boudicca, queen of the Iceni (East Anglia); revolted against the Romans in A.D. 61; defeated by Suetonius Paulinus

Brigantēs, -um, *m.pl.,* Brigantes, a very powerful tribe which lived in northern part of Roman Britain

Britannicus, -ī, *m.,* Britannicus; title conferred by the Emperor Claudius on his son after the invasion of Britain in A.D. 43

Burrus, -ī, *m.,* Burrus, Prefect of the Guard and adviser of the Emperor Nero

Calēdonia, -ae, *f.,* Caledonia, the name given to the territory beyond the line of the Forth and Clyde rivers in Scotland

Capua, -ae, *f.,* Capua, chief city of Campania, noted for its luxury and wealth

Cassius (Dio), -iī, *m.,* Dio Cassius (A.D. 150–235), author of a 'Roman History' in Greek

Claudius, -iī, *m.,* Claudius, Roman Emperor A.D. 41–54

Cleopātra, -ae, *f.,* Cleopatra (68–30 B.C.), queen of Egypt; famous for her beauty and charm; took her own life in 30 B.C.

Cogidubnus, -ī, *m.,* Cogidubnus, king of the Regnenses; one of the first British kings to collaborate with the Romans; appointed Roman Legate

Cōnstantīnus, -ī, *m.,* Roman emperor A.D. 306–337; baptised as a Christian shortly before his death

Cōnstantius, -iī, *m.,* Constantius, father of Constantine

Cūmae, -ārum, *f.pl.,* Cumae, a Greek colony in Campania

Dēiphobē, -ēs, *f.,* Sibyl or prophetess who lived in a cave at Cumae

Diāna, -ae, *f.,* Diana, goddess of hunting and of the moon

Drūsus, -ī, *m.,* Drusus, son of the Emperor Tiberius; designated to succeed him, but died in A.D. 23

Eborācum, -ī, *n.,* York

Eusebius, -iī, *m.,* Eusebius (A.D. 265–340); wrote a biography of Constantine

Formiānus, -a, -um, belonging to Formiae, ancient city of Latium

Galerius, -ii, *m.,* Galerius, emperor A.D. 305–311

Germānicus, -ī, *m.,* Germanicus, son of Drusus

Gothī, -ōrum, *m.pl.,* Goths, a tribe from northern Germany

Hamilcar, -aris, *m.,* Hamilcar, Carthaginian general, father of Hannibal

Lepidus (Marcus Aemilius), -ī, *m.,* triumvir with Antony and Octavian

Luguvallium, -ii, *n.,* Carlisle

Massilia, -ae, *f.,* Marseilles

Maxentius, -ii, *m.,* Maxentius, proclaimed emperor in A.D. 306; defeated by Constantine at the Mulvian Bridge in 312

Mediōlānum, -ī, *n.,* Milan

Megara, -ae, *f.* (also **-ōrum,** *n.*), Megara, a Greek town on the isthmus of Corinth

Minerva, -ae, *f.,* Minerva, goddess of crafts and wisdom

Mōns Albānus, Montis Albānī, *m.,* the Alban Hills, 20 km S.E. of Rome

Mōns Palātinus, Montis Palātīnī, *m.,* the Palatine Hill, one of the seven hills of Rome

Mūciānus, -ī, *m.,* Mucianus, who wrote a book of geographical **Mīrābilia** from which Pliny the Elder borrowed freely

Mulvius Pōns, Mulviī Pontis, *m.,* the Mulvian Bridge, at the point where the Via Flaminia crossed the Tiber

Mytilēnēsēs, -ium, *m.pl.,* the inhabitants of Mytilene, chief city of the island of Lesbos

Nerō, -ōnis, *m.,* Nero, emperor A.D. 54–68, a man of considerable talents, but cruel and brutal

Nicomēdēnsēs, -ium, *m.pl.,* the inhabitants of Nicomedia, capital of Bithynia (Asia Minor)

Nōla, -ae, *f.,* Nola, an ancient city of Campania

Noviomagus, -ī, *f.,* Chichester, capital of Cogidubnus, King of the Regnenses

Nūceria, -ae, *f.,* Nuceria, a city of Campania

Ōceanus, -ī, *m.,* the great river which was supposed to encircle the earth; the Atlantic Ocean

Octāvia, -ae, *f.,* wife of Nero

Octāviānus, -ī, *m.,* Octavian, the adopted son of Caesar; later known as Augustus

Octāvius, -ii, *m.,* Octavius, father of Octavian

Orcades, -um, *f.pl.,* the Orkney Islands

Orcus, -ī, *m.,* Orcus, the underworld, the dwelling place of the dead

Oriēns, -tis, *m.,* the east

Pictī, -ōrum, *m.pl.,* the Picts, the ancient Caledonians

Plinius (C. Plīnius Secundus), -ii, *m.,* Pliny the Elder, who perished in the eruption of Vesuvius in A.D. 79

Plinius (C. Plīnius Caecilius Secundus), Pliny the Younger, governor of Bithynia A.D. 111–113; famous for his ten volumes of letters written on a wide variety of subjects

Poenī, -ōrum, *m.pl.,* Carthaginians

Portus Itius, Portūs Itii, *m.,* harbour in N. France, probably Boulogne

Regnēnsēs, -ium, *m.pl.,* the Regnenses, tribe who lived in S. England (Sussex), chief town Noviomagus (Chichester)

Salernitānus, -a, -um, belonging to Salernum (now Salerno)

Seneca, -ae, *m.,* Seneca (the philosopher); writer on many subjects; tutor of Nero

Sevērus, -ī, *m.,* Severus, emperor A.D. 193–211; set out for Britain in A.D. 208; worn out by sickness, died at York in A.D. 211

Sibylla, -ae, *f.,* Sibyl or prophetess associated with Cumae

Siculī, -ōrum, *m.pl.,* Sicilians

Stōicus, -ī, *m.,* a Stoic philosopher. Stoic philosophers maintained that to be virtuous was the only good

Suētōnius Paulīnus, -ī, *m.,* Suetonius Paulinus, governor of Britain A.D. 59–61; crushed revolt of the Iceni under Boudicca; recalled because of his severity

Syrācūsae, -ārum, *f.pl.,* Syracuse, a city on S.E. coast of Sicily

Thrax, -ācis, *m.,* a Thracian; a kind of gladiator, so called because of his Thracian equipment

Tiberius, -iī, *m.,* Tiberius, emperor A.D. 14–37

Tigellīnus, -ī, *m.,* Tigellinus, a favourite of Nero, upon whom he had a very bad influence